Scavenging Beauty

SCAVENGING BEAUTY

A MEMOIR IN WALKS

Angelica Glass

RIVERHEAD BOOKS
NEW YORK
2026

RIVERHEAD BOOKS
An imprint of Penguin Random House LLC
1745 Broadway, New York, NY 10019
penguinrandomhouse.com

Book design by Amanda Dewey

LIBRARY OF CONGRESS CONTROL NUMBER permalink:
https://lccn.loc.gov/2025044526
ISBN 9780593855348 (hardcover)
ISBN 9780593855355 (ebook)

Printed in the United States of America
1st Printing

The authorized representative in the EU for product safety and compliance is
Penguin Random House Ireland, Morrison Chambers, 32 Nassau Street,
Dublin D02 YH68, Ireland, https://eu-contact.penguin.ie.

*For my wife, Ellen, my taproot,
and for my beloved sons, Kita and Miles,
who don't need an explanation, but deserve one*

MOST OF THE CHAPTERS in this book revolve around long walks and some of the many topics I pondered while out wandering. Throughout the book, I have condensed aspects of multiple walks and related experiences into single outings. Conversations and experiences related to my childhood are recounted as I recall them. My stories move between both time and place. I've done my best to smooth these transitions.

The stories regarding people connected to the child welfare system do not reflect actual individuals: They are composites of different circumstances I encountered during my twenty-two years working in that system. While I refer to some of my siblings' childhood experiences that provide context, there are some that I don't expand upon, as they are not my stories to tell. Throughout the process of writing this book, I met with my brothers and sisters regularly. Initially, I interviewed each of them individually about their childhood experiences; then we met as a group via conference calls. During weekly calls, I read each chapter aloud. This process has strengthened our bonds and given us a chance to gain a much fuller understanding of the depth of the chaos we were raised on. I've heard stories of writers for whom memoir writing has caused deep rifts in their familial relationships. I am honored and fortunate to be a part of a sibling group full of frank and honest people who support me wholeheartedly in telling my story.

Names and details of some of the people I write about have been changed or omitted to protect their privacy.

While my mother was diagnosed with manic depression, which is now called bipolar disorder, not all of her actions are directly attributable to that condition. I want to make explicit the fact that plenty of people, including many whom I know and dearly love, manage life, including parenting, with bipolar disorder without becoming violent or completely alienating their families. Like all major mental health conditions, it's a complex and multilayered issue, the specifics of which manifest differently in each individual impacted by it. No individual is wholly defined by the disorders or conditions we contend with, just as no disorder or condition can account for all behaviors, actions, and decisions.

I did roughly three quarters of the walks alone throughout these seven years and fifteen pairs of shoes of slow travel, and for the sake of streamlining, the story is told through solo walks. But I also had the distinct pleasure of walking with various friends and family members who gamely joined me for a trek or two, or in the case of a few friends, many.

CONTENTS

Scavenging Beauty

Chapter 1

Stepping Out

quaquaversal *adjective* \\¦kwākwə¦vərsəl\\:
dipping from a center toward all
points of the compass

I'M SOAKING IN A HOT BATH, attempting to relax after an
arduous day at work, when I have the rumble of an
idea. My wife, Ellen, comes in to brush her teeth.

"I think I'm going to walk every street in Santa Cruz,"
I tell her.

"City or county?" she asks without missing a beat. She
knows—and has known for quite some time—that walking
is becoming my go-to for regaining perspective after particularly challenging workdays.

"County," I reply. "I think I'll do the whole thing."

Outside, the sky is clear and darkening into evening, but
the air is cold. I've made a sauna of the bathroom, fogging
up mirrors and leaving a layer of beading moisture on every
conceivable surface, the very thing I nag my kids about,
admonishing that it will create mildew and cause the paint

to peel. But slowly breathing in these clouds of warm water vapor is so precisely what I need right now that I can live with being a momentary hypocrite.

It's so relaxing, in fact, that I don't even bristle when Ellen uses a hand towel to wipe the steam off the mirror, leaving streaks that only Windex and blue shop towels can eradicate. Instead, I add a couple of drops of eucalyptus oil to the water and agitate it with my hands to disperse the refreshing, woody scent. Ellen breathes in the essence, makes an encouraging comment about my walking scheme, and plants a kiss on me before heading out to the living room in her flannel grizzly-bear pajama pants and Mickey Mouse T-shirt to catch the evening news.

As I continue to hatch my plan on this November evening in 2013, I know there are two truths I need to confront: I need more exercise in my largely sedentary lifestyle. And I must have a release for work-related stress. In this screen-focused, information-saturated world, my bubble, like those of so many people I know, has narrowed to a handful of places: my job, home, my younger son Miles's school, the grocery store, and the homes of my older son, Kita, and a few close friends. That's it. I need to shake up my life, get outside, and stir up the dust.

This same unsettled feeling visited me many months ago and propelled me to incorporate weekly walking into my life. I started by inviting a group of six coworkers to go for early morning strolls on Sundays. We met in the parking lot of Kelly's French Bakery, a few blocks from my home, at 5 a.m., to minimize the loss of precious weekend time with our families. Strolls quickly gave way to brisk six-mile, then eight-mile, then ten-mile walks, but we still managed to take our walk, have breakfast together at the bakery, and return home by 10 a.m. when most of our families were just starting their days.

We were an effusive group, never short on topics to discuss. Conversation flowed seamlessly from Little League games to current events to easy-to-prepare recipes. During the week, we shared a high-stress workplace as social workers, supervisors, and program analysts in a child welfare agency, and though we tried to steer away from too much shop talk, the walks sometimes served as times to debrief particularly challenging events from work that we rarely got a chance to discuss in depth during the week.

One chilly spring morning, on the asphalt walking path in Wilder Ranch State Park, just two miles from my home, our group of seven moved along like a hive of buzzing bees. There were multiple conversations going at once and plenty of cross talk between. Suddenly, my friend Melissa grabbed my shoulder urgently from behind, stopping me. I looked up to see a mountain lion crossing the path just several feet in front of us. We all fell pin-drop silent as we watched the sleek cat glide by, ignoring us completely, and vanish into a row of bushes. We remained quiet as we collectively absorbed the moment, startled and awed by the fluidity of the animal.

We recounted the experience a hundred times in the

ensuing days when we ran into each other around the office, sculpting our few-seconds brush with wildness into an unforgettable memory.

For a variety of reasons, all involving happily expanding families (including a set of twin boys, a baby girl, and a few impulse puppies), the weekly walks dwindled to monthly, then fizzled out altogether. But each of us kept a photograph of a generic mountain lion taped to our office walls long after the group walks stopped.

I wasn't ready to give up taking long walks. I'd grown attached to moving at a pace that allowed me to see parts of the world that I missed when I drove or even rode a bike. And the quality of conversations is greatly enhanced when ambling with a friend down a country road, through the woods, or along the beach. I rarely go out for meals with friends anymore. Whenever possible, I'll opt for a walk or hike.

I went over to my friend Jo's house one October afternoon and asked, "Will you walk to Los Gatos with me?" Los Gatos is a small city, a sliver of which lies within Santa Cruz County while most of it is in neighboring Santa Clara County, in the foothills of the Santa Cruz Mountains in central California.

Jo sprang up from her chair on her sunny deck, went inside, and leaped for her computer. Before I knew it, she was printing out pages of United States Geographical Survey maps and cutting and taping them until we had a narrow five-foot strip of a map.

"I'll take that as a yes," I said.

A couple of days later, I picked up Jo and we drove to the base of Bean Creek Road in Scotts Valley with day packs full of water, snacks, and sunscreen and set off on what could have been an eighteen-mile walk but stretched to twenty-two miles when we went astray, wandering along the edges of the Lexington Reservoir. The route wove us through neighborhoods, wetlands, and open spaces each of us had driven by for years but had never set foot in. Every now and then, we'd roll our long scroll map out on the ground to check our progress. By the end of the adventure, we both were so tired and hungry that we inhaled hamburgers and ice cream sandwiches, then crashed on park benches while we waited for our friend Jesse to pick us up. I elevated my feet, propping them on the arm of my bench, and chuckled to myself thinking of Miles, who has since become an avid hiker, at age three, when Ellen and I took him for a short hike in a local park. He loved it, but after a mile or so, he announced, "I need to take a break. My shoes are tired." I craned my neck to tell Jo, over on her bench, but her eyes were closed. If she wasn't asleep, she would be before Jesse arrived. Over the next several weeks, I repeated the walk with my friend Melissa, then a third time with my brother Jerry and my elder son, Kita, and a fourth with my friend Nancy, forging slightly different routes each time.

After our Scotts Valley–to–Los Gatos hike, Jo and I took a walk of roughly the same distance from Aptos, a town of small beach communities and old-growth redwoods about midway between the cities of Santa Cruz and Watsonville, to Moss Landing, a historic fishing village in

Monterey County with an active harbor where otters and sea lions can be spotted frolicking among the boats. We walked along the beach the entire way, crossing the mouth of the Pajaro River where the water was hip high, necessitating that we hold our day packs over our heads and step carefully through the rushing current.

Now I steep in the tub, mulling my new strategy to incorporate walking more consistently into my everyday life. As the idea develops, so do the objectives around which a detailed project begins to take shape, emerging from the bathtub steam like a friendly apparition. The thought comes to me that I could photograph something beautiful on every street. I know nothing about photography, and I haven't given much thought to what might qualify as beauty, but I know that just as I crave more physical activity in my daily life, I also crave more beauty, a need more desperate than profound. Without consciously doing so, I've added a new dimension to what I'd thought would be simply a physical pursuit.

I craft a tidy plan for organizing my walks. I make a list of what I expect to take with me on each trek and what I will need to keep track of my adventures—the notebooks, the running shoes, the maps, the spreadsheets, the photo albums. And all goes as planned during my first several walks. Within the first ten days of my adventure, I explore fifty suburban streets in Santa Cruz, a city of sixty thousand people on the Pacific Ocean about seventy miles south of San Francisco, including many I've never heard of before. Already familiar roads are made fresh as I visually scour my surroundings, taking in gardens and paying attention to architectural details I have never noticed. A towering heritage tree here, a whimsical chicken coop there. Crumbling headstones and overgrown railroad tracks. Then, over the course of 2,878.51 miles, something unexpected and transformative happens. Walking becomes an antidote to a long-standing sense of disconnection from my early life, helping me to remember and reconstitute the past enough to gain a fuller perspective, while photography becomes a nepenthe, soothing past heartaches and patching the resulting holes with resplendent beauty.

IN MANY WAYS, I already know Santa Cruz well. I've lived in the county since 1979, and I've worked many jobs over that time. I delivered newspapers (back when people wanted "the paper" in physical form); scooped ice cream for a local company; sold natural-fiber children's clothes in one retail store, previously owned children's toys, clothes, and books in another, and "women's" apparel in a third; packaged textiles for an import/export company run out of a tiny run-down garage; cleaned houses; took care of children in day care centers, preschools, and private homes; provided sign language interpretation for grade school kids; and ultimately became a social worker, a career I would maintain for thirty years.

I've been a recipient of social services, such as Aid to Families with Dependent Children (AFDC)—what people call "welfare"; Women, Infants, and Children (WIC), a supplemental nutrition program; the state's Medi-Cal health insurance program; food stamps; and employment training programs. Later, in one of the social services agencies from which I had once received assistance, I worked as a frontline social worker, a supervisor, and finally a manager in the field of child welfare. I've developed a tight-knit group of longtime friends, and my sons were both born and raised in Santa Cruz. With each of them and their schools and activities, my social network expanded further until it was unusual for me to even go to the grocery store without stopping to chat with people I knew.

For reasons I can scarcely imagine now, I was tentative and embarrassed about telling my friends and colleagues about my plan to walk the length of every street in the county. As excited as I was to get started, I feared that it might seem odd, frivolous, or self-indulgent. At the time, I'd never heard of anyone organizing walks so systematically. But as soon as I started, people began telling me about a man who had walked every street in New York, and another who walked every street in San Francisco. Over the years since, especially during the COVID pandemic, I've heard of others. Each time, I feel a kinship.

It helped that Ellen, Kita, and Miles were all fully on board. When I told my friend Jesse about it, Jesse's response was "I wish I'd thought of that!" Other family and longtime friends were similarly supportive. Their encouragement gave me plenty of fortification against some of the less favorable responses I received, such as "Why in the world would you do that?" "Isn't that a bit extreme?" and "Is this work related? Are you going to be paid for your time?"

One coworker told me that I should steer clear of the mountain areas because "there's nothing but trees up there. You'll be bored out of your mind!" A common response was "Are you going to listen to books on tape as you walk?" Another was "Won't you be scared, walking alone?" (To no one's surprise, this question is often asked by women and accompanied by cautionary tales of women being attacked while walking in the woods alone and predawn assaults in otherwise perfectly "good" neighborhoods. It's well meaning and well founded, but also heartbreaking and infuriating.)

But with all due caution, I start walking. I branch out into areas I've never explored, some of them mere blocks from home. Training myself to pay close attention with all my senses, I begin to notice what's around me—and I find myself smiling at the unforeseen. Creative homemade mailboxes, for example. An octopus, a fire engine, a lighthouse, a giant chicken. I appreciate the objects themselves, but I also begin to sense the longing behind the creations, the reach for beauty or lightness or maybe just someone's internal landscape demanding to be turned inside out and made visible. What I'm seeing tugs at a long-standing wish I have for more creative expression in my own life.

Each place of worship I pass leaves me feeling less defensive and more pleasantly pensive than they once did, given past negative experiences with organized religion. And eventually, making my way around new neighborhoods, if I come across someone who greets me, I stop and talk to them, sometimes for several minutes.

Step by step, block by block, my understanding of my community begins to expand. On Swift Street—a neighborhood of breweries, surf shops, single-family homes, a Head Start program, and a grade school—I come across a woman getting out of a pickup truck with a flat package wrapped in butcher paper. She looks positively glowing.

"Something fun?" I ask as I walk past, nodding toward the package.

She beams. "My first time selling one of my paintings!"

The exchange is brief, but it sticks with me. I've just witnessed a hope realized, perhaps the start of something life-changing.

I'm in the middle of something life-changing myself, although it takes me a while to fully realize it. Walking begins to shake loose new thoughts, untapped dreams, and unattended memories. After decades of rarely remembering my dreams, I wake up regularly with detailed recollections of the previous night's images.

Triggered by something I see or hear or feel during a walk, I begin to remember stray details from childhood: a little perfume-filled brooch in the shape of a skunk that my friend Julie's mother, a beautician and Avon lady, gave me when I was heartbroken that my older sisters got to go to a birthday party at the skating rink and I wasn't invited. Or more troubling memories, such as the sound of shoes scuffing hardwood as you might hear in the echoes of a gymnasium—only it was my mother's feet, and mine or one of my siblings', struggling to get away from her. During scuffles she often stationed herself at the top of the stairwell and occasionally managed to shove one of us down it, unheeding of the poster pressed haphazardly with thumbtacks into the wall above the landing that proclaimed "War is not healthy for children and other living things."

Memories first come in staccato fits and starts, but soon they begin to pour like spilled glitter. Seeing geraniums planted in someone's garden as I walk a side street in my neighborhood, I recall that when we were young, Kevin, the fourth born of our sibling group of eight, used to insist that geraniums smelled like caterpillars. This tiny detail brings to life that seven-year-old boy, three years older than me, with his close-cropped dark hair coming to a point in a widow's peak at his forehead. For a split second the memory feels less like a foggy image that I'm trying desperately to pin down and trap under glass, and more like a real-time moment when heat radiates off the stucco wall of the house where the geraniums grow around the gray metal of the 1960s electricity meter. I feel the warmth of the sun and I smell . . . caterpillars. Kevin's childhood earnestness, his very essence, is fleetingly palpable, then gone.

It's remembering, and something more than just remembering.

I start making connections, some painfully obvious in retrospect, between my early life and some of the struggles I carried with me into adulthood. I begin to realize that I've been living with a bottleneck, a clot in my emotional arteries, for so long that I haven't noticed the subtle hiss of lost oxygen. I'm not unhappy. I've had the good fortune of being surrounded by fun, intelligent, loving people throughout my adult life. But I begin to see that my tendency to strong-arm my emotions and wrangle them into submission, rather than deal with them head on—rather than feeling them—has had consequences. I have worked so hard over the course of my adult life to separate myself from my past that I feel amputated from my roots.

At age thirty-eight, I met Ellen and fell madly in love. I sensed she felt the same way. During our first few months together I thought she had an eating disorder. We'd go out to eat and she'd take two or three bites of her food, then push her plate aside. Finally, after several dates, I gingerly broached the subject of her eating habits and she laughed out loud and said: "My appetite is huge. You just distract me from my food!" Twenty-seven years and several thousand shared meals later, it still makes me chuckle to think that I could ever have been concerned about her caloric intake. She is the best person to cook for.

As our relationship evolved, there was quickly a solidity to our connection that felt like a shared taproot. Sometimes I was able to sink into it and trust my senses. Other times, I'd panic to find myself relaxing into what looked increasingly like the long-term relationship that I both longed for and feared, and I'd subconsciously find ways to sabotage and push her away. Ellen would stand by while I spun out and, without engaging my anxiety, wear a loving look that, to me, read "Whenever you're done spinning, I'm here just waiting for you."

On our ten-year anniversary, we married before our

friends and family when gay marriage was not yet legal. Ellen's father walked us both down the aisle. We married again, when it became legal, at our county government center and were among the first gay couples in Santa Cruz County to be legally married.

FROM A YOUNG AGE I strived to be tough, to not need anyone or anything. Though my edges have softened considerably over the years as a parent, a partner, and an employee, it wasn't until I had these long stretches of silence while walking that I sensed the last vestiges of that identity sloughing off, leaving me simultaneously uncomfortably exposed and pleasantly expectant.

Until now, admitting to any need made me feel needy, exposed. I always counted my tenacious self-reliance as a strength, my best-developed emotional muscle. There's always been plenty of tacit mutual care and support in my relationship with Ellen, but we had been together for seventeen years before I ever asked her to bring me a glass of water. I was flat on the couch recovering from shoulder surgery. The words came out strained because they signaled a level of vulnerability that left me queasy.

My deeply ingrained assumption was that the less I relied on others, the more readily I could manage when life crumbled around me—as it had in the past and as I feared it would again. In hindsight I can see that this mindset, this defensive outlook, stunted my emotional growth. It prevented me from fully developing the give-and-take I need to sustain healthy personal relationships. I understand now that I don't get any extra points in life for appearing to have no needs, no gold stars for holding people at arm's length, no shortcuts to heaven for storing my tears on the inside, away from prying eyes.

ONE OF THE first significant indicators that my walking is turning into something more than I bargained for emotionally is when Ellen points out several weeks into the project that I'm crying more than she's seen me cry throughout all our years together to that point.

My initial reaction to this observation is defensiveness. I'm not a crier. My very fiber is designed to repel neediness, weakness, and vulnerability. But Ellen is right. And those are only the tears she witnesses during our time together, when I cry over a poignant video of a dog being reunited with its long-lost owner or I tear up when a friend serves us massive bowls of chicken soup with egg-size matzo balls. It's just so kind. So warm.

ALONE ON MY ADVENTURES, I leave dewdrops of grief and amazement at any number of sites. A walk in Scotts Valley, a city in the mountains north of Santa Cruz, brings me through a large open meadow where I sit on a pad of poured concrete that was once the doorstep to a miniature house at Santa's Village, an amusement park my family once visited when I was very young, which fell into disrepair in the '80s and stood abandoned for years until it was torn down to make room for housing. Now only a few relics of the original park remain, and there are large signs posted indicating that construction will be underway soon.

As I sit on the abandoned doorstep, I remember the gigantic painted-concrete mushrooms that dotted the park, which my brothers, sisters, and I climbed on and slid down. With little warning, I have a surge of sadness and I miss my siblings terribly. The wind goes out of me in the same way it did when I was nine and thought if I launched off my top bunk with a pogo stick in our house in Fremont—a small city in California's East Bay where my family moved from Oakland shortly before I was born—I'd be able to jump unbelievably high. I stuck the landing, but then I took the full force of the upward thrust of the handlebars under my ribs and fell to the floor in pain and shock. I crawled from my downstairs bedroom to the base of the stairs leading to the upper floor, gasping for help. Some now-blurred combination of siblings who'd been watching television upstairs came to the rescue and had me sit on the steps and put my head between my knees until the pain ebbed and I could breathe normally.

On the concrete slab, as memories of Santa's Village swirl around me, I gasp out my siblings' names and cry unabashedly until I hear behind me a couple and their dog wandering through this Christmas wasteland. Sobbing, I pull myself together and extend a greeting to them, hoping they didn't hear me.

IN HIS BOOK *The Body Keeps the Score*, Bessel van der Kolk, MD, explores the ways our brain's neuroplasticity can be put to work to "palliate or even reverse the damage [caused by trauma] to help survivors feel fully alive in the present and move on with their lives." He describes several approaches, such as talk therapy and medication. The one that strikes a particular chord in me is "allowing the body to have experiences that deeply and viscerally contradict the helplessness, rage, or collapse that result from trauma."

For me, the experiences van der Kolk refers to take the shape of long, strenuous walks, close observation of the natural world, and hours and hours of silence and introspection. As a result of these walks, I am more settled and comfortable in my body, more emotionally integrated, and more content and joyful than I have ever been over the course of my life.

This project is a braided journey: a project of the body and an accidental pilgrimage of the mind, leading me to rediscover wonder and reframe the fragmented recollections from my early years into a cohesive whole-life story. It's an object lesson in holding past, present, and future in their delicate balance. It is a school.

My quaquaversal rambles take place in a state of mind that feels untethered from time. Concepts that to me were once just words attached to hokey meanings—timelessness, immersion, oneness, communion—have become profound, urgent, almost tangible. More and more I reach for language to describe the experiences—the walks and all of the unfolding lessons within them—and the words hover just out of reach. This book is my effort at translation.

Fleshing out my own story becomes the catalyst for reconnecting with my siblings, the three brothers and four sisters I grew up with. As I've pieced my own memories back together, I've begun to wonder how they have each made sense of our family. I nervously ask each of them if I can interview them individually about their childhood. To my surprise they all agree. With each phone call I gain a more complete and more heartbreaking understanding of the long-term impacts of our childhood and my parents' actions and inactions. I also get nourishing infusions of their candor, humor, fortitude, and intelligence in ways that I've never fully experienced before.

In addition to meeting with each of my siblings individually, we begin to meet as a group via video conferences. During the initial call, we realize it's the first time in twenty years that all eight of us have been in the same *place* at the same time. Each time we meet, I read aloud a chapter of the manuscript of this book and we discuss the thoughts and memories it evokes in us. Chapter by chapter, sentence by sentence, we slog through the muck of a dysfunctional family and meet each other with peals of knowing laughter, tears of relief at the chance to speak what has been left unspoken for too long, and even random rowdy outbursts of song. It is a wonder to hear the eight sides of our collective truth and to begin to decipher the road maps of our respective lives, revisiting where we've intersected or run parallel for a time and where we've diverged. And we celebrate this reconvergence.

Chapter 2

Pieces of Eight

---

welkin *noun* \\'welkən\\: the vault of the sky:
firmament

Fɪʀsᴛ ᴀ ʙɪᴛ ᴏꜰ ɢᴇᴏɢʀᴀᴘʜʏ. If you look at a map of the United States, California is the slightly bent arm along the Pacific Ocean, and Santa Cruz County is just below the outer elbow. Nearly its entire length runs between the Santa Cruz Mountains, with their towering coastal redwood trees, and the Pacific. The county covers roughly 445 square miles of land, or 607 square miles if you get out in a kayak and explore the areas covered by salt water.

When I begin to plan my walks, I am surprised to learn that the Santa Cruz Public Works Department can't provide me with a precise number of streets within the county, but I quickly understand why. With old roads falling out of use and new ones being built, the number is dynamic—it's a moving target. When I collect the maps I use to organize my walking, I see roads indicated that were planned but never developed. And there are roads I've walked on that I can't locate on a map. There are trails that are called roads, and roads that are called trails, such as Ohlone Trail. So at the outset of the project I have only a guess gleaned by counting the streets listed in the street name indexes of various maps. By the time I walk the last road of my project, seven years after I started, Silver Mountain Road, home of the Silver Mountain Vineyards, in 2020, I, of course, have a much clearer count: 4,121.

Nearly half of the roughly 270,000 residents of Santa Cruz County live within four incorporated cities that, combined, cover only 24.1 square miles and include a total of 1,295 streets. Capitola is the smallest city at 1.6 square miles with 118 streets. Scotts Valley covers 4.6 miles and has 212 streets. Watsonville is the second largest with 411 streets in 5.9 square miles, while the city of Santa Cruz, the county seat, is 12 square miles with 554 streets. The remaining residents live in the unincorporated areas of Santa Cruz County, which, combined, cover 299 square miles and include 2,825 streets and roads.

The San Lorenzo River, the largest watershed fully within the county, originates in Castle Rock State Park, in the highest reaches of the county at twenty-five hundred feet above sea level, and travels through rugged mountains, suburban neighborhoods, and several small to midsize towns before it runs brackish where it blends into Monterey Bay, at the river mouth along the Ferris wheel end of the Santa Cruz Beach Boardwalk. A portion of the thirty-mile-long Pajaro River, which snakes through three additional counties, runs through Watsonville. There are ten major watersheds within the county, more than two hundred named creeks, and numerous unnamed creeks.

In the course of a day walking through the county, I can move through stretches of dry chapparal rooted in sandy soil that bring to mind the old westerns that were sometimes on TV after school as a kid, moist forests teeming with life, shady oak groves dropping acorns, rolling hills, steep cliffs buffeted by ocean breezes, and a range of neighborhoods.

The inaugural walk of the project, on December 8, 2013, a pleasantly cool Sunday afternoon, is only a mile long. All the same, it holds significance.

I ask Ellen and Miles to join me in walking our own three-block street and two of its side streets, and they agree. We set out from our house, Miles on his skateboard holding Izzie's leash, sometimes walking her and sometimes being eagerly pulled by her, and Ellen beside me, holding my hand. Ultimately, I'll take most of the walks solo, but having them with me to mark the beginning of what will become an epic adventure sets the tone perfectly.

At the time of the first walk, Ellen and I have been together for fifteen years. Miles is thirteen, and Kita, who was fourteen when we first got together, is now twenty-nine and has long since been on his own, living and working in Santa Cruz. Ellen and I were both nearing forty when we met, and early in our relationship we realized that if we wanted to have a child together, time was of the essence. Ellen had never so much as changed a diaper, but she wanted to be a parent and approached it as she approaches everything she commits to, with gusto, dedication, and uncommonly detailed planning. Once we agreed to have a baby, she put a down payment on a house, swapped her sportier car for a Subaru Outback, and practically memorized the book *What to Expect When You're Expecting*. At each prenatal visit, she asked the doctor a long list of questions and wrote notes in the margins throughout every appointment. We had a darling six-pound, seven-ounce baby boy, whom we named Miles, in our arms before we celebrated our second anniversary. We were both so excited to have a baby in our lives that we often got ourselves jammed up in the doorway to his room, trying to be the first to get to him when he woke up from a nap.

OVER THE WEEKS following the first walk, I squeeze as many additional walks as I can into the short winter days, before and after work and on the weekends. I wander around our neighborhood and fan out into adjacent areas. I walk along the streets themselves, but I also trek through adjacent alleyways, campgrounds, parks, and beaches. This gives me some material to work with as I start practicing using my spreadsheets and figuring out how to keep track of the walks and the photographs I take as I go. In addition to writing in notebooks a few details of what I see and experience on the walks, I keep a spreadsheet into which I enter information after each outing. While I'm putting together this spreadsheet, I'm also learning how to process, store, and organize my photographs electronically. The learning curve on that is equally steep. I purchase archival quality photo albums with black pages, and white pens to write the street name below a photo for each street, which I affix onto the albums' pages with old-fashioned photo corners.

Just weeks into the project, I close the front door behind me and step out into the predawn morning. I try to carve more hours into the day by slipping out before the world is awake. I am ostensibly making my way to work, roughly six miles to the south, but somehow, I'm walking in precisely the opposite direction. Since I've begun these walks, I've discovered an irresistible vantage point from which to see the day begin: a clifftop above Natural Bridges State Beach.

I walk-race the half mile and arrive in the still-dark. Settling into a patch of ice plant, I gulp first light and sea air greedily, like a drink of water after thirst. Waiting for the sun, I resist the urge to lift my hands and conduct its rising. Instead, I sit quietly and observe the world around this place, which comes to life slowly, deliberately: in shifting clouds that rearrange brilliant rays as the light curves over the horizon and spills buckets of color across the sky. It astounds me that before these walks I had never given much notice to the sun or the moon, nor felt their welkin masterpieces etching my eyes.

The beauty is too much to bear alone. I want to call a friend. But it dawns on me that they have all likely already noticed that the sun rises and sets. I save myself the awkwardness of rousing someone from a dead sleep to say, "Um, hi. The sun rose again!"

Instead, I pry myself away and start my walk to work

along West Cliff Drive, a three-and-a-half-mile road with an adjacent walking and cycling path that hugs the coastline. A relaxed pace should put me at my desk—with its incessantly ringing phone and overflowing inbox—in roughly two hours.

I look to the shoreline below and spot dozens of sanderlings, moving as a single organism, charging brazenly toward the incoming waves to snatch up sand crabs, small fossorial crustaceans, then retreating on comically fast-moving tiny legs before the waves catch them. They are well tuned to each other and to this ritual: It's how they survive, and it's amazing to see how efficiently they work.

A curve of the road delivers me to one of Santa Cruz's most famous surf spots, Steamer Lane. I watch the action of the few surfers who've already tossed their boards into the chilly water and are now at its mercy, bobbing at the rise and fall as they wait for a good ride. A bird lights on a fence post, the night sky painted in stars and hearts across its licorice breast. I fall under the spell of the starling as the morning sun strikes just so, sending the full spectrum of color cascading down his feathers like liquid, head to tail. I admire him until he lifts off into the air, reminding me that I, too, should be on my way.

West Cliff Drive draws locals and visitors alike to the cliff edges to mingle or amble or sink into a wooden bench and gaze at nature manifest in the mesmerizing repetition of waves. It's said that Steamer Lane got its name from a surfer, Claude Horan, who, in the 1930s, appreciating the wake created by passing steamships, entertained the idea of hiring steamers to cruise back and forth along the "steamer lane" to generate more waves for surfing. I get lost in thought for a few moments, pondering the power of naming. This surfer made what I imagine was an off-the-cuff comment, and the resulting name is a household word for thousands of people almost a century later. The name far outlived the man.

When I was seventeen, I found and adopted an abandoned kitten and called him Kintar. Six years later, I named my first son Kita. Both were names I made up, but it was only many years later that I registered that my cat's name included the word *kin* and that the name Kintar also contained the name Kita. Well after I named him, I learned that *kita* is also a Japanese word that means "north." I named him before he was born, and I have to wonder if he took his name literally. He was born breech, heading north.

I try to imagine my parents choosing a name for me. They landed on Angelica Felice, which translates to Happy Angel. Were they expressing a wish for me? Did they have a hunch? Did they name me for someone they knew? Which of them suggested the name? The answers are lost to history. I never thought to ask my parents before they died and they never mentioned their reasons.

My eldest brother, Jerry, didn't start out with his current name. He was a junior, named for our father, Frederick. He chose a new name for himself in sixth grade, smack in the middle of the '60s: Jeremiah, which he later shortened to Jerry before one more person was compelled to sing to him the Jeremiah lyric from the Three Dog Night song

"Joy to the World." Though, truth be told, that doesn't stop his siblings, to this day, from belting it out from time to time when we're with him.

Debbie, my eldest sister, was given my mother's middle name, Jean. Of the additional children, only Edie, the fifth born, was named for someone. Our maternal great-grandmother was Edith. Our list of names isn't conducive to a smooth mnemonic, but when we were young, we'd compete to see who could say our names the fastest, youngest to oldest, until it became a single utterance of "MargaretJohnAngelEdieKevinCathyDebbieJerry." To the outside world, we were often referred to as a group: the Glass kids, the Glass menagerie, the troops, the brood.

With our long, unruly hair, bare feet, filthy house, and constant fighting, we were out of place in the middle-class neighborhood in Fremont we moved into when I was six. On a continuum of television families from the Brady Bunch to the Gallaghers in *Shameless*, we fell roughly between the Addams Family and the Gallaghers, somewhere between odd and unhinged. My father worked as an assistant to an electrician. My mother took occasional part-time work as a nurse's assistant, a substitute teacher, and an assembly line worker at a plastics factory. Mostly she stayed home with the brood.

MY PARENTS MET in high school in the city of Alameda, which, like Fremont, where I grew up, is in Alameda County. Shortly after graduation, they married and started a family. They lived together for over twenty years, and during the thirteen years that I lived with both of them, I don't recall once seeing them express affection for each other. Not a hug or a kiss or a hold of the hand. I can scarcely conjure any memory of them even talking to each other. They clearly had some sort of relationship, as they had two more children after me. But there was an unbridgeable abysm between them that I and my siblings witnessed growing up. They did share one trait: If my father, who blew up only occasionally, had an anger management problem, my mother could be better described as having a fury problem.

FROM LIGHTHOUSE POINT, the cliff where surfers jump in at Steamer Lane, a short meander reveals a classic swath of Santa Cruz, including the municipal wharf, both of our local lighthouses, the Santa Cruz Beach Boardwalk, and the famous "Surfer Guy" statue, an important fixture on West Cliff, particularly when he dresses for the occasion: Each Halloween someone puts a jack-o'-lantern over his head; at Christmas, he wears a red Santa hat; the day of the Women's March in Santa Cruz, he donned a "pussy hat"; during the COVID crisis, he sometimes wore a face mask, with a bottle of hand sanitizer at his feet; and while the devastating fires burned thousands of acres in Santa Cruz County in 2020, he was dressed in full firefighting regalia replete with a badge reading "Hot Stuff."

THIS AREA, rich in surfing history and local pride, is the site of the O'Neill Cold Water Classic, which started in 1985 and is now the longest-running North American surf contest. Modern wetsuits were developed by Jack O'Neill, a longtime Santa Cruz resident and surfer, and Pat O'Neill, his son, is credited with inventing the surfboard leash.

One of the largest bird migrations of the northern hemisphere, that of the sooty shearwater, can be witnessed right from the sidewalk along the beach. By itself a single sooty shearwater is a small, unassuming bird, dark in color, with lighter underwings. Bigger than a common blackbird, smaller than a bread box. When they collect as a flock, they form what looks like a near-solid wall of moving animation, skimming just above the water in a massive figure eight that can be seen through the northern and southern hemispheres. They can fly as much as forty thousand miles in a year.

It was the sooty shearwater that inspired Alfred Hitchcock, who owned a home in Scotts Valley, to include Santa Cruz in the 1963 movie he directed, *The Birds*. Local legend goes that a dense fog fell over the sea during the migration, setting the birds off course. This caused an avian catastrophe as birds crashed into buildings and died in untold numbers. The *Santa Cruz Sentinel* printed the story in August of 1961 and it captured Hitchcock's imagination. And the rest—a generation of ornithophobes to rival the galeophobes born of the movie *Jaws*—is history.

From this spot, just blocks from home, I can observe otters floating on their backs, each with a large rock stationed on its chest, and listen to the *crack crack* as they break shells against their stones, which they keep in a loose fold of skin on their forearms, like a pocket. This frees up their paws while they dive to hunt for food and swim back to the surface with it. I've sat on benches along the cliffs, eating lunch or checking work emails, to look up and see a humpback whale spouting or breaching, or a pod of dolphins performing a synchronized leap and dive.

The atmosphere is tinted orange today. This shade of morning sky, which I've heard surfers call *orange crush*, makes me feel as if I'm swimming through a substance thicker than air. The temptation to walk in slow motion is strong.

As kids in Fremont, my best friend, Melinda, and I invented different walks as we made our way through Montgomery Ward or Mervyn's department stores. We would take turns announcing the walk, then move through the store, or a field, or an orchard, or wherever we were. One of our favorites was "the Ostrich," which required us to pull our heads way back while one leg moved in a huge arc forward, then stretch out our necks dramatically and thrust our heads forward as the other leg started its arc. The annoyance of those around us—including our families—only fueled our delight. Every now and then, out on my walks, when there's no one in sight, I allow myself a moon step or an ostrich walk, or I swim my arms, slow motion, through the tinted morning air. It's a nod to a friendship that made my early life more bearable.

I venture among some of the city side streets just inland of the cliff and spot a street sign I've never noticed. I say the name aloud, Via Riva Trigoso, and repeat it. The words feel important somehow, rife with meaning. Geoffrey Dunn, a local historian, recounts the story of Cottardo Peter Stagnaro in his book, *Santa Cruz Is in the Heart*. Stagnaro was a young seaman from Riva Trigoso, Italy. He jumped ship in 1874 while docked in Santa Cruz. Over the following years, he slowly brought one family member after another to Santa Cruz, creating an expansive community focused around the Santa Cruz Municipal Wharf, the longest timber pile wharf along the US coastline, where an impressive fish market still stands. I wend my way to the wharf and walk its half-mile length out over Monterey Bay.

I can't count the bowls of clam chowder I've ordered at this open-air fish market and enjoyed on a bench overlooking sailboats, sea kayakers, surfers, and paddlers, with my jacket zipped to my chin against the ocean breeze. Nor the number of times I have stood at the deck openings at the end of the wharf to watch the sea lions that park themselves on the wooden planks between the pilings below. I've stood there with my sons, nieces, nephews, and godchildren, pointing out starfish clinging to the pilings, admiring the fishermen, and cheering for seagull fledglings testing new wings.

Santa Cruz has been my home since I was eighteen, and standing at the end of the wharf, I am reminded that it's been a part of me since even earlier in my life. I'm flooded with memories of being here with my parents and my siblings. I remember the times my father would pay the man at the bait shop a quarter for a paper cup full of small fish, which we'd toss down to the sea lions. We'd laugh at how quickly they'd gobble up the fish and how dejected they looked when we ran out.

I look across the water to the Santa Cruz Beach Boardwalk, and vivid memories wash over me of riding in the back seat of our red Volkswagen van down what I now know to be Ocean Street and listening to my older siblings excitedly point out the big roller coaster on the far side of the river levee.

I recall the sensation of being a small child trying to identify a specific detail within a visually overstimulating landscape and having my brother Kevin, the fourth born, place his hand on top of my head and turn it in the direction of the Giant Dipper, the oldest wooden roller coaster in California, a fixture at the boardwalk since 1924.

My limited and likely selective memory has always held me back from talking in depth about my upbringing or even thinking about it fully. I've never felt like a person with a cohesive story; I feel more like a waif with a box of fragments that I cannot piece together. My siblings, I've learned as an adult, have the same experience.

But as I've aged and begun these walks, I find myself tumbling the past in its own coarse grit and find that memory is only one factor preventing me from articulating my story. Another boils down to a dichotomy as powerful as it is simple: Focusing on the good stuff makes me feel as if I'm disregarding the bad, ignoring or minimizing the ways that my siblings and I were hurt by our parents. Focusing on the bad makes me worry that I'm betraying them, dismissing their efforts, not recognizing their struggles or the historical context within which they were raised and developed their respective idiosyncrasies. The two strain against each other like twin ends of a drawstring cinched tight across my larynx.

Before the walks, I wasn't able to fully tell the story, even to myself, of a mother who was rageful, violent, and profoundly depressed, but who also attended as many back-to-school nights as she could manage, took us to the library, and oversaw as many of the small moments she could, such as stringing popcorn and cranberries for Christmas tree garlands and pressing cloves into oranges to fill the house with a distinctive smell.

My mother was a fighter in two senses of the word. She had the disposition and the propensity to fight physically—and she did, regularly, especially with her own children. But she also had the determination and courage to speak up for her beliefs and to advocate for what she needed.

Being a fighter came with risks and opportunities. For example, when I was around twelve, I overheard a series of telephone conversations that she had with a social worker from Crippled Children's Services, a state program later renamed California Children's Services.

The agency had agreed to cover the cost of orthodontia for one child in our family, while my parents would be responsible for any additional orthodontia. But for my mother that wasn't enough. She was relentless. I suspect that she just eventually wore them down because the agency ultimately agreed to provide free braces for two of her children. I was one of the recipients. I don't know how she determined which of us would get the free braces. (I suspect it was based on the condition of our teeth.) Besides a surgery to repair receding gums when I was twelve, I don't have any recollection of what shape my teeth were in or of feeling bad about them.

I did need extensive dental work as a young adult that was partially covered by Medi-Cal, and I continue to have complications, but the braces my mother fought for allowed me to go through life with straight teeth, a luxury that some of my siblings didn't have. Most of the Glass children have dental problems as adults. About half have full dentures or missing teeth. So far, I have all my original teeth, though almost every one of them has required work. Even with stringent daily dental hygiene, they seem to be set in increasingly shifting soil, but they still look more or less straight after all these years.

When the Head Start program started in the mid-'60s, my mother signed up those of her children who met the age criterion. She also signed many of us up for Girl and Boy Scouts and negotiated fee waivers and scholarships for dues and activities.

I believe I have uncovered a memory from before I had language. I was being bathed in the tub. Someone had me lean my head back under the running faucet. I got shampoo in my eyes and panicked at the sting of it. Someone put a towel on my face and helped me wipe my eyes dry. Someone was right there, recognizing my need and prepared to help me. I have no memory of a voice or appearance, just the relief from pain and the secure feeling of having someone understand that I needed help and responding instantly. It was likely my mother. When I talk to my sister Cathy about it, she points out that it was just as likely that it was her or Debbie, who would have been six and eight at the time and were expected to help with the younger kids. I clearly remember all of us girls taking care of Margaret, but it had never dawned on me that they had also helped care for me.

At my core, I feel both like the small child to whom a dry towel was proffered at my first whimper and like the girl whose mother shoved her head into the dining room cupboard for getting in the way of her Christmas gift-wrapping efforts. For a split second the whole world narrowed to a bright white light in the shape of a jagged "kapow!" speech bubble in a comic book. My mother checked the damage, reassured me that the copious blood was due to the fact that there are a lot of blood vessels in the head, taped my forehead with green-and-red holly berry tape as if I were another of the packages she was wrapping, and sent me marching. I feel both an internal foundation of security that I don't believe I could have if I hadn't been taken care of as a young child, even if I don't vividly remember receiving that care, and a deeply felt sense of groundlessness and unsafety in the world.

Further complicating my desire to draw a timeline from early childhood to the present is the unreliability of memories. Memory is always distorted by one's perspective and by all that one has learned and heard from others in the intervening years. In what must be my earliest clear memory of my mother, a moment that has always felt like a smudged film frame in the background of my life but was only recently explored more fully, I was at Natural Bridges State Beach with my family. I was probably three years old. My mother and I were standing in the surf. She held both of my hands and jumped me over the tiny waves. Without warning, a larger wave came in and the world was suddenly upside down. The water pulled at me and roared in my ears. I couldn't breathe. I was spinning. Disoriented. Terrified. She still had one of my hands and she yanked me up. She looked blurry through the salt water in my eyes and my sputtering cough, but I could see she was laughing. I've always held it as a cruel laugh and wondered if she had deliberately let me go under.

Many years later, I was holding Miles on my hip and holding the hand of a friend's toddler as we played at the water's edge at Twin Lakes State Beach. I didn't notice that the swell coming toward us was getting a little bigger, and the incoming wave knocked over the toddler. I leaned down and swooped him up, but not before he was tumbled in the water like a towel in the washing machine. I laughed nervously as I reassured myself and him that he was OK and looked around for his mom.

I realize now that I might have misunderstood my mother's intentions and attitude in that situation all those years ago, and I've happily reclaimed this as a tender memory. It's a challenge to reconcile this recollection with my overall experience of her. But I have made the conscious decision to store it with my other good memories of her, tiny moments that were specific to me. The time she told me that I sounded like Precious Pupp, the cartoon dog I loved, when I snickered. That bowl of Froot Loops she made for me as a kindergartner.

For now, this handful of images constitute my positive memories of her.

Not all of my remaining memories of my mother are of her more horrendous moments. Most are simply neutral. There are several aspects of my personality that I attribute, at least in part, to her. My sense of humor, for example—she could be very funny with an unexpected quip. My convictions around human rights and dignity—my mother loudly and proudly supported people who might be perceived as underdogs or treated as "less than." My love of and protectiveness toward animals—such as the time my girlfriend and I rescued a dog that had been the victim of a hit-and-run car accident, rushed it to an emergency vet, and agreed, without due consideration, to take financial responsibility for the treatment if the dog's owner didn't show up. (We were grateful he did, thousands of dollars later!) And my mischievousness. But the trait I can most clearly trace back to her is my passion for singing.

Wherever we went we sang folk songs and union songs. We sang about our proud Irish heritage and about political strife. We knew church songs and love songs: "Sons of God," "Molly Malone" ("alive-a-live-o"), "The Skye Boat

Song." We used lively hand gestures to "Rise and Shine," the story of Noah's ark, and gave one resounding clap, twenty hands in unison, to "Dona, Dona," the tale of a calf being led to slaughter.

Singing allows us to travel in place, to dwell in the yearnings, passions, and heartaches of another, as if they were our own. It conveys history in the language of emotion. Songs are ghosts. They haunt us and hold us captive until we lend our breath to restore them to life.

Both of my parents sang. When she was a child, my mother attended Catholic summer camps sponsored by social service programs. This is where her passion for singing first ignited. My father sang with equal exuberance, sometimes soft-shoeing around the kitchen as he cooked, singing songs like "I'm Called Little Buttercup." They taught me by example that you don't need to be trained, you don't have to have a *good* voice, to feel your singing reverberate in your bones. It costs nothing and means everything.

If we were ever happy as a family, it was in these moments, spontaneously breaking into song as we sat in our living room, cramped in a vehicle full of camping gear, or gathered around a popping fire singing into the dark. My brothers and sisters and I cut our teeth on so many songs that over half a century later my wife, Ellen, frequently hears me singing a tune and asks, "Another one? Where did this one come from?" Often, I can't recall myself: The words and melodies lie dormant deep in my brain until they emerge as needed and prompt me into song—to myself or to a group, quietly under my breath or at full volume.

Neither of our parents was a big storyteller, besides in song, so we knew little about the specifics of their childhoods or upbringings. While we know that my mother grew up poor in Alameda, California, I suspect my father, who also lived in Alameda as a child, was better off, at least initially. According to a yellowing newspaper clipping from the 1940s found in my father's belongings after he died, my paternal grandfather worked for a paleontologist. He died while my father was still in elementary school, around twelve years old, and my grandmother didn't feel capable of caring for him, so she placed my father in an orphanage. Whether this was due to the sudden loss of income or something else is, like much of my family's story, lost to history. Whatever the case, she eventually retrieved him, but the experience scarred my father emotionally, and he carried remnants of those wounds throughout his life.

My mother's background is similarly unclear. The way she yelled in our faces things like "I'm going to tan your hide and tack it to the garage door!" and "I'm going to knock you into the middle of next week!" makes me wonder where her parents—the people I assume taught her such behaviors—came from. She stood five feet tall, plus an inch, but her physical stature did not minimize her effrontery: She was blunt, even caustic. I was eleven when I plucked a wiry hair that was sticking straight out of my forehead and held it up for my mother's inspection. She took a good look at it and then announced, "Yep! A misplaced pubic hair. They don't call you 'fuckhead' for nothin'!" Even when her barbs stung, I couldn't help but admire their originality.

Before I came along in the early 1960s, my family lived in a housing project in Alameda. Jerry—who like the rest of us has limited memory of childhood—does have a preverbal memory of sharing a very small windowless space—such as a closet or a pantry—as a bedroom with Debbie. In a rare exception to my mother's typical reluctance to talk about her past, she told me when I was in my thirties that an order of nuns regularly visited the units, wearing capelets from under which they would surreptitiously remove food items and leave them on the kitchen counter without a word. My mother took what she absolutely needed, then gave the rest to a neighbor, who was so poor that she regularly put her kids to bed in the afternoon and let them sleep as long as possible in the morning to conserve their energy and minimize the number of meals she had to provide each day.

I was delivered at Kaiser Hospital on MacArthur Boulevard in Oakland in 1961 and my parents brought me home to a small house on Jamestown Road in a little town listed on my birth certificate as Irvington, though it had long since been incorporated into the city of Fremont. My parents had a friend from the church we attended, St. Leonard's, who made a tidy sum in the clothing industry and wanted to move from working-class Irvington into a more affluent area. He offered to sell his home to my parents, who reflexively declined. Combined, they made an income that could have modestly supported a family with three or four children. With eight children, life was a struggle.

The church friend persisted, proposing that my parents purchase the home over time with payments they could afford on their limited income. His generosity launched my parents into homeownership—the only way they could have afforded it. Several years later, before I entered first grade, my parents sold the little flattop on Jamestown Road and we moved into a larger, two-story house that had an intercom system and a backyard with a swing set. We felt like mansion dwellers. When we moved in, we ran up and down the bare wood stairs, our laughter and cheers echoing through the new expanse. It was exhilarating to be in a big house in a nice neighborhood where the fathers worked at the nearby General Motors plant and the mothers were teachers or Girl Scout leaders or gave painting classes to neighborhood children out of their garages.

We discovered a dismantled soft-sided swimming pool in the back of the carport, left behind by the previous homeowner. My father put it together and built a small wooden deck around it. I loved being in the water. Even after the filter system broke, leaving soggy leaves and a layer of sediment, it was a luxury to be able to "swim" in your own backyard. Apparently, our baby sister, Margaret, liked water too. One day as a toddler she stepped off the deck and splashed into the pool. My little brother, John, eight years old, was close at hand. However, he had a brand-new pair of shoes on and was not about to spoil them. He sat down to take off his sneakers while my mother, not moving a muscle, yelled at him from the upstairs window to "get in that pool and get your sister!" John saved his sister and his shoes while my mother, Barbara, spared herself the effort of walking down the ten steps.

My mother had a menagerie of pets and readily obliged when one of us kids wanted to add to it. She had two giant tortoises; a chinchilla; a rat named Ratso (the older siblings insist his name was Rato); mice; rabbits, including a wild one that Edie and John caught in a nearby field with a simple homemade trap of a box and rope; a duck named Wilbur that John "rescued" from nearby Lake Elizabeth, though Margaret swears to this day that he was her duck; snakes; and lizards. We also had dogs and birds, and too many cats to keep track of, several of them giving birth to a litter here and there, in a dresser drawer left open too long or on top of stray laundry under someone's bed. If we counted kittens, there could easily be over a dozen cats in the house at any given time.

My mother once found a baby owl, fallen from its nest, and raised it in the garage. She loved animals more than people and reminded us of this frequently. "*Animals* can be trusted," she'd say. The implication was not lost on her children. She kept algae-clouded aquariums of guppies and black-and-white-striped loaches in the kitchen. They captivated her. She would coax them out of their hiding places behind rocks of black pumice or under the colorful gravel lining the bottom of the tank and catch them with a tiny green fishing net so she could admire them. Once, while trying to get a closer look, she dropped one of her loaches into a basket of potatoes that we stored below the aquarium. She rescued it deftly, moving more quickly and efficiently than I'd ever seen her before, removing dusty potatoes, one at a time, and inspecting them for the escaped fish before adding them to a mounting pile on the kitchen floor. When she finally reached the now-struggling animal, she picked it up with her hands and gingerly, as if she were rescuing a flailing child, placed it back in the water, cooing and reassuring between puffs of relief, her cheeks flushed red with concern.

Some neighborhood children were forbidden by their parents to come into the Glass home. One girl once told me that her mother said my siblings and I looked like urchins. It was clear she meant it as an insult. But I liked sea creatures.

Another told me that her parents described our house as a "filthy birdcage." All the same, everyone in the neighborhood knew that if a baby bird fell from its nest or if they had second thoughts about a guinea pig or hamster purchased from some shopping center, they could take it to Barbara Glass. I think now that people in our neighborhood were a little afraid of her, but when it came to rescuing animals, maybe they also had a little respect.

LYING ON THE couch watching *Donahue* one afternoon in the early 1970s when I was twelve, I heard my mother pull into the driveway in her two-tone blue Ford Pinto. She came through the front door and made her way up the stairs. She had been to the doctor and was so excited to announce her new diagnosis that she didn't wait for another adult or one of the older kids. She just blurted: "I'm a manic-depressive. I have to start taking lithium, effective immediately!" She seemed positively ecstatic about the news. Maybe having a name for the internal chaos she felt made it seem more manageable, or maybe she felt less alone in her struggles knowing that there was an authority who had decisively categorized her symptoms: lethargy, suicidality, grandiosity. I had no idea what a manic-depressive was or what lithium was, but they sounded important and like good news.

Several days later when I left for school, the upstairs bathroom was its usual white, with a houseplant in a basket on the floor. When I returned home that afternoon, my mother had painted the walls black and hung a fluorescent light, illuminating a neon poster of an enraptured couple, a man and woman in an intimate pose with the words "Light My Fire." If anyone else noticed or cared, I wasn't aware of it, but it lodged in me as a marker of changing times. I wasn't disturbed by it particularly. But something about it made me pause.

Lots of parents use the opportunity of driving alongside a police car or running into an officer in the community to socialize their children to law enforcement: "Say hello to the nice policeman," they might say. My mother had her own take. "Flip off the pig," she'd say, or "Give him the bird." We'd all dutifully turn in our seats and flip off any cop unfortunate enough to be driving behind us.

Over the course of my life, I've accumulated precisely two written items from my mother: One, a typewritten three-page letter signed simply *Barbara* from July 20, 1988, was specifically to me. The other was a list, titled "25 Things About Me," that she posted on social media when she was in her seventies. When I saw the list of twenty-five things, I read it with interest, dying to know if having children made the cut. We were there, item number seventeen, hovering somewhere between Robert Frost and her desire to go scuba diving. It wasn't a particularly flattering reference, but we were there: "17. I have eight children and 16 grandchildren." And Jerry got an additional mention: "21. My oldest son says I'm like a porcupine, looks cuddly, but don't rub it the wrong way."

I also had a cassette tape of an interview I did with her as a school project when I was a student at UCSC (University of California, Santa Cruz) more than thirty years ago. With memories now pouring out of me on my walks, I was eager to listen to it after having not heard it in many years. Rather than take Ellen's advice and wait to have someone transfer it from cassette to a more current audio format, I bought a cheap cassette player and sat smugly listening to my mother's voice brought back from the dead. I got about halfway through the recording before the tape broke.

Her one letter to me was in response to one I had sent her trying to broach the subject of "What the hell happened to our family?" Her response included a few nutshells—bombshells, really—of her understanding of her early childhood, like this one:

> "I was born four months after my teenage parents (16 & 19) got married. . . . My father left for

the next five years . . . I was "cared for" by my great-aunt "Midge" . . . cared for is in quotes . . . I was alone in a hotel room in San Francisco for eight hours a day, 6 days a week for the first two years of my life. It's not bad to cry, I suppose . . . but what if you cry and nobody comes . . . to this day, I can only show feelings if someone digs them out of me . . . and then, I rarely forgive the "digger."

I WAS TWENTY-SEVEN when I first read these words—the same age she was the year I was born. I'd crafted my letter to her carefully. I had worked hard to be as honest as I could be without being hurtful, and laid out the questions I had for her about our family and my childhood: Was she aware that my father had started drinking heavily after she left? Did she know that our father had poor physical boundaries? Did she realize that her emotional distance impacted her children? She barely responded to the issues I'd raised in my letter. Instead, her letter minimized the experiences I'd faced as a child and used her own childhood to explain away her challenging behaviors and her lack of insight into our father's issues.

At the time, her letter irritated me. I was only looking for what was *missing* in her response. But over the years, I revisited the letter from time to time and I began to see what *was* in the letter, what she was trying to communicate to me. I hadn't known that she was born to teen parents or that her great-aunt had helped raise her. But the part about not showing her feelings and not forgiving those who dug feelings out of her, I knew in my bones. I was raised on it.

THE FIRST ITEM on her "25 Things" list was about her love of California. Number two says, "Grew up a project brat, mean and hungry, clawed my way into college and the teaching profession when I was almost 40." Her father was an alcoholic who dropped out of family life for years at a stretch. Her mother had multiple men around the home, many of whom abused her and my mother, both sexually and physically. My mother suffered from malnutrition as a child and for the rest of her life had a complicated relationship with food and weight, perhaps accounting for the fact that she kept much of our family's food under lock and key and doled it out only when she chose to.

When I was a child, I often heard her boast loudly about not being able to participate in therapy because the therapists always "fired" her. I don't know how differently our lives might have gone—for her and for us—if she'd gotten help sooner. She made several suicide attempts over the course of my life, starting when most of my siblings were still in grade school, and eventually she ended her life in her late seventies due in part to mounting health complications.

After my parents married at seventeen and twenty—not as young as my mother's parents, but close—they moved from California to Saint Louis, Missouri, for two years, where my father was stationed in the army prior to being deployed to Korea. My mother was pregnant with her first child at twenty. She was twenty-seven when I was born, her sixth child. I supplanted number five, Edie, while she was still in diapers, and number seven, John, came along before I was out of diapers. Number eight, Margaret, trailed several years later.

ON MY WALKS, memories return in unexpected ways. I go back to the wooden pews in the two Catholic churches I attended as a child, St. Leonard and Santa Paula, both in Fremont, their armrests at either end and their seat backs polished by the oils of many human hands. I remember being amused by the stereo hiss of dozens of parishioners reciting Our Father, their *s*'s overlapping each other so the church echoed with "forgive ussss our tresspassessss assss we forgive thossssse who trespassss againsssst ussss," and the noisy transition back to sitting, hymnals closing with a barrage of snaps, and children and purses rearranged just so. In the 1960s, as a result of the changes brought by Vatican II, the Catholic Church loosened up on women having to cover their heads in church, though the language was not expressly changed until the 1983 Code of Canon Law came into effect. But required or not, my mother made squares of fabric edged with rickrack into headscarves for each of us girls. Folding them on the diagonal, she'd put them around our heads and tie them firmly under our chins. And the eight of us followed behind her into church like a row of ducklings, taking her cue to stop and cross ourselves with holy water before trailing her to the pews, where we knelt before taking our places beside her.

Given her devastating childhood, my mother made strong efforts to do what she thought a *good* parent should do. But most of her efforts fell flat in the face of her constant state of preemptive self-defense. She was perpetually braced for battle, and it took little to provoke her. Annoyance could blossom into rage and escalate into physical violence without warning. And she was not a fair fighter. She kicked and punched and slapped. She hit us with fly swatters, belts, brooms, anything she could get her hands on. She pushed and shoved and yelled in our faces. She once attempted to hit Debbie with the handle of a broom. She swung it so hard that when Debbie jumped out of the way, my mother couldn't stop the momentum in time to avoid injuring herself. This enraged her.

She had a special zeal for pulling hair and employed a specific technique she proudly described to anyone who would listen. "It's best on people with thick hair," she'd pronounce. Being the thickest-haired of the bunch, I would reflexively try to compress the spaces between my neck vertebrae whenever she got mad at me. "Spread your fingers like a big comb and jab them at the person's forehead so you can slide them through their hair at the roots, grab and twist, then yank straight up," she said. Each of us got a taste of the approach and no one could argue its effectiveness.

During the summer between fifth and sixth grades, I

asked my mother if I could spend the night at Melinda's house and she distractedly agreed. Melinda lived a few blocks closer to our school, Brier Elementary, than I did, and we knew that the following morning lists would be taped to the metal shutter slats of the windows of the street-facing classrooms indicating which kids would be in which teacher's class. We planned to go together the next day to see if we'd have the same teacher.

That night, without warning, my mother barged through the front door after Melinda's family had all gone to bed. Melinda and I were on the brown-and-orange-plaid couch watching TV in the otherwise dark living room with Schnappsy, her dachshund, at our feet. Without saying a word, my mother wedged herself between the coffee table and the couch, grabbed me by the hair, and dragged me to her idling Pinto. My feet flailed for solid ground as I tried to keep my head as close to her hand as possible to avoid the feeling that several thousand hair roots were being tugged from my scalp. She offered no explanation, no apology, no excuse.

My mother shoved me into the passenger seat and slammed the door. I had no idea what I'd done wrong until she pulled away from the curb and launched into a tirade about my unruly behavior. I didn't bother defending my-self. During the three-block drive from Melinda's house back home, the volume of her voice cranked higher and higher. From the rant, I gathered that after everyone had gone to bed, Edie woke up my mother to let her know that

I wasn't home. Everyone knew that if I wasn't home, Melinda's house was the first place to look for me.

THAT NIGHT MY scalp was screaming and my dignity was destroyed. She had managed to pull not only strands of my hair but also a tiny patch of scalp. But it was nothing compared to what had happened several weeks before when I, along with some of my siblings, witnessed a scary, noisy scuffle between my mother and a young man who stayed at our house sometimes, who, like my mother's live-in boyfriend, was not much older than my eldest brother. She pulled out a big handful of his hair, enough to draw blood, and he fled through the front door, leaving her staggering and breathless but holding up the clump of hair like a trophy.

Years later, I learned from older siblings that the man whose hair my mother had pulled was one of her sexual partners and she was in a jealous rage because he was also pursuing a relationship with my father.

My sister Cathy remembers the man fondly because before the fight on the stairs, she had been sick in bed for a few days with an elevated fever and our mother, though aware she was sick, wasn't tending to her. The man went downstairs, scooped Cathy from her bed, carried her up the stairs, and delivered her to our mother, who was lying on the living room couch. Our mother apparently felt pressured to finally take her to the emergency room, where Cathy was diagnosed with meningitis.

I REALIZE THAT I'm walking fast—too fast. My brain is roiling and my feet are trying to keep up. I take a long inhale, like a reset button, intentionally slow my steps, and try to absorb the sights and sounds around me. Delivery trucks on the pier are restocking stores and restaurants, workers are preparing the kayaks and boats that will be rented and lowered over the edge of the pier throughout the day, and the ceaseless cries of seagulls fill the air. A large flock of pigeons have settled on the wharf railings, and I catch a shot of them silhouetted black against the amber orb of the morning sun, still low in the sky. There's undoubtedly something I can do about the white balance in my camera to make the colors less stark and more reflective of the much subtler hues that my eyes perceive, but for the purposes of this image, the drama works. The pigeons hurry off as if they've remembered that they're late for an appointment, then immediately circle back and land in the same spot, where they kiss each other's beaks and mumble coos before making their rounds again.

At the end of the wharf, I descend the stairs to Main Beach, along which the Santa Cruz Beach Boardwalk runs parallel. I'm looking at it all with new eyes. I frequent the wharf regularly, but I rarely venture onto Main Beach, except when we have big storms with their promises of strange, washed-up treasures, and as the kids are grown, I no longer have occasion to visit the boardwalk.

As I walk the beach, breathing in the layered scents of seaweed and salt air, I'm inundated with memories I haven't thought about in decades. The dime toss where I could win mismatched cups and plates. The distorting mirrors in the fun house. The chocolate-dipped soft-serve ice cream cones Melinda and I had when we spent a day here in our late teens. Suddenly I must have one right now, but to my dismay the amusement park is closed.

I stop in my tracks as I approach the bandstand where free Friday evening beach concerts and movies take place in the summertime. Here's another connection to Santa Cruz that somehow feels monumentally more significant now, and it knocks the wind out of me. I realize that I'm standing in the area where my father died.

Shortly before I turned sixteen, about three years after my mother had moved out of our house with her boyfriend, I'd insisted that my father participate in a support program called Parents Without Partners. To my surprise, he complied. I have no recollection of how I knew about the program, but I remember my relief when he joined. He quickly met another single parent, and before any of us saw it coming, they were engaged and we were suddenly facing the prospect of merging two distinct families who barely knew each other. The program hosted an outing to the boardwalk for single parents and their children.

At that point, I was living in a foster home in Berkeley, a mutually agreed-upon arrangement between my father and me because he was tired of being called away from work whenever I got in trouble at school, and I was done with his drinking and depression. The rest of the kids who were under eighteen—Edie, John, and Margaret—continued to live with my father in the house on Ogden Drive. But I was visiting my siblings in Fremont the night before the board-walk event. When I got ready to walk to the Bay Area Rapid Transit (BART) station, part of the primary public transportation in the greater San Francisco Bay Area, to get back to my foster home, I shouted a goodbye to my father. He was in the shower and asked me to wait until he was done so he could say goodbye.

"I have to go," I shouted down the hall.

"Are you sure you don't want to go to the boardwalk with us tomorrow?" he asked.

I hesitated but yelled back, "I can't." I had no way of knowing in that moment, but he said the last words I would ever hear from him: "OK. Goodbye, Angel."

Edie, who went to the boardwalk with him (along with Margaret, John, and Melinda), saw that our father was napping in the sand. She playfully snuck up on him and poured water on his forehead. When he didn't respond, she thought he was messing with her, but when she splashed more water in his face, he gave a terrifying gasp and Edie jumped up and ran for help. The ride Margaret was on had to be stopped so she could be escorted down to the beach while our father was taken away by ambulance. Our father was declared dead on arrival at Community Hospital on Frederick Street in Santa Cruz at the age of forty-eight.

I walk along the edge of the water through the wet sand, dodging the incoming waves as I used to with my siblings when we were young, making my way toward the train trestle with its cantilevered walkway that connects the boardwalk and the surrounding Beach Flats neighborhood to the Seabright neighborhood, then I follow the San Lorenzo River to Ocean Street.

I recall several occasions when my father determinedly said that he would always keep his children together. It seemed a given to me, like congratulating yourself for getting out of bed in the morning, but I didn't know at the time that he'd essentially been given away by his mother when he was twelve while still grieving for his dead father, and that such a proclamation by him was of profound importance.

I'm struck by a wave of guilt. He had worked so hard to keep us together so we wouldn't have to experience what he lived through, and my behavior and attitude had made it impossible for him to keep me. Had it devastated him to break his promise to himself? Had he given up hope because I wasn't participating in school? Because of the Valium I got caught taking? Because I was hurting myself? I've always been led to believe that my brothers and sisters and I had ruined our mother's life by our very existence. Had I ruined our father's too? And what about the fact that when I moved out, Edie and Margaret and John were left behind with him?

I'm suddenly so disgusted with myself for never having considered this in all the years since that I want to shed my skin and start over. But I remind myself that I was young too, and that I didn't know until well into adulthood that my father had a history of having sexually abused two of my siblings.

Turning down a side road off Ocean Street, I'm pleasantly surprised to find an unfamiliar neighborhood of cottage-style homes with flourishing gardens spilling over picket fences. I stop to take some close-up shots of clematis and foxgloves and Canterbury bells, allowing myself to be charmed and momentarily distracted, allowing my heart to relax back into a steady, dependable pace. In silence I beg the petals for absolution and the honeybees, weighted with saddlebags of pollen, for a murmur of benediction.

I find the quiet footpath that runs along Branciforte Creek and follow it toward the street my office is on. The water is slow-moving and a couple of mallard pairs drift along, lazy and aimless. I spot a mother duck and her string of tiny hatchlings trailing behind her like a child's pull toy and I wait for them to reach me. I count the babies and I'm delighted to discover there are eight. I count them again to make sure I'm not just hoarding symbolism and there are precisely eight. Adorable, fluffy ducklings, all in a row. After a few attempts, I catch a shot where all eight babies are clearly visible, then I turn away from the water and head toward work as they continue, following their mother, carried along by the current.

I remember the day my parents brought Margaret home from the hospital. All of us were sitting around the living room and we each got a chance to hold her briefly. She wailed and I imitated the rhythm of her cry with the sharp little breaths between each syllable: "Wah-hoo, wah-hoo, wah-hoo." The others were there when I was born, no doubt, except for John, who arrived when I was too small to remember, so in my conscious memory he, like my five older siblings, has just always been there.

A distracted hum from a childhood ditty about ducks slowly builds in me and becomes a vocal trance, one song after another. The more upbeat the tempo, the louder I sing and the faster my stride becomes, until I have to stop to catch my breath. It dawns on me that I always sing in the combined voice of the seven other humans who comprised my earliest ecosystem. Cathy and Jerry sing from their souls. John looks on bemused. He and Edie pretend to simply endure the singing, but their straight-line grimaces and skyward eyes cannot conceal their joy. The same parents who gave me song as a lifeline shamed Edie into believing that she should never try to sing, or even to whistle. Instead, she became the keeper of the lyrics. She talk-sings and cues us when we lose our way. Kevin sings heartfully to God. Debbie sings as salve, and Margaret uses her voice to plead to the past and the future.

A squirrel skitters up a scrub oak and without a thought I slow my pace to a children's song: "Gray squirrel, gray squirrel, swish your bushy tail." My memory travels back and I can see and hear my mother singing it gently to John and Margaret, my younger brother and sister, as small children, demonstrating hand motions to accompany the lyrics. I remember her fashioning a drum for John out of an empty Folgers coffee can with a shoelace strap so he could wear it around his neck and pat the plastic lid as he marched through the house. Only now, looking back through decades, can I see the effort, the intention in her. She wanted to be a good mother, I think. Allowing for this is somehow as painful as acknowledging the ways she hurt us.

I keep singing as I walk, but my pitch thins and my voice grows spongy around the lump in my throat.

"What have I done to her memory?" I beg the air. "Have I flattened her to simply a *bad mother*? Robbed her of dimension?" Why hadn't I been able to apply the tenets of compassion and acceptance that I practice as a social worker to this woman who was scarcely an adult herself before she grew one baby after another until her battered uterus collapsed and had to be surgically removed? Now she's gone.

I feel as if I'm conducting an emotional autopsy, testing and weighing answers, but I can't settle on a cause and I can't shake the worry that I was somehow part of it, that there was something I could have said, or done, or been that would have extended some small measure of hope to her and changed her course. I let the tangled emotions wash over me and ply myself with desperate reminders that I am a basically good person.

I arrive at the office a few minutes late and sit down at my desk. Through my window I can see a single tree in a grassy plot. I think to myself, *I've already done my work for today.* But I turn on my computer, listen to voicemails, arrange documents to align with the forthcoming series of meetings, and begin my day. Again.

I power through the hours determined to leave the office before the sun starts flagging so I can walk home by the shortest route and get dinner on the table at a reasonable hour. I visit Vendi, my nickname for the vending machine in the hallway outside my office that keeps me in Diet Cokes, and pour some caffeine into my bloodstream. It always feels wrong to drink a soda so early in the day, but I never developed a taste for coffee.

The walk home is all business. I chart the quickest possible course. No striving for memorable photographs, no hunting for unusual bugs or flora. I make a beeline for Ocean Street, which becomes a virtual parking lot during the summer months when the boardwalk and surrounding beaches draw droves of visitors. I'm walking fast but my mind wanders and my thoughts turn to my brothers and sisters, who've been background music to my day since I saw the eight ducklings this morning, which by now feels like eons ago.

Each time a new child joins a family, the configuration of relationships grows. I've heard parents of three joke that when the children outnumbered the adults, their home life became exponentially more complicated. The more children, the less it's a joke. For a family of ten, strong alliances forge and fade, shifting along seemingly invisible fault lines. When I was a child, since our bedrooms were gender specific (as we understood gender at the time), I generally knew my sisters better than my brothers. And since interests are often influenced by age, I generally knew the younger kids better than the older ones. As we became adults, the connections continued to shift and change, but they were no longer delineated by age or gender.

After our father died when Jerry was twenty-four and Margaret was ten, there was no longer a home for our family. No physical location where we could find each other. Cathy, the third born, who by that time was twenty years old, married, and raising children, still lived in Fremont, not far from our childhood home, and she felt a sense of responsibility, especially toward the siblings who were displaced by our father's death. She made her house a gathering place for the holidays. She prepared Christmas dinner, baked cookies, and put a tree up in her living room. She facilitated a new gift-giving practice of each of us picking a sibling's name from a hat and then purchasing a small gift for that person.

Despite Cathy's efforts, each of us drifted off in our own direction to tackle life. Some of us stayed in touch in smaller groups of two or three, while others lost contact for long stretches at a time. It took years for all of us to find our way back to each other as a group after many attempts ended in yelling, spitting, and even physical altercations. As kids, we took our cues for problem-solving from our mother, devolving into violence easily. Becoming adults didn't magically correct that tendency. It took conscious, sustained effort. Some of us embraced it more readily than others, but eventually we all tamed ourselves.

As I turn right onto Laurel Street, which will eventually connect back to the west side, I try to think about each of my siblings individually. I conjure my memories of each, my relationship to them over our lives, the life lessons I've learned from them, the assumptions I've made about their experiences in our family, how they see the world, their politics. I challenge myself to remember how I formed my opinions about them and when I last made any effort to update or fine-tune my understanding of them. If I'm operating on old information, I vow to myself mid-stride, I will try to get to know these seven people as they are today. I close my eyes and take a mental snapshot of us. Now.

Chapter 3

Discovering Snowflakes

formosity *noun* \fȯr'mäsətē\: beauty or a
beautiful thing

I TYPICALLY PLAN MY walks the evening before I take them. Sometimes I base the location on practical factors, such as how much time I will have or what part of the county will be most conducive to getting some errands done before or after the walk, sometimes on whether I want to be in a more rural or more populated area. There are times when I start out on a planned walk and end up far afield because I spot something interesting or surprising that leads me into a different neighborhood than I intended.

Mindful that only about thirty miles of the walks will take place right along the cliffs and beaches, I try to plan my ocean outings sparingly. When it comes time to start venturing into the mountains, about two years into the project, I'm both nervous and excited. My chances of seeing wildlife improve greatly, but I will also be in remote areas, most of which are not familiar to me. With this in mind, I start with mountain roads I already know in the area, including some I traveled during my multiple walks from Scotts Valley to Los Gatos, along a roughly west-to-east axis with some twists and turns to avoid the highway.

I map a rough course for a motionless spring morning with a plan to leave the house early enough to be at my starting place just before the sun rises. I start on Mountain Charlie Road, a narrow, winding, paved road that rises to the summit north of Santa Cruz, running parallel to Highway 17, the thoroughfare that connects Santa Cruz with the booming Silicon Valley. It doesn't take long before I'm on a cartoonishly steep stretch, walking at an unnatural angle to avoid the feeling that gravity is going to take me down. There's no stopping to catch a breath; momentum, I have learned, is key on inclines. I've walked this road several times, but walking alone in silence in the early morning, I see it with new eyes.

Just as I reach a more reasonable grade and work to regulate my breathing, I make my first acquaintance with a tiny spring azure. "Blue butterfly!" I whisper-shout to no one. I have heard that there are blue butterflies in the world but I have only half believed. Now what first looks like a flake of stray ash drifts into my realm in apparent free fall until a barely perceptible flap reveals grayish underwings opening to a shock of vivid color. The azure's presence is so startling, so captivating, that I might as well have awoken to find the full moon resting in my hand.

Mountain Charlie Road was named for an early settler in the Santa Cruz Mountains, Charles McKiernan, who built the road in the mid-1800s. It was the first route by which wagons could travel between Santa Cruz and San Jose about thirty miles north. McKiernan was a pioneer whose head, legend has it, was disfigured in an encounter with a grizzly bear, resulting in the need for a metal plate to be put in his skull. *Ursus arctos horribilis* once roamed this area in numbers. I spook myself trying to imagine looking up to see this six-hundred-pound giant lumbering through the redwoods toward me as he considers his lunch options.

I hear Steller's jays bossing each other from treetops. Their squawks bring me back to camping trips I took as a child with my parents and siblings. We had a massive army-issue tent, a canvas house really, with wooden poles thicker than broomsticks and windows cut out of the canvas, panes of nothing but trees and sky. With sardine-packing precision, my parents could fit my entire ten-person family into the tent, a toddler wedged between two preteens here, the baby-of-the-moment snuggled into a corner there. We would wake up, encased in musty, flannel-lined sleeping bags, to the sounds of these feisty birds with their fancy mohawks, their royal-blue feathers, and their food-stealing ways etching indelible symbols of camping. But sometimes we preferred to be out under the stars.

It was these pockets of California wildlands that allowed my parents to escape suburban Fremont, a soul-crushing place in the '60s and '70s for two young adults who would have much preferred to be activists for peace and the rights of poor people in a more liberal, but regrettably less affordable, place like Berkeley. Out camping, they would set free their disheveled brood to pursue scorpions, blue-belly lizards, and garter snakes.

We had an old green camp stove with rusty burners, which a blue-and-white-speckled enamel coffee percolator stood on, taking what seemed hours to reach a boil, and a cast-iron griddle from which browning pancakes shot breakfast-scented aromas through the pine-tinged morning air. When we camped near a river, my father always put a full-to-bursting melon in the water and built a simple retaining wall of stacked stones to hold it in place, singing one of his favorite camp songs, as he did it: "Just plant a watermelon on the top of my grave and let the juice slip through." When the sun struck noon, we'd have chilled watermelon with slippery, onyx-black seeds to spit into the creek with all the power that our lungs could muster while pink nectar snaked down our chins and arms in sticky rivulets.

This is how it starts. I'm out walking and something so simple as a party of jabbering jays sends me tumbling back to childhood. I notice a ladybug on a wheat stock, which brings to mind Margaret, who invariably tried to join us bigger kids in a game of hide-and-seek where she would "hide" behind a sapling narrower than her, thinking that since she couldn't see us, we couldn't see her. I laugh and something in me opens, a portal to fall into, as I watch memories braid themselves into the sights and sounds of my walk in the present.

Psychology professor Dacher Keltner defines awe as

"the feeling of being in the presence of something vast that transcends your current understanding of the world." At first blush, there's not much vast or transcendent about six-mile Mountain Charlie Road, let alone my three-quarter-inch butterfly, but this definition holds. The vastness dwells in the fact that I might easily have gone my whole life without ever seeing a spring azure, but on this sunny day both of us happen to be out in the world wandering and our paths have crossed. Vastness lies in the fall-in blue of the butterfly's wings and in the very fact of wings, of flight, of butterflies, for whom the collective noun is *kaleidoscope*, for the thousands of reflective scales on their wings.

There are countless paths to awe. Some people actively go in search of it in places of worship, or they travel great distances to see untold billions of stars from the darkest reaches of the planet, or they use hallucinogenic plants to transport them to different levels of consciousness. Others stumble clumsily upon it. For stumblers like me, awe is joined by joyous incredulity.

The deceptive solid line representing this road on my paper county map gives no indication of elevation gain, and in my haste to get out into the morning air, I've failed (as I often do) to bear in mind that this part of the county called the Santa Cruz *Mountains* requires some serious hoofing. The exertion of reaching the summit leaves me content but physically spent, and the memory of cold watermelon in the stream has reminded me of the fruit in my camera bag. I find a little spot between two trees to rest as

I snack on Fuji apple slices and goat cheese on crackers, then pack up and get back in motion.

In her book *Wanderlust: A History of Walking*, Rebecca Solnit posits that "walking, ideally, is a state in which the mind, the body, and the world are aligned, as though they were three characters finally in conversation together, three notes suddenly making a chord." I have found this so. The conversations I have had can play out in wafts of pine, a wind ripping through the canopy, or a moment where I'm in the presence of a deer or a bobcat when both of us seem to have forgotten to be frightened or startled by the other and instead we simply regard each other, as if we both belong where we are. I feel present and attentive in these moments in ways I had not experienced before the walks.

My mind has become a floor-to-ceiling, wall-to-wall apothecary cabinet of drawers brimming with vivid curios: objects observed, instances witnessed, gifts given and received. A glimpse of a pileated woodpecker in flight as it takes off from a shabby knobcone pine, the orange shaft of a flicker feather found on the forest floor, a homegrown spaghetti squash from a neighborhood farmer—now bring unexpected meaning to my every day.

There is an apothecary drawer in my memory just for birds, from which I can pull out a recollection in minute detail of the first bluebird I saw on my walks. It was perched on a telephone line on densely wooded Old Graham Hill Road, a rural byway of pleasantly spaced houses in the hills north of downtown. I had no idea before that moment that there were bluebirds in Santa Cruz County, but since then I've seen dozens.

My first cedar waxwing, with its black eye mask and bright yellow tail tip, I came across on Corralitos Road, the main byway through the rural town of Corralitos, surrounded by acres of open farmland and vineyards. Before I set off on my walk that day, I parked in front of the charming Corralitos Market & Sausage Company, a family business that has operated in Corralitos since the 1880s. I ordered the zesty apricot sausage sandwich, added the requisite ketchup, mustard, and onions, and headed out to the tiny park across the street to sink my teeth into the perfect ratio of texture and flavor—chewy, squishy, sweet, and savory with a kick of heat. Sated, I set off on foot. I'd walked the length of a few tractors when I looked up into a leafless persimmon tree, its orange fruit like Christmas tree bulbs, and watched as one cedar waxwing was joined by another and another until a great high-pitched, persimmon-eating party commenced.

I saw black phoebes, dressed in their formal attire of white shirt and black jacket, on Old Chittenden Road, a country lane in Watsonville just at the crossroads between Santa Cruz County and neighboring San Benito County, where chickens and guinea fowl, escaped from a timeless-looking homestead, strut about clucking and pecking in the dirt outside an old produce stand.

Spotted towhees, green flycatchers, varied thrushes, grosbeaks, thrashers, sapsuckers . . . Presumably they've always been here. It's unfathomable to me that until these walks, I had never noticed them. I snap photos so I can learn their names, recognize them next time. I can't pronounce my own name in birdsong, but I sometimes hear it now in dreams.

There's a drawer in my mind devoted to fungi, some with a benign appearance that belies the truth revealed in their foreboding monikers: death cap, destroying angel. Others, like the *Amanita muscaria*, with its bright red umbrella cap and white polka dots, bring to mind gnomes and fairies. A drawer for the spores and seedpods and their endless array of delivery systems. The yucca plant with pods in spheres that can be opened and quartered like slices of an orange. Inside you find columns of flat black seeds stacked like perfect Pringles in a can.

Milkweed, God's gift to monarch caterpillars, dries to reveal little pockets full of tidily situated seeds attached to a bundle of fine, hairlike threads. When the pocket dries up and splits open, the seeds fall out, and the strands blossom like the canopy of a parachute, the slightest breeze lifting them up and delivering them to a new home. The bugs that compel me to pull out my magnifying glass for a closer look to whom I say, "Are you even possible?" Feathers. Stones. Seaweed. Bones.

The road's incline has tapered off and I'm reveling in moving through the world at my own pace. I adore walking with friends and family—the shared experience of exercise and conversation is one of my favorite ways to connect with a loved one—but there's something elemental and sustaining about neither straining to keep up and missing details nor holding back when I want to devour a hill to reach a vista.

I spot a few rotting tree trunks off the side of the road and without giving it much thought, I pull up a patch of loose bark, having learned that the odds of encountering a colony of ants, a salamander, or a centipede are far greater than a winning hand at Pai Gow, my favorite poker game. I pry off a piece of the outer bark and barely have time to register what I've seen before I reflexively put the bark back in place because what's under it recalls some complex fiber network or even brain cells, something not meant to be exposed. Yet my curiosity persists. I pull the bark back open slowly, as if it were a door on hinges, and take a closer look. Maybe very fine, etiolated plant roots? But they seem too spongy.

Later that evening, I search for more information and learn that mushrooms are simply the fruiting body of mycelium, the filaments of a fungus. Far from being the odd little stand-alone plants I've always assumed them to be, mushrooms are but a suggestion of a massive, interdependent network. They are not technically plants, but comparing them to a plant, the mushroom is equivalent to a flower and the mycelium the roots. In *Finding the Mother Tree*, Suzanne Simard provides a fitting description of fungi: "The mushroom is the visible tip of something deep and elaborate, like a thick lace tablecloth knitted into the forest floor. The threads . . . fanning through the litter—fallen needles, buds, twigs—searching for, entwining with, and absorbing mineral riches."

The more I dig in the dirt, study decomposing tree

trunks, and read about the ways fungi and plants help facilitate the delivery of nutrients to other plants or compete with others for sunlight and nutrients, the more I realize: It's all interconnected. We're all interconnected—interdependent. As Merlin Sheldrake observes in *Entangled Life*:

> Spores are carried upward by a current of wind generated by mushrooms as water evaporates from their gills. Fungi produce around fifty megatons of spores each year—equivalent to the weight of five hundred thousand blue whales—making them the largest source of living particles in the air. Spores are found in clouds and influence the weather by triggering the formation of water droplets that form rain and the ice crystals that form snow, sleet, and hail.

Now that I know where to look, I always keep an eye out for mycelium when I'm exploring in the woods. I can't sit long enough to watch it grow, but I can sense its aliveness. It feels ethereal, like finding life on another planet, but it also feels as if I'm looking into my own brain, my own mysterious network of fine filaments that weave and cross and rewire to remedy short circuits. I'll never get to see myself objectively, of course, but after thousands of hours of consciously observing the world around me, I begin to better understand my *self* within a larger context.

With the benefit of hindsight, I can see the point in my

life where I no longer needed armor to feel safe in the world. I could have off-loaded long ago the mounds of fear and the outdated storylines of toughness and lack of intelligence, but I was too far into these beliefs to see them. I'd formed an identity around disguising my needs. It would have been like trying to separate Simard's lacework of mycelium from its environment intact.

When I finally do start to shed layers of the old armor I'd forged, I'm shocked, almost disappointed, by how easily those years of buildup slough off. I don't need them any longer but they are familiar, which makes their absence a peculiar kind of loss. It feels like what I imagine hermit crabs must experience, an exposed interlude between upgraded shells.

Nature's unflagging acceptance and concurrent utter indifference toward me neutralizes my self-judgment when I'm out among the trees. The deep lines in my face that take me aback when I look at a photograph of myself or see my reflection in the mirror are no more problematic here than the yawning grooves in the redwood's bark.

The fallen tree doesn't take offense when mycelium devours it. Plants don't mean any harm when they crowd out other plants to absorb the sun. It's just dispassionate survival. I try this on as a way of thinking about those who blocked my sun as I was growing up. To my surprise, it helps.

This realization doesn't magically cure me of the bitter envy that I swallow when people go on about how their mother is their best friend or my urge to accidentally trip someone when they tell heartfelt tales about going fishing with their father. I'm not a plant, after all.

But in the peace of these long walks, I begin to relax. I start to see how tightly I've been holding myself, how I've been trying to keep all my pieces together. On these walks, I begin to allow myself to grieve for what I missed, for who I might have been, what more I might have achieved in my life if I had known how to use the energy I'd poured into surviving toward thriving instead.

SEVERAL MONTHS INTO my project, after I had begun to walk as much as thirty or forty miles a week, Ellen proposed a trip to Lake Tahoe, a four-hour drive from Santa Cruz. I'm excited for some long, lazy days with Ellen and Miles, but I'm a little reluctant about leaving town for more than a day or two, afraid I might miss something on my roads or forget how to scavenge beauty. I'm still developing a habit that feels elusive, tentative, as if it might slip out of my grasp if I loosen my grip or avert my gaze. But once we arrive in Lake Tahoe and settle into our cabin, I'm delighted to be sitting near our fireplace with an expansive view of the snowy valley below.

I fill our home away from home with the aromas of homemade chicken noodle soup on the stove and blueberry hand pies in the oven. We challenge each other to pool games and racquetball in the nearby lodge and sit in the hot saunas breathing in eucalyptus steam, then walk back through the snow in the dark. Early one day, while Ellen and Miles sleep, I steal out into the cold morning. I feel compelled to get outside and walk.

Within moments I am on a narrow forest path that opens into a stark graphic of white snow, brown tree trunks, green canopy, and billowy clouds in a blue sky. The scene is so bold, so blunt, that it is a caricature of itself, like a drawing done by a precocious child that's affixed to the refrigerator by a doting mother.

There is a quality of silence here that I haven't experienced before. The stillness and the absence of sound create pressure on my eardrums. I strain to hear beyond the quiet while snow begins to fall.

On the sleeve of my black windbreaker, I notice that the white dots of flakes are jagged around the edges, not perfect circles. I fumble in my jacket pocket for my reading glasses and discover when I look more closely that they take the shape of tiny stars. I then switch lenses on my camera, replacing the wide angle with my macro lens. I take a close-up shot of a snow-drop. Looking at the LCD screen on the back of the camera, I zoom in on the image: tiny fragile crystals arranging themselves in delicate patterns. Tiny details of impossible beauty. Yet here they are. I feel bewildered. Overcome. I sit on the cold ground, winded, and photograph snowflake after snowflake. I desperately want to show Ellen and Miles but I can scarcely pull myself away.

When I finally make my way back to our lodging, I find they've left in search of breakfast. I go out onto the balcony and sit in the snow, catching and photographing the tiny gems on a drinking glass, an ice cube, my camera bag.

When Ellen returns, I ask her in a dazed whisper, "Did you know?" I must look deranged, perched gloveless in the now-driving snow, hands red and numb with cold, neck and cheeks clenched against chattering jaws. If snowflakes falling from the sky really do look like the snowflakes I made as a child with paper and scissors, what else have I missed?

"Did I know what?" she asks, bringing my attention back to my question. "About snowflakes," I say, reverently turning the image on the LCD screen toward her, poised to reveal the biggest secret I'll ever uncover. "Oh yeah," she says. "Pretty." "Pretty?" I echo indignantly and think, *This is the frozen essence of beauty itself, fragile crystal cut from all the colors of light, this is a formosity*. But then I remember that she grew up with snow, and the delicate shapes, while interesting, are no surprise to her. Nor to Miles, who trails in a few minutes later and sweetly compliments my macro shots.

I think about snowflakes every single day for the next two years. They still cross my mind. I buy myself a cheap little snowflake brooch that I know I will never wear because I don't wear brooches. But it makes me smile.

When we return home from Lake Tahoe, I tell everyone I see about snowflakes. I am disappointed that no one is really surprised by what I have learned. I know I would not have discovered them if I hadn't been in the throes of observing nature. The walks are stirring up a sense of wonder that is warming my heart to thawing. It's impossible to be hardened while pondering ice crystals that have traveled from over ten thousand feet above the earth while shaping themselves into intricate discs of ephemeral handiwork.

A friend tells me about a man known as Snowflake Bentley of Jericho, Vermont, who in the nineteenth century was one of the first photographers of snowflakes. After reading about Wilson Alwyn Bentley, who lived from 1865 to 1931, I purchase a book of his images, *Snowflakes in Photographs*—page after page of nothing but ice gems of mind-boggling variety. Seventy-two pages of snowflakes. I "read" it again and again. Sometimes the world needs to just stop for a minute so we can all marvel at ice crystals.

A short film, *The Snowflake Man*, describes how Bentley figured out how to attach his camera to a microscope in 1885, when photography was only about twenty years old. This was before electricity, so he had to work outside in freezing weather to make use of sunlight. He worked with long exposures of twenty seconds to two minutes. His family and neighbors were perplexed by this man who put off chores around the farm in favor of running around in fields catching snowflakes on swatches of black velvet. Learning all of this, I wanted to travel back in time and tell him that we are kindred spirits, that I, too, fell hard for those gossamer masterpieces.

A snowflake's six points are caused by the shape and interaction of water molecules, I learn. Each molecule includes three atoms, two hydrogen atoms bonded to a central oxygen atom, like little arms. Additionally, two more "arms," or spokes, called lone pairs, adhere to the oxygen atom. When water molecules connect in the clouds, their various arms fit together efficiently into six-sided shapes, called plates. Each plate whirls and races around in the clouds, gathering weight and dimension until it gets too heavy and falls to earth. As it falls, the plate continues to expand and sprout points that grow symmetrically, dictated by its hexagonal shape.

At times, I have had to practice restraint when I'm in public to not yell, "Hey! Water molecules are made up of three atoms and they make snowflakes! Did you know that?" Instead, I practice on Ellen, who does a pretty good job of absorbing my enthusiasm. "This is made up of atoms," I tell her, holding up a tile from our set of Bananagrams. "So is this," I add, showing my Fuji apple before I take a bite. "I'm eating atoms. Atoms make up water molecules. Water molecules make snowflakes!"

It turns out there's a limit to how much people would like to discuss snowflakes. Now I carry my knowledge of them like a giddy secret—that atoms swirl and gather and form into ice crystals as they have since time began and will continue to whether humans are here to witness it or not— but it still takes effort to keep it to myself. Sometimes I consciously keep my lips sealed so snowflakes don't fall out.

Kids typically start learning about atoms and molecules in sixth or seventh grade and continue to learn about them in high school chemistry classes. I checked out, academically, before that point in my education. I have certainly heard over the course of my life many of the terms, but I have very little reference for understanding their meanings or applications. The experience of discovering snowflakes, then learning more about them, gives me a comfortable, even enjoyable, way to make some basic connections about the natural world around me.

It is on this trip that I begin to understand that all that the project is teaching and showing me is geographically transferable. I had to step away from Santa Cruz County to see that all the details I've come to notice and cherish—the mushrooms, the newts, the expanding sense of community—are not specific to a place. Perhaps more to the point, that this place inside me, this practice of seeking beauty, connection, and true belonging, is portable. The word *portable*, first used in the 1400s, derives from the Latin term *portare*, "to carry." We visit *place* and we carry *place* with us. The spot where I discovered snowflakes is a physical location that I can return to, but it also dwells inside me and stays with me wherever I go.

Chapter 4

Sitting in the Dirt

---

griffonage *noun* \¦grifə¦näzh\: careless
handwriting: a crude or illegible scrawl

THROUGHOUT MY SCHOOL YEARS, I longed to go back to kindergarten and start fresh. I desperately wanted a do-over. One of the constant themes of my life is the sense that I'm behind, that I'm missing basic, foundational information, that intellectually I don't belong. Among close friends and family, where I feel accepted and embraced and my gaps of knowledge are no surprise and have no impact on how I'm perceived, I can maneuver between the criss-crossing ropes of conversation and add my input, unself-consciously ask for history or context, try on an opinion, or bow out of a conversation and just listen. Outside of that comfort zone, I often feel as if I'm on the sidelines of a double-Dutch jump rope game, trying to pick up the rhythms so I can leap into the game without tripping over my own feet.

After nearly three decades together, Ellen is accustomed

to the peaks and valleys of my knowledge base. In the first few years of our relationship, she might make a comment about the US Constitution, and I'd ask, "Is the Constitution the one that starts 'Four score and seven years ago'?"

"You're joking, right?" she'd say.

I wasn't.

She has tried countless times to help me remember what many consider basic knowledge, such as the three branches of government, information she learned young and accepts as something everyone knows. No sooner do the words leave her lips than my brain stubbornly repels them. There are three branches of government in the United States: executive, judicial, and . . . I know it . . . I just had it . . . it's the one that develops laws . . .

Remembering the branches of government is hell on earth for me. Learning the branches of madrones and redwoods is effortless, enthralling, all-consuming. Madrone branches have a layer of papery bark that cracks and peels like old paint, curls up like shavings, and falls away with a brush of my hand, revealing smooth, mottled, red-and-olive-toned flesh.

Along the coast there's a small seabird, the marbled murrelet, that nests in the towering redwood canopy near Sempervirens Creek in Big Basin Redwoods State Park and makes a twenty-mile round-trip journey to the ocean each day to . . . Legislative! This is my brain on walking. Learning through observing and interacting with the natural world, with zero pressure, boosts my confidence and buttresses the knowledge that already lurks shyly in the folds of my brain.

Trying to take in details for which I have no reference point is challenging, almost impossible, for me. I need to be able to make direct connections. Numbers and equations, for example, have always been intimidating. But now that I've sat quietly on beaches in the course of my walks, sorting pebbles into piles by color or size or markings, feeling both their physical weight and their conceptual weight, forming a visceral understanding of the roots of counting, weighing, and tracking cycles and the basic exchange of rocks, shells, and metals for goods, the precursor to modern money, I'm ready, even eager, to give mathematics another shot.

I've always been perplexed by the fact that Jerry occasionally purchases a book about calculus or statistics or some similarly torturous subject.

"Why?" I ask him incredulously, browsing the titles on his bookshelves.

"It's fascinating. I just want to understand," he replies matter-of-factly.

Maybe I'm beginning to understand. Knowledge and information, I'm learning, can be exhilarating. They don't have to be a source of pressure, anxiety, or embarrassment.

I still flush when I think about an incident soon after Ellen and I first acknowledged that we had growing, mutual crushes on each other. We'd worked together on securing a grant that would bring a new approach to our local child welfare system to more fully involve families in their own safety planning process. All these years later, she still playfully holds that she *got me* through a Packard Foundation grant.

At a department-wide meeting when our proposed program was on the agenda, my supervisor asked me to say a few words since I knew the details of the program. And while I despise speaking in public, I thought I could choke out a few explanatory sentences. People streamed into the largest conference room in our office building until it was standing room only.

When the facilitator asked me to introduce the program, I started, "Family group conferencing originated in New Zealand, where it . . ." I stopped to take a breath and delayed just long enough that people who'd been only half paying attention looked up to see what was happening. The room went silent. Dead silent. I opened my mouth to continue but my brain went blank. I knew no language. I scanned the room for an anchor and met Ellen's compassionate eyes. A lash of hot shame coursed through me like a fueled wick.

One of my colleagues quietly moved her chair closer to mine and asked in a whisper if she should try to finish my comments. I looked at her but couldn't answer. Finally, my supervisor stepped up and saved me by summarizing the grant proposal and moving on to the next topic. After the meeting, I turned to the social worker who'd tried to help me and asked if my face had turned bright red while I was mute.

"No," she replied frankly. "You went ashen."

I managed to get myself back to my office and shut the door before simmering self-loathing reached a full boil. I was convinced that everyone in that room would now realize what I'd worked so hard, for so long, to conceal: that I didn't belong there, that I didn't deserve the job, that I could barely string a sentence together. My catastrophizing mind sent me careening off its rails, plunging me into an abyss, alone. My stupidity was laid bare, my graduate degree, licensure, and career disintegrating faster than a snake can strike.

It has become clear to me over the years that I'm not actually stupid, but a missed beat in a conversation, a simple fact not readily at my fingertips, or freezing when it's my time to speak can be a direct route back to the familiar lost, rudderless feeling that I had when I was a child.

I was never a great student, but up until fifth grade I'd been able to meet the basic requirements for moving to the next grade. Then suddenly my school performance dived. I stopped retaining new information, and tasks I had mastered, such as cursive writing and the multiplication tables, were now out of my grasp. My reading skills plummeted, and I stopped participating in class at all.

I started being called out of the classroom regularly to see the school psychologist, Mr. Noble, who conducted tests on me. In one, he held up a horizontal spiral-bound book of images, flipped the pages, and asked me to name the objects depicted in a simple graphic. Or he'd give me a worksheet with a drawing of a woman and a child preparing something in the kitchen, with a fill-in-the-blank sentence:

"Mrs. Smith and her daughter are __________." I'd fill in the blank with "fighting," even though I could clearly see they were making cookies. The unfamiliar tenderness of having an adult sitting next to me, trying to understand me, made me desperate to hold Mr. Noble's attention. But after a short visit he always said, "OK, then, back to class with you," way too soon.

Mr. Noble tried in earnest to figure out what was wrong with me. He had the school nurse test my eyes. I could see the letters on the charts clearly, but I wasn't about to give up the attention, so I read them wrong. Based on the school's tests results, I was legally blind. The school insisted that my parents take me for a more thorough vision test and a scan of my brain, a new technology at a clinic connected to Stanford, possibly a precursor to a CT scan. After the scan, I had an EEG, an electroencephalogram, where suction cups connected to wires were placed all over my head and connected to a machine. Next, I had a spinal tap, where I had to lie curled like a snail so a doctor could draw fluid from my spine with a gigantic needle, or so my imagination conjured. (I never saw it.)

After three or four visits, the doctors finally arrived at a diagnosis for my unusual condition. I imagine they used a more sophisticated term, something like *malingering*, but my dad translated: "You're faking," he said, yanking me by the wrist and marching me out of the doctor's office.

I was both embarrassed and indignant. I wasn't faking. Not exactly. A ten-year-old doesn't know how to say, "Hey, your parenting is causing behavioral problems and poor academic achievement." Instead, I muttered to my father: "I'm not faking. I just forgot everything."

I'M HEADING DOWN Seventh Avenue and memory is a layered cake. Childhood memories often surface when I'm out walking, sometimes consuming me, other times simply hovering in the background. And walking every street in the county means that eventually I pass by each of the thirteen houses I've lived in since I was eighteen years old, each of the nineteen places I've worked as an adult, the bars I snuck into that have since become restaurants or live music venues, the stores I stole from, the bus stops I waited at.

I'm walking in Live Oak, an unincorporated neighborhood parenthesized by two significant land features, Arana Gulch and Rodeo Gulch. As with much of the Santa Cruz coast and mountain range, the area was for millennia the dwelling place of the Awaswas-speaking Ohlone people. But in the mid-1800s, the three-square-mile area was divided into two ranches, Rancho Arroyo del Rodeo and Rancho Los Esteros, owned by two brothers.

This neighborhood was once my own stomping grounds. I've lived in several different houses in the area. When I stop in front of the two-story shingled A-frame on Thirteenth Avenue where I lived with a single mom and her daughter when I was nineteen, I'm flooded with detailed memories that I haven't thought about in years. My housemate's weaving loom, her sewing machines and colorful textiles, the walks to the end of the road that leads to a clifftop with a broad view of the ocean, and a fling I had with a neighbor a few doors down. I try to wedge this period into a spot along the timeline of my personal history, like Flashback, the weekly *New York Times* quiz where you try to put historical events in chronological order.

If I was nineteen, Michele and I were still together, so why would I be having a fling? It must have been while she was in Austria visiting relatives. Oh yes, it was *because* of my affair that she invited me to join her in Europe, to get me away from the neighbor. And come to think of it, if I'm brutally honest, I was partially having the affair in reaction to Michele visiting an ex-girlfriend while she was abroad. So then it was *after* Michele and I had moved into a house on Branciforte Avenue—an accessory unit in the backyard of our landlord that, reputedly, one of the Doobie Brothers had once rented, which we shortly moved out of when our roommate caused a fire with her witchy candle ritual—and *before* I moved into the living room of another single mother with a daughter on Capitola Avenue. *After* Michele went swimming in the San Lorenzo River with the woman who drove the red-white-and-blue Vega and kissed her while they sunned on the boulders, but *before* I started making regular visits to the reclusive poet who lived over a garage on California Street with a big fluffy dog she found wandering on the beach, which clearly was *before* Michele moved in with said poet and started a monogamous relationship. Details. Details.

On Sixteenth Avenue, I linger on the sidewalk outside a house that I stayed in with Michele while I was between homes myself. It was a revolving-door rental where many people I've now known for decades lived for at least a spell in the late '70s and early '80s. The man who would a few years later be Kita's donor dad lived there along with his partner at the time. I try to place this historical event on the timeline. Was this the last place Michele and I stayed together before we broke up?

Planning my walks, I focus on covering the streets. It never dawns on me that I will stumble over reminders of my young adulthood at every turn. The path from childhood to adulthood lives in me as a chaotic, fragmented, untenable mess. Walking into the past, catching glimpses of forgotten moments, retracing the roots of lifelong friendships, learning compassion for my younger self, I can see that though my route was circuitous, it has all amounted to a life that I love.

On Seventeenth Avenue I notice an elementary school set back from the road and remember that I worked there as a teacher's aide during summer school one year in the early 1980s. Since school isn't in session now, I wander around the campus, where I'm charmed by a set of murals by a favorite local artist, created in collaboration with students. Fantastical creatures rendered in bold colors. I notice a small cluster of ladybugs on a nearby plant and step in for a closer look. There are much smaller insects among the ladybugs and I take out my macro to see the details of the minuscule creatures. They're orange in color and appear to have six legs. They haven't grown into their spots yet, so I imagine that develops over time. I gasp at my good fortune of seeing mama ladybugs tending their young. I'm so absorbed that I don't register that there are other people around until a father and his little rainboot-clad daughter are standing next to me, curious about what has captured my attention. As if seeing baby ladybugs wasn't a bedizened crown to top off my day, a small child has arrived to share the wonder.

"Do you see the ladybugs?" I ask her, gently bending the leaf toward her.

She nods vigorously.

"They're taking care of their tiny babies," I tell her. Simultaneously, her heels come up off the ground and her neck telescopes upward.

Her father reads her wordless cues seamlessly, scoops her up, leans in close, and announces firmly: "Those are aphids. I imagine the ladybugs are eating them, not taking care of them."

My mounting sense of confidence in my ability to learn suddenly feels as if it's built on a house of cards that's about to topple. I am unreasonably embarrassed, mortified to be exposed as a fraudulent naturalist. The man walks away with a barely discernible grunt of farewell, his wide-eyed, well-groomed, and clearly adored child in tow. I want to scream after him, "I probably know things you don't know too!" Instead, I stand in front of the elementary school, a raw nerve, holding an invisible blinking neon sign: DUMB. I'm having a painfully familiar attack of stupidity, a close relative to the anxiety attack.

Weeks later, walking in Wilder Ranch State Park, I find

a strange little black bug with orange markings. It looks armored by black ridges along the length of its body. The underside of a ladybug comes to mind, but it has no wings. Later, at home, I get online to identify it and quickly learn that it's a ladybug in its larval stage.

WHEN I WENT to junior high, I started in regular classes, but I was placed in Learning Disability Group (LDG) a few months into seventh grade and stayed there through eighth grade, learning and relearning rudimentary math, and reading from sets of slender illustrated booklets with color-coded bindings denoting level of difficulty. Under the wing of my teacher, Mrs. Johnson, I was able to find some of what I'd lost, my vision problems resolved, and my penmanship edged from griffonage back toward legible, though it never fully recovered and continues to be a source of embarrassment, with its tendency to fall drunkenly off its prescribed lines and elude attempts to be read, including by me.

I have learned to conceal the depths of my anxiety around my intelligence in most settings. Sometimes I even forget about it, but my handwriting feels like a dead giveaway—a window into my rawest insecurity. I routinely destroy everything I write by hand—grocery lists, reminders on Post-its that I leave for my wife or my sons, notes from trainings at work—and I do my best to ensure that no one else sees them. I rarely send birthday cards or letters.

Still, I loved the quiet safety of Mrs. Johnson's classroom. I never figured out if I was, in fact, learning disabled or if I was still "faking it." I wanted to know but I didn't know who to ask. Being able to participate in school activities like choir was a highlight for me. I cherished being dressed like everyone else in a black robe with a wide, shiny gold collar. Pulling it on over my own clothes meant a brief reprieve from the self-consciousness about my stained, wrinkled, and ill-fitting clothing for the time I sat among rows of students, everyone's attention focused forward, our voices merging to one mighty hum, bouncing off basketball backboards, ricocheting off the high gymnasium ceilings, and sprinkling back onto us like bounced light. We wore down the old folk song "Scarborough Fair" to a smooth chamois.

I don't know if there was a discussion between my parents and the school or between the junior high and the high school, but when I finished eighth grade and entered high school, I had no extra educational supports, yet somehow I managed to survive freshman year without flunking out. But partway into sophomore year, I was transferred to the first of several of what were called "continuation schools." Also known as alternative schools, continuation schools are designed to provide options for students who are at risk of not graduating from a traditional high school for a range of reasons, including poor grades and behavioral issues. At my first continuation school, there were still classes, but no one cared if you participated. The primary measure of success, it seemed, was for us students to remain on campus for the duration of the school day. I got through each hour-long class by numbering the lines on pieces of binder paper

1 through 60 and filling each line with sixty repeating shapes—stars, flowers, smiley faces, triangles—so that by the time the lines were filled, the class would be over. Occasionally something a teacher said broke through and I actually listened, which distracted me momentarily from my self-assigned doodling.

Between my sophomore and senior years, I lived with three families besides my own and attended five different high schools before I left without graduating. When I was fifteen, my father arranged for me to stay with a neighbor, Mrs. Rogers, her husband, a long-haul truck driver who was frequently gone for days at a time, and her three daughters. I don't think my father ever explained to me why I was going to stay with the Rogerses, but it didn't matter. I was thrilled.

Looking back at that time through the eyes of an adult, I can now see several reasons he might have had for farming me out. My mother moved out of the house with her boyfriend when I was thirteen, leaving my father a single parent to the five remaining kids, ages six through seventeen, who were still living at home. I don't know if my father had any advance warning that she was leaving. I don't remember learning about it until I saw her packing up her things.

At fifteen, I was constantly challenging him, insisting that he get help for what I perceived to be alcoholism and depression—neither of which he would acknowledge. At the same time, I was regularly in trouble at school and twice ended up in the hospital, once after taking too much

Valium and then slumping against the lockers while the gym teacher tried to teach us how rugby is played, and again when I told my counselor over the phone that I was going to end my life, then left the house with a butcher knife in my shoe held against my leg with my red-and-white argyle knee sock. I had no intention of killing myself: I was hoping she would come and talk to me. Instead, my counselor called the Fremont Police Department, who located me in a nearby field and took me to the hospital ER.

The counselor was part of an effort to extend support services to teen girls in Fremont, an attempt to balance out the fact that boys were served through the Boys Club while there was nothing for the girls. The boys had a building, sports equipment, and a range of community activities. Funds were short, so a seemingly random bunch of girls who were deemed to need help were assigned a counselor. But we had no set place to meet. Instead, the counselor had to find spare classrooms at various schools and inform us each time the location changed. Usually, three to six girls attended. We'd just hang out and talk or make things out of Popsicle sticks. The counselor taught us about hygiene, social skills, and nutrition. She encouraged us to talk to each other, support each other, and teach each other any skills we had. We listened to her because she was fun and cool. She wore overalls, drove a Volkswagen van, and talked to us as if we were her peers. She had springy, curly hair and an overall attitude so full of pep that my sister

Edie took to calling her Tigger, the bouncy tiger in the stories of Winnie the Pooh. She became a friend. When I told her I thought I might be gay, she let me know that she was too. Before long we started seeing each other romantically, though she was also in a long-term relationship. I can only imagine that my dramatic butcher-knife-in-the-sock incident put her in a terribly awkward situation.

When several days after her call to the police I got out of the psychiatric ward at Kaiser Hospital in Richmond, California, I milled around the neighborhood alone, trying to figure out what to do with myself. I wandered onto the elementary school playground and walked straight to the jungle gym, a metal structure that kids climbed on at recess. I slammed my right wrist against it over and over with all the force I could muster, trying to fracture the bones in my hand, but I managed only deep bruising.

I used to stand in front of a mirror sometimes and punch myself in the face until the hard ridge below my eye turned starkly red, which would later bruise into a black eye. Sometimes I would sit in a field of high weeds and use a shard of glass to scrape shallow crisscrossing scratches into my skin and watch blankly as beads of blood formed on my arm. I never thought about why I did any of these things. I didn't experience them as decisions or even as choices. I felt compelled. Self-injurious behavior, I learned much later, is relatively common among teens. A 2018 *New York Times* article estimated that roughly 18 percent of American high school students have participated in self-harming behavior, in some states as many as one in four girls. Psychologists view it as more of an attempt to *relieve* pain than to *inflict* it. This behavior is seen as *attention seeking*, as opposed to injuries inflicted with the intention of ending one's life. It's a useful distinction for therapists and doctors to determine what type of intervention is needed, but it does little to describe the complex emotions that can lead to such desperation.

Until I began these walks, whenever I thought of my younger self, I regarded her with the same blank, unfeeling stare I'd tried to perfect as a kid.

I LEAVE THE elementary school on Seventeenth Avenue and as I do, I absently wrap my left hand about my right wrist and apply pressure. Clearly my left hand is administering first aid, but to no obvious injury. Standing in the middle of the quiet street, I kiss the knobby bone on the back of the wrist that I brutalized so many years ago. "I'm sorry," I whisper.

There's a mounting late afternoon breeze, and unexpected tears feel like ice crystals, cold against my cheeks otherwise flush and warm from hours of adventuring. The thought enters my mind that I left my younger self abandoned in that schoolyard and started a new life without her, severing a sense of connection and continuity across my lifespan, and that through the walks I'm circling back to pick her up.

I ADORED LIVING at the Rogerses' house. The days were neither amorphous nor endless as they were at home. Every meal was shared around the little dinette set in their kitchen and everyone sat down together. The house was clean and you could find what you were looking for in designated spots: the broom, towels, soap. Each weekday morning, Mrs. Rogers sent me and her two daughters off to school with bagged lunches and hugged each of us as we left the house. I acted indifferent and shrugged off her hugs, but I secretly loved it when she'd say, "You will never be too old for me to hug."

After several weeks, without explanation, Mrs. Rogers told me it was time for me to go home. I returned begrudgingly, walking the half block and the million miles back. At home nothing had changed: My father's drinking and depression continued to suck all of the air out of the house. At night he'd sit in a wooden rocking chair in the living room, a jug of cheap wine at his feet. He'd rock slowly back and forth, his head thudding against the wall over and over. Sometimes he'd still be in the chair with an empty bottle at his feet the next morning when I left for school.

One evening my mother called me from her home in Berkeley. She got straight to business. "If you don't start behaving better, your father is going to die and it will be on your shoulders." She didn't specify what I was doing wrong or how I could avoid harming him in the future, and I didn't ask. I just took it like a spoonful of vinegar, sour and astringent, and got off the phone as soon as I could. A few days later, my father took me aside himself and told me that if one day he didn't get up for work, I should open the safe in his bedroom closet, where I would find some papers that would explain what I needed to do.

I grimaced and told him I thought he was being a little dramatic. He'd had a heart attack in the past, sure, but he was only forty-seven years old. I sarcastically suggested that he quit drinking to see if that might improve his health and resumed my campaign to get him to go to AA. He may have had a similar conversation with Edie, who was the eldest of the siblings still living at home, but she and I never discussed it.

He told me that I should move out if I didn't like it at home, and that if I didn't move, he'd have to make me "a ward of the state"—a term that was commonly used when his own mother placed him in an orphanage after his father died when my father was young.

I knew some girls my age who had been living on the streets in the Bay Area after running away or being kicked out of their family homes for being gay. They were involved with a nonprofit social services agency that arranged foster placements for gay youth. After I told my father about it, he signed the necessary paperwork to arrange a placement for me. My father had no problem with the fact that I was gay. In fact, his first response when I told him was "I've had gay experiences myself." I did not venture to inquire further. I didn't want to know.

My mother's response, when I called her to tell her I

was gay, was similarly nonchalant. She said, "I've known that since you were asked, at age six, what you wanted to be when you grew up and replied, 'I will be a big man and I will ride a motorcycle.'" That was before the nuances of sexuality and gender were well understood. Still, in the late '70s she was ahead of her time.

At sixteen I moved into a foster home in Berkeley with two lesbians who each had a school-aged daughter. Several months later, my father died suddenly from a massive heart attack. Cathy, the third born, called to inform me of his death, and I remember throwing the phone across the room—as if that could undo her words. Only in retrospect have I come to wonder whether part of his reason for letting me go was that he knew that all the kids remaining at home would need places to live; he knew that he was going to die. If this was the case, I realize for the first time, the stories I've told myself about why he so readily sent me off to foster care were not necessarily accurate. Maybe he was simply trying to ensure that I had a place to be after he was gone.

It wasn't until we were adults that Cathy and I realized that we'd both lived through the same quiet hell of believing that we'd had a hand in our father's death. I told my siblings during one of our group Zoom calls about my phone call from our mother just months before our father died. Cathy confided that she'd had a nearly identical conversation with our mother, and then I could finally see the absurdity of us kids essentially being preemptively pinned for manslaughter.

The evening of my father's death, I took the BART

train from my foster home in Berkeley to Fremont, to be with my siblings. All of us were together—from Jerry, who was twenty-four years old, to Margaret, who was ten. We wandered around the house in a daze, unsure what we should do next.

Our mother refused to take any of us home with her, even for the night, while new arrangements could be made. Instead, the siblings who had still been living at home went their separate ways. Edie, the fifth born, went to stay with our uncle Bob in Oakland. John, the seventh, moved from one neighbor's home to another's, then at seventeen enlisted in the navy. Margaret went to live in a commune in Oakland with some friends of my father's.

Shortly after my father's death, I moved out of the foster home in Berkeley and into a third foster home in San Francisco, with Sue, whom I'd first met when I was fifteen. She was one of the therapists running the counseling agency that was placing gay youth in foster homes with gay adults. I was embarrassed to be in placement, as I believed myself too old to need care, and it bothered me that I needed an adult to help me navigate getting into a new high school. It didn't help that Sue was as close in age to me as she was to my mother, but she found ways to show she cared without threatening my need to feel autonomous. Whenever she went to the grocery store, she'd come home with a big red apple and give it to me like a carefully chosen gift. I loved those apples. They sent a message of care and concern for my well-being that I could receive.

Once, walking with Sue through a San Francisco neighborhood full of Victorian homes, I marveled at the intricate woodwork and stopped to admire their dramatic color schemes. I was mesmerized by one building that was painted in relatively drab colors except for the underside of the eaves, which were painted in a vivid blue.

"I like how they painted this one," I said. "Look how strong that blue is because it's surrounded by more subtle colors."

As we continued walking, Sue said, "You know, I've noticed that you really pay attention to details."

I can't imagine that it was the first time anyone had paid me a compliment, but I pondered it again and again. I do think it is my first conscious memory of having someone notice and name a personal strength in me.

When I aged out of foster care at eighteen, I was accepted into a trades training program through Alameda County social services, got a job at an ice cream store on Telegraph Avenue in Berkeley, and rented a room from an older lesbian couple in an old Craftsman house on the border between Oakland and Berkeley. The idea that I had to leave home when I turned eighteen had been so deeply ingrained in me by my parents that I never considered asking Sue if I could stay a little longer. Almost everything about my life to that point had taught me that self-sufficiency was my only hope, but very little had helped me develop skills to become self-sufficient.

My father's job throughout my childhood was primarily assisting electricians, so when I was presented with my options for the trades program—plumbing, carpentry, etc.—I selected electronics, thinking that it must be roughly similar, given its first six letters.

But then I met Michele.

I was on Natural Bridges State Beach in Santa Cruz visiting my friend Melinda, who had moved to Santa Cruz to attend boarding school when we were fourteen. She had buried me up to my head in the sand. Melinda noticed a friend walking by and called her over. I worked my arm through a mound of damp sand to shake Michele's hand and introduce myself. Several weeks later I was waiting to board a Greyhound bus in San Francisco to head east to the Michigan Womyn's Music Festival, sort of a rite of passage for a young lesbian, and through the crowd of passengers Michele and I spotted each other and locked eyes. We sat together on the bus and spent the following two years together. At eighteen, without giving notice at the ice cream store or informing the trades program, I moved from the East Bay area to the relatively small town of Santa Cruz to be with Michele. I remember walking around the neighborhoods and thinking to myself, *What the hell do people do here?*

Michele and I had a lot of great times together during those two years and, as good friends, in the forty-five years since, but my all-time favorite memory of that time was when I decided to take Michele to meet my mother in the home she bought for herself in Pittsburg, California, after selling our family home. I reached into the cage of my mother's double yellow-headed amazon parrot, Charlie, and coaxed him to perch on my hand as I'd done dozens of times when he lived with us before my mother left Fremont. Charlie bit my hand with his powerful beak, and as I assessed the damage, my mother snapped, "You're a stranger to him now, dummy! He has no idea who you are!" Michele turned sharply, made direct eye contact with my mother, and said firmly, "Angelica is not dumb." Time stood still.

I GOT INVOLVED in the CETA (Comprehensive Employment and Training Act) program, which offered subsidized jobs and training for up to two years to low-income people. I was sent to early childhood education courses and was assigned to jobs in two different local childcare centers as a cook and a teacher's assistant.

During my first two years in Santa Cruz, I was asked regularly in the grocery store or at social events whether I was a student at UCSC. I had no idea what UCSC was and could not figure out what it was about me that made so many people think I was somehow associated with the place. It would be ten years before I drove onto campus as a student, shortly after my thirtieth birthday, in a baby-blue diesel Volkswagen Rabbit. The same car my ex-girlfriend taught me to drive in when I was twenty-two, a demo model with no radio or air-conditioning, which she kindly gave to me when she bought herself a new work truck.

When Michele and I broke up, I gave away my few belongings, slung a day pack over my shoulder, stuffed my canvas bifold wallet in my back pocket with all the money I had, maybe a hundred dollars, and walked downtown to the Greyhound station, where I read the bus schedule like a menu and ordered up a ticket to Sonoma, an hour north of San Francisco. I was restless and anchorless. My time with the CETA program was up. I was working multiple part-time jobs and barely piecing together enough money to rent the room I was living in.

Several hours later when I arrived at the bus terminal in Sonoma, I was the loneliest I could recall ever having been. As the sun set, I became increasingly nervous about finding a place to sleep. Two storefronts down from where I sat on a cold cement curb, a woman stepped out of a small community grocery store, locking the door behind her. I summoned all my courage to ask her, "Do you happen to have a place I can stay for the night?" She ran her eyes over me and replied, "Sure." Then, gesturing as she pointed down a side road, she said: "I'm Rebecca. I live a few blocks this way." She made me a delicious veggie melt and told me I could stay a couple of nights in her spare room.

The next evening she invited me to a party in nearby Point Arena, where I met a woman named Annabelle and her nine- and eleven-year-old daughters. The three of them were living in a big blue box van, a delivery truck, and Annabelle suggested I move in with them. We changed locations from night to night, washing our clothes in gas station sinks or sneaking into trailer park bathrooms for a shower. The van broke down on Thanksgiving Day and the owner of the nearest repair shop we could find took pity on us. We slept in the van parked inside the Point Arena Garage eating cold food out of cans I'd lifted from the one grocery store we found open. I was already practiced at shoplifting and it came in handy as a way to contribute to my new household. We skipped giving thanks.

On my twenty-first birthday, I lay on my back in a damp, weedy field near the box van listening to the music of crickets and gazing up at the stars thinking, *What am I doing? If I have enough intelligence to figure out how to get by, I likely have enough to earn my CHSPE*, the California High School Proficiency Exam. I didn't leave right away, but a few weeks later when Anabelle decided that she, her new girlfriend, and her daughters were going to pack up and head to Vermont, I boarded a bus back to Santa Cruz.

I wanted to do something different, be someone different. I didn't know what specifically that would entail, but I resolved that it wouldn't involve stealing and scamming. By that time I had graduated from simple petty theft to purchasing traveler's checks and having a friend spend them while I reported them missing, then splitting the spoils of the replacement checks.

I managed to rent a room in an old farmhouse back in Santa Cruz, got another job scooping ice cream, and started Monday school, a social services program geared toward helping young people prepare for the CHSPE. At twenty-one, I was the oldest person in the class.

IT SEEMED AS good a time as any to have a baby.

I wanted to be part of a family, so I would make one. A sound plan for who I was at that moment.

Numerous people cautioned me to hold off until I was a little older and in better shape financially. I didn't think that would ever be the case. So at age twenty-one, I started the journey of becoming someone's mom. We would be poor, my baby and I, but we'd be happy.

I had heard that a few lesbians around the Bay Area, and at least two in Santa Cruz, were getting pregnant through artificial insemination. I knew very few men socially, but Jesse talked to a friend of hers whom I barely knew, and I talked to Rabbit, an acquaintance of mine. Both agreed to be donors. My initial plan was to use two donors so neither they nor I would know which of them was the biological father. But before I got started, Jesse's friend dropped out. I tried for nine months and finally, in June of 1983, at twenty-two years old, I learned that I was pregnant. Nine months later I gave birth to a nine-pound baby boy, Kita Wilder Glass.

It is appalling and embarrassing in retrospect, but until Kita was about a year old, I kept to myself the fact that one of the donors had decided not to participate. At that point, I let Rabbit, the sole donor, who was becoming a friend, know that I knew who the father was, and I asked him if he wanted to know. He did. This required explaining that I'd withheld the information, which he took with both surprise and generous grace.

The older I get, the more I see how ill prepared I was for motherhood. I understand now why some friends were concerned. But I raised a well-loved child, and, to my surprise, an incredibly intelligent one. Learning to parent, especially without the help of parents of my own, was humbling. I swore I would never hit a child, and I never have. Not once. But the fear that I would slip and revert to what was familiar to me was a persistent cloud that hung over me. In the child development courses I took at Cabrillo College when I was eighteen and nineteen, I heard repeatedly that children who are abused grow up to abuse their own children. The intention, no doubt, was to discourage people from using physical punishment and educate students about generational violence, but it made me feel doomed.

One day Kita had a classic toddler meltdown because I was decidedly not a competent tie-er of shoes, and anyway, he didn't want shoes, but yes he did, so put them back on NOW! But with no socks! No socks! No socks! It was big, dramatic, and exhausting.

He desperately needed me to help him regulate his emotions, which I sensed but had neither the words nor the skills to do. His frustration and anger ballooned. I didn't feel any temptation to hit him, but I felt out of my league and in that moment I feared that what I was feeling must have been what my mother felt before she lashed out at us. So I picked him up, kicking and screaming, put him in the small rectangle of dirt we called our backyard, locked the sliding door so he couldn't get back into the apartment, and went upstairs and stared at the wall. I believed I was protecting him from myself. He cried louder and louder, gasping between squalls, until he finally ran out of steam.

I went back down and picked him up, his face flushed

and tear-streaked, and brought him back into the apartment. We sat on the couch quietly together, he in my lap, until we both fell asleep. It took time, there were stops and starts, but I learned to trust that I wasn't going to hurt him, and he learned to trust that I wasn't going to walk away from him. Forty years later, I can barely recall those moments without feeling that my chest is going to cave in and I fight the urge to apologize to him . . . again.

I raised him with the help of his other mother, Mardi, the original owner of the Volkswagen Rabbit, and a host of friends, partners, and ex-partners. Mardi and I never lived together and we split up when Kita was a toddler, but she and her wife of nearly forty years, Mel, remain in his life today, as do his biological father, his wife, and their grown children—a far-reaching, unlikely, and dynamic family.

It was Mardi's strong reaction to my stealing some sunscreen at Longs drugstore by putting it in the basket of Kita's stroller that finally got me to taper off shoplifting. She was furious at me, which I found odd. I mean, I was trying to protect his skin! Stealing wasn't a great idea, but it was something you had to do from time to time to get by between monthly checks. Mardi pointed out that if I'd been caught, Kita would have been impacted too. After that I stopped stealing. Mostly. The last thing I stole was a Christmas tree in 1988 out of a grocery store parking lot on Soquel Avenue. I was flat broke and there was no way my four-year-old was going without a tree. He got plenty of gifts from friends and relatives.

While Kita attended a state-funded preschool in Santa

Cruz, I took more child development and sign language classes at the local community college and landed my first full-time job, complete with health insurance and paid leave, as a special education specialist for the Santa Cruz County Office of Education, providing sign language interpreting for two children who were deaf in a mainstream classroom.

Being back in a grade school setting stretched my nerves like taut rubber bands. Everywhere I looked there were reminders of a time I didn't want to revisit and of people I preferred to forget. The lonely clang of tetherball chains against their metal poles rang of alienation. The unkempt child with dirty nails, dried snot trails across the backs of his hands, and the sour stench of unwashed hair and stale pee was a looking glass I did not want to stare into. But the advantage of being in a learning environment with an inspired educator, the classroom teacher, Patty Partch Lovato, quickly became clear. I was able to listen to lessons every day for two years without the pressure of being a student. I learned about basic machinery, plant anatomy, mathematics. During quiet times in the classroom of twenty-five ten- and eleven-year-olds with their heads in books, I practiced my penmanship on preprinted sheets with the same letter repeated across the page. I did my best to listen and interpret classic fifth-grade books like *James and the Giant Peach* as the teacher read aloud.

In my second year at the school, one of the teachers, Nahara, took me aside and said, "You're too smart for this job. It's a dead end." I had clawed my way into that job, and it far exceeded any expectations I'd had for myself. I assured her that I was content with my work and that a college degree was out of the question for me.

Nahara concentrated years of parenting and educational advice into a single pill, placed it on my tongue, and refused to step away until I'd swallowed it. She told me I needed to make a six-year plan. I guffawed. I could barely plan what I was going to make for dinner that night. When she said we should make a list of the pros and cons of my going to college, I replied that I didn't know what a "pro" was and I didn't know what a "con" was. I thought I saw a flicker of surrender in her, but she explained the concept, got out a sheet of paper, and handed me a pencil.

At age twenty-eight, I capitulated, and with Nahara's help I mapped out a plan. Two years at the local community college, Cabrillo. Two years at UCSC. Two years in a graduate program. And at the end I'd be trained as a social worker.

Attending Cabrillo College, the first step in Nahara's three-step plan, was challenging but also thrilling. I took a class in cultural anthropology from an instructor who used humor to engage his students and spark interest in the subject he was most passionate about. He would get up on a long row of classroom tables and walk along it like a model on a catwalk, showing us his impressions of how different hominids walked and lived over the millennia. From another teacher, I learned about astronomy. As a class, we went to an observatory.

I didn't know the word *sociology* when I began, but the

academic counselor at Cabrillo told me it would align with my ultimate goal of becoming a social worker. I wish I could say that it was my challenging childhood that led me to choose a career in the helping professions. The plain truth is that I chose a topic on which I believed I had a head start: I knew this world from the inside. (Or so I thought at the time. I had a lot to learn.) In retrospect, there are plenty of areas I could have succeeded in, but starting off with the *belief* that I had a leg up likely tilted the balance toward success.

Based on Nahara's advice, I became a full-time student for six years. I got financial aid, loans, AFDC (Aid to Families with Dependent Children), and worked under the table cleaning houses to manage financially. I tried to juggle my schedule so that Kita was either with Mardi and Mel or participating in an after-school program on my longest days. When that didn't align, I called on various friends to help me with child care, and occasionally I took him to school with me.

With my associate's degree in hand, my next step was UCSC, City on the Hill, as it's called locally. The academic counselor at Cabrillo helped me get connected with the women's reentry program at UCSC, which smoothed my transition into a university.

I had started dating while I was at Cabrillo, and by the time I was gearing up to start at UCSC, I was in a full-fledged relationship that spanned the next seven years. It was the longest relationship I'd been in at that point in my life and by far the longest I'd ever imagined myself in.

I loved the beginning of relationships. It was the part I was good at: the electric connection. The lusty joy of two people presenting their best selves, dressing a little better, standing a little taller, being more open to new ideas. The mesmerizing vortex of getting to know a new person inch by inch over the canvas of skin and story by story over their singular lifetime.

I loved the elusive potential of a lasting relationship just out of reach and the yearning effort to claim it and all the settled comforts I imagined it could bring. I craved familiarity, but I also treated it like a catching virus. As soon as I felt passion turning to expectation in myself or my new person, some part of me started preparing for the dissolution.

KITA WAS SEVEN and had already been through several moves, starting when I had to leave the farmhouse where he was born, before we finally settled into an apartment on Seabright Avenue. Over the course of his first seven years, I'd cycled through multiple brief relationships. I didn't want to disrupt his life again, so I didn't move in with Lisa until we'd been together for a couple of years.

In my eyes, Lisa was a real adult. She had a professional job, owned a home, and drove nice cars. In addition to her hard-earned successful business, she had the financial support of her family in going to college, buying her vehicles, and purchasing her home. I had never seen close-up what looked to me like a life of unimaginable luxury.

Lisa introduced Kita and me to worlds we'd never dreamed of: skiing, snowboarding, travel, fine dining, scuba diving (snorkeling for Kita; he wanted to learn to scuba dive, but I couldn't stomach the risks). Lisa was extremely generous and extravagant in her gift giving. When we moved in together, I declined to merge our money. I was afraid of becoming dependent on this new way of life. I paid a small portion of Lisa's mortgage payment and contributed toward utilities. But my financial contribution to our life together was a pittance.

I tried to act nonchalant about our new lifestyle, but Kita, at seven not concerned about making an impression, sometimes gave us away. The first time Lisa took us to the lodge at Squaw Valley, her preferred resort, near a house that she and a few friends had purchased to make their frequent ski trips less of a hassle, she asked Kita, "What do you want for lunch?" He looked at me perplexed. On the rare occasions when he and I ate away from home before I met Lisa, I would order one thing and split it with him. When she asked him what he wanted to drink, he replied, "Is the water free?" Lisa read to him all the options on the drinks menu: milk, apple juice, soda, milkshake. He looked at me quizzically. Only when I nodded encouragement did he quietly voice his choice: apple juice.

I was still on cash aid from the county and receiving student loans, but I was now wearing diamond earrings and a soft leather jacket. I started going to a small salon to get my hair cut instead of to the students at the local beauty college. Whenever Lisa went clothes shopping for herself, she always brought something back for me. For the first time in my life, I was amassing a wardrobe that I was proud of. When Lisa rounded up all her work clothes to take them to the dry cleaner, she took mine too. They came back to me clean and perfectly pressed, on crinkly paper-covered metal hangers and wrapped in thin plastic.

If a car malfunctioned, it immediately went to the mechanic. If something broke, it was replaced with something of equal or greater quality. When I went to stores like Macy's or Nordstrom, the clerks now knew me and readily offered their help. My association with being in department stores was of feeling I was being eyed suspiciously (with good reason), left over from my shoplifting days, or of being assessed by my clothing as someone who was not likely to make a purchase.

Lisa loves dogs like few people I know. For the period we were together, Kita joyfully became part of a puppy pile of four with her wonderful, spoiled canines. When he was eight, she brought home a dog just for him. Suki was a chow, pit bull, and Akita mix, all breeds with reputations for aggressiveness. But Suki was the most docile, loving dog I've known, except when she was reacting protectively. When I took her on evening strolls, if a passerby so much as said hello to me, she would pull on her leash and growl. I had only to return the greeting for her to turn from an apparent killing machine to a tail-wagging angel. I had never felt so safe as I felt with her beside me.

A SIMPLE REDWOOD sign reading UNIVERSITY OF CALIFOR-
NIA SANTA CRUZ announces the campus. Trying to find a
name for the unfamiliar emotion welling up as I drove by
the sign on my first day of classes, I landed on *pride*. Even
alone in my car, I blushed at the idea that I might be proud
of myself, that anyone might be proud of me. Where Cabrillo felt sufficiently familiar when I became a full-time
student there, everything about UCSC threw me into a
swivet: the parking, the transportation around campus, the
etiquette. (I'd mustered the courage to compliment a wom-
en's studies professor on her beautiful silk scarf and she
practically bit my head off, expounding on women's value
being minimized and reduced to appearance. I quickly set
a rule for myself: Only address professors if they talk to
you first.) I had to fight the urge to walk away from my education plan frequently.

When I graduated, Lisa had a big party for me. She ordered a cake in the UCSC colors, gold and blue, and gave
me a gorgeous leather satchel to take with me to San Francisco State University (SFSU) the following fall, step three
of my academic plan.

I continued to take housecleaning jobs in addition to
being in school full time, but having a partner made life
monumentally more manageable. On the days that I had to
be in San Francisco for classes, I would get up early, pack
an ice chest with the day's food, and head north along Highway 1. I liked that though school was seventy-five miles

away, my driving directions were "Turn left onto Mission Street/California Highway 1. Turn left into the parking lot of San Francisco State University." I had both morning and evening classes and didn't get home until 8 p.m. Lisa would pick Kita up from school on the days he wasn't staying with his other mother, Mardi, make dinner for him, and get him ready for bed so I could spend some time with him and read to him before he went to sleep.

When I graduated from San Francisco State, Sue and Lisa had another party for me at Sue's house in San Francisco. They invited my mother, and to my surprise, she came. We didn't have much to say to each other, but I liked that she was there.

Lisa and I had some good years together. But as small problems between us grew more prominent, we grew increasingly discontented until we grew apart altogether. With distance, I can see what a transformative period of my life those seven years were. Lisa helped me get a taste of what it is to live in a world that doesn't feel one blown head gasket or missed rental payment away from homelessness.

BEFORE THE WALKS, I would simply have said that the home I grew up in was chaotic, that my mother's belief that her children were intellectually inferior and my father's apparent inability to intervene on our behalf, as well as the willingness of both of them to talk to and about us using words like *retard* and *imbecile*, hurt our confidence in educational settings. My parents' name-calling was indiscriminate and wide-ranging, such as the time my father chased Edie down the street yelling, "Get back here, you retard!" in front of our neighbors, and the many times my mother referred to me as "dummy," as if it was my name.

Sometimes my mother tried to diagnose us. I have a memory of seeing my sister Cathy sitting on the orange-and-white vinyl couch downstairs crying. I asked her what was wrong. She explained that she had overheard our mother telling our father that Cathy was retarded. Cathy doesn't remember that, but she remembers our mother determining that she was "hysterical" and convincing a doctor to prescribe medication to address the problem. Cathy's new medication, phenobarbital, went on the refrigerator shelf next to John's (the seventh born's) ADHD medication.

While the name-calling and shaming were cruel, they were also deeply entrenched learned behaviors for my mother and her own mother. With my mother's death a couple of years before I started the walking project, her story, besides the small fragments of information she imparted to some of her children, was lost. I will never know where this pattern of debilitating self-doubt or its potent perpetuation started. All I know is that it was seemingly permanent and immovable within her.

Marilyn Brookwood's devastating history *The Orphans of Davenport: Eugenics, the Great Depression, and the War over Children's Intelligence* lays out the disturbing period of racist and class-biased thinking about how people acquire intelligence, and why during my parents' childhoods it was commonly held that intelligence was inherited and fixed and that traits such as inferior intelligence could be bred out of society. A group of psychologists at the Iowa Child Welfare Research Station, dubbed the Iowans, produced studies that revealed that both heredity *and* experience influence development and intelligence. The author notes that "stark political and ethical consequences followed psychology's denial of the Iowans' discoveries. Potential reforms in education, child psychology . . . and parents' encouragement of their children all lost ground to the persistence of hereditarian ideology." I can only guess that my mother's cruelty was in part a manifestation of her fear that her "dumbness" begot ours. She matured into adulthood at a time when getting married and having children were expected, and in her case it was an acceptable avenue to get away from a tumultuous family life. By seventeen she was married, and within a couple of years her first son was born.

When my mother was in her mid-thirties with eight children, a friend of my parents, recognizing her intelligence, urged her to go to college and earn a degree. It was the 1970s, the women's movement was in full swing, and my mother started to understand that by following the status quo when she was younger, she had limited her options. To prove to herself that she was in fact intelligent, she started taking classes at the local community college, and later focused on studying English at Cal State Hayward. When she went back to school, she began to challenge our spelling and vocabulary, and if the dictionary proved her wrong, she questioned its accuracy. Soon she was regularly correcting our grammar and chiding us more than ever for doing poorly in school.

My mother took a formal IQ test, and since she suspected that my brother Kevin, the fourth born, was also smart, he got an IQ test too. He and my mother both scored at the genius level. Kevin was studious, rarely emerging from his bedroom, where he kept his books and writing materials. His entire identity became focused on academic achievement, at the expense of a social life and outdoor activities. He worked two jobs and as a senior in high school received multiple scholarships and attended the University of California, Berkeley. He received no financial or emotional support from our parents, and regardless of consistent, concrete evidence to the contrary, he continued to doubt his intelligence well into adulthood.

Margaret was put in the Gifted and Talented Education (GATE) program in her elementary school but was still labeled "troubled." Being a Glass kid seemed to be synonymous with being troubled in the eyes of some of the school staff and our parents alike. Our mother told her that she was the kind of girl who would end up a teen mother and admonished her not to waste her life by getting pregnant. Why our mother thought she understood what kind of girl Margaret was perplexed me even then, and the fact that she felt at liberty to voice her opinion still infuriates me. Our mother's opinion made Margaret doubt herself. At age seventeen Margaret *was* pregnant with her first child. She returned to school at the age of forty-one, and earned her bachelor's degree at forty-five, with her children in the audience at her graduation.

Many of the Glass children followed the same path our mother had, being certain that college was not an option for us, then figuring out later in life that we were capable. Each of us had to forge our own path to overcome generational insecurities about ourselves on our own timeline. Some of us went to college in our thirties or forties. Edie, the fifth born, earned a degree and started her career as a special education teacher in her early sixties. She was in special education programs throughout her own schooling, which gave her insight into her students' lives that strengthened her effectiveness and commitment as a teacher.

I would like to believe that interspersed with our mother's legacy of self-doubt is one of perseverance.

SINCE I STARTED the walks, I frequently wake deep in thought, as if my brain has been churning as I sleep and I'm simply eavesdropping on myself. At first, strings of words and phrases would run through my mind, not all of which I knew the meaning of: *phosphorus, common denominator, nitrogen, carry the two, igneous, photosynthesis, Constantinople.* Information I'd held at bay since I *forgot everything* in fifth grade gushed forth, slipping through the metaphorical cracks in my subconscious, breaking down walls. Basic concepts I'd struggled to understand for years and ultimately given up on—such as directionality, the four directions—suddenly began to make sense.

I'M WRAPPING UP my walk so I can pick up Miles from his friend's house on my way home. I find my way through a maze of side streets back to Seventeenth Avenue. Out of the blue it dawns on me and I say aloud, "Oh, the four directions are fixed, but left and right are relative to where I'm standing." It used to repel me to hear people talk to themselves; it looked like a shameful lack of self-control. Now I understand that it can also be a bubbling brain overflowing its banks. I think nothing now of giving literal voice to a surprising revelation, greeting newts like long-lost friends and complimenting dragonflies on their color combinations. (As it turns out, dragonflies don't have ears, but I still talk to them.)

The combination of hating to ask for help and not understanding directionality has led me far afield many, many times. Today I bring out my phone, open the Notes app, and add to an ever-growing list of books to read, hiking gear to procure, and questions about the natural world to research: *Compass. Book on navigation.*

One upside of having missed out on some of the basics when I was young is that now I get to experience the wonders of nature and the deep wells of history at a point in life when many people my age take them all for granted—or worse, forget about them. There is the unadulterated joy of expanding my mind, but unlike the unwitting process of taking in new information as a child, I've been able to consciously observe the process of my own learning. I am both learning and learning how to learn. I revel in both.

Throughout the project and beyond, I've marinated in immersive information gathering, or as I call it, "sitting in the dirt." I repeatedly find myself taking a close look at a fallen nest, scat, or an animal bone, or wading in the murky shallows of a river to watch bugs, fish, or crawdads. Quietly, calmly, patiently, I watch long enough to notice patterns and habits. A friend who is a teacher gave me another term: field study. I wear it like a badge.

I have finally gotten my do-over. I am building a stable foundation upon which to layer new knowledge and information. I can't begin to quantify all that I've learned from this project, or what I continue to learn building upon that foundation. It's common knowledge among mental health and child development professionals that the first five years of life is the period in which the human brain sees the most growth. The brains of babies and preschoolers make millions upon millions of neural connections every day. Parental involvement, preschool, and other early childhood intervention services are increasingly recognized to be of critical importance. Those first five years are long gone for me, of course, but this decade from my early fifties to my early sixties is the closest second for intake and processing of information that I could ever have hoped for.

I COME UP against reminders every day that I am not a native tech user, and I often resent the ways technology has infringed on our daily lives. For example, my sister Margaret and I once went camping in Oregon. We got online to buy tickets to visit nearby Multnomah Falls, but after entering the necessary personal information, we got a pop-up message saying something to the effect of "Sorry, the system cannot verify that you're human." We were prevented from using our hard-earned dollars to observe a naturally occurring feature because a computer system had doubts as to our humanity. It was boggling. Still, sometimes I feel an urgent need to know whether a newt I've spotted is a rough-skinned newt or a California newt, and I rejoice at being alive in the time of this indispensable miracle of the modern age, my cell phone. I search for answers to questions like: What colors do ladybugs come in? Where do mountain lions sleep? Why are there fossilized sand dollars in Scotts Valley, 560 feet above sea level? What's another term for forest duff?

There are, I've learned through walking and research, five thousand types of ladybugs in a spectrum of colors. Mountain lions like to sleep in caves and among dense brush. Scotts Valley was once underwater. *Mulch, detritus, O horizon*: these are words you can use if you get tired of saying "forest duff"—though I don't get tired of saying "forest duff."

Walks lead me to searches, and searches lead me to books. The contents of my bookshelves have changed more radically and become more geared to new interests and passions in the past decade than in all my previous years combined. Books on walking, writing, photography, tide pools, forests, history, dreams, butterflies . . . If you told me when I was twenty (or fifty) that I would one day read with rapt attention a book about mushrooms, I would have sneered.

My voracious new appetite for information brings to mind a day many years before the project started, when Kita was four years old. I'd picked him up from preschool and as we drove down the highway, he flung his arms with an exasperated huff. I asked him what was up. "Argh!" he groaned earnestly. "There are too many things I want to learn!"

"What kinds of things do you want to know about?" I asked him.

"Well, like steam shovels . . . and foxes," he replied.

I wanted him to know that I cared about his frustration, so I kept my glee to myself. *I was raising a child who was eager to learn!* We made an emergency stop at the library. Dinner would wait. With the help of a kind librarian, we found a book on foxes and another on large machinery, including steam shovels. Kita was happy. This was the beginning of a lifelong love of learning.

Making discoveries on my own, then seeking out information about them to gain a fuller understanding, is an entirely different experience for me than reading something in a book, then going in search of it with someone else's impression already in my mind. Both can be enriching, but the former greases the cogs of my brain and sends me on a life-changing treasure hunt for my own steam shovels and foxes.

IT BREAKS MY heart now to remember how I actively practiced being invisible as a child, consciously breathing shallowly to take up the least possible space. Now when I'm hiking alone, my ability to be still, and even disappear, is an asset when it comes to observing nature: the animals, plants, birds, fish, and bugs. It works best on long solo hikes when I have plenty of time to transition back into the ways of the forest, when I can become one of the creatures in it, less of an outsider.

The once-stark barriers between past and present, vulnerability and security, damage and healing, toughness and tenderness, soften and blur as the walks unfold, and continue to resolve as the rifts are sutured and replaced with an unfamiliar but welcome sense of internal integration.

I study geometry in spiderwebs, history in tree rings, science in a butterfly's proboscis. There are songwriting lessons in sun-saturated meadows, and economy lessons in the bay laurel leaves that I pick from fallen branches, break in half to inhale their rich, camphoraceous medicine, then fold carefully into my wallet like a fresh, new currency. Among redwood fairy rings, serpentine roots on the forest floor, and burrows of small mammals in the hillsides, I sense the mother tongue of fairy tales and poetry. The open-air cafeteria serves dew-kissed miner's lettuce, warm blackberries, and liquid morning light. Map reading and wayfinding are requirements. It's all recess. It's all a kind of theology.

Chapter 5

Put the Moon Where You Want It

omnium-gatherum *noun* \\,ämnēəm-
ʼgatḫərəm\: a miscellaneous collection

FROM THE START of the project, my plan is to take a snapshot of something beautiful on each street as a way of documenting my progress. I unearth a camera I bought a few years ago, filled with great intentions of creating family photo albums. The settings and controls on it had intimidated me, so I turned to the owner's manual, which only complicated matters, then I quickly stuck the whole lot in the back of my closet, with a promise to myself that I'd give it a try *another day*.

In 2013 when I start these walks, I resolve to absorb the information in the manual if I have to read it a thousand times. As I work to understand the basics of composition and framing through reading, videos, and practice, I leave the camera on its automatic setting, reducing a relatively pricey digital single-lens reflex to a glorified point-and-shoot. When I'm ready to branch out, I switch to aperture priority, where the user selects the aperture size, the opening in the lens that controls how much light is allowed in, and the camera automatically adjusts shutter speed. Next, I try shutter priority, where the user selects the shutter speed, or how long the light enters the camera, and the camera does the rest. In both settings, ISO, which controls the sensitivity to light, is automatically determined by the camera. Looking not just through my own eyes but through an additional lens puts space between me and objects of interest. Over time, this leads to looking at the outside world in a new way and eventually translates to looking at myself in a new way. With enough remove, I am able to see my past and the ways it impacts me more clearly.

I've never tended bar. I have never even had a cocktail. I stopped drinking alcohol at age twenty-one when I still drank straight from the bottle, not a staid glass. But I have a rough understanding, thanks to grappling with shutter speed, aperture, and ISO, of the art of the mixed drink. Pour in a little light, allow time for the light to linger, tweak the sensitivity. Too much of one element requires adjustments to the others. Add the skewer, the olive, the onion: subject, focal length, composition. The trick is in acknowledging and accepting that there is no perfect concoction. You strive to find a balance that moves you, and hopefully, especially for the bartender and for the professional photographer, what moves you will also move others.

In the beginning, spotting images—details in nature,

unexpected encounters, the interplay of light and shadow—
to snap a picture of is simply fun and entertaining. It takes
active effort, boring visually into my surroundings to find
the shiny penny in the gutter, the furled frond of a fiddle-
head fern. I look with such concentration that I come home
spent after walks. Eventually it becomes my default vision
noticing fine details, spotting movement in the distance,
and using my telephoto lens to zoom in on a bobcat, a kes-
trel, a coyote, a blue jay with a giant green katydid in its
beak. It reminds me of a game I used to play with my siblings in the 1960s and '70s where we'd take the Christmas
catalog from Spiegel, a Chicago mail-order store, and each
of us had to pick one item on every page, even if our only
choice was a three-pack of men's dress socks or an alarm
clock. Each of us took our time, earnestly selecting the most
desirable, practical, or valuable item.

As the miles of my walks accumulate, my practice of
moving through the world window-shopping for beauty
leads to my increasingly fine-tuned discernment of what
moves me, trying to answer the question everyone asks
themselves: What matters to me? I came to feel that beauty
spotted me first. At some point, I begin to notice that I'm
no longer scouring but simply zeroing in on the moments
and details that resonate. Or maybe almost everything has
turned beautiful through my new eyes so everywhere I gaze
beauty is gazing back at me.

Looking through my lenses—whether the macro that
can capture and delineate details far more accurately than

my eyes alone; or the telephoto, which collapses space to dramatic effect; or a fixed lens with a range similar to that of the human eye—I find myself bombarded with visual stimuli. I am scarcely able to filter out the way low evening sunlight can set a splash of water caused by a small boy's skipped stone ablaze or raise a lustrous display of color to rival the stained glass of a dragonfly's wings.

I begin to experience the correction to perception one hopes for from new glasses or eye surgery: crisp definition of lines and edges, acuity of detail, clarity of color. I devour my world through discs of sand, soda, ash, and limestone, compressed and melted at over 2,000 degrees Fahrenheit. My camera lenses. Lost in fine detail or sweeping vistas, I observe my surroundings like a stranger; everything I lay my eyes on is brand-new.

Reflections in the bumper of a car in front of me stopped in traffic have me trying to pull out my camera and snap before the light turns green. I try to take pictures of anything that appears to me: light itself, the blank slate of a blue sky, the instant that water emerges from a spigot, bubbling soup stock, the steam rising off hot pasta, and laundry spinning in the washing-machine drum. I try to detect the split second between on and off, flipping a light switch repeatedly while snapping images, and doing so reminds me that I did the same as a child, without a camera.

I ride the swell of a tsunamic wave of curiosity. My mind and my computer swim with an omnium-gatherum of images that require only internal curation. I even try to take photographs of things I can't see. After picking a stupid argument with Ellen one night, I sit in the dark at the kitchen table, brooding, way out of proportion for our petty exchange. (Pizza toppings? The vital importance of rinsing dishes before you place them in the dishwasher? I can't remember.) I put my camera on a tripod and try to take photos of my gloom hanging in the air. The images look like nothing but grainy gray or stark white, of course, but the process of trying turns me inside out. The attempt can be more revealing than the outcome.

During one late afternoon walk, I sit marveling at the way sunlight hits a fence, forcing radiant spotlights through knotholes and setting the moss growing between the boards aglow. Even after dozens of attempts, I don't capture what I'm after, but that green, that gem of moss and light, fuels my budding desire to develop photography skills, to move past the casual snapshot. On another walk, I notice a patch of towering matilija, also known as fried-egg poppies, growing at the edge of a field at nature's whim—volunteers, as some call these flowers that spring up without human planning, gracing us for a fleeting season or setting down roots and permanently altering the landscape.

The moon is still visible in the morning sky and I lament that the flowers aren't situated so that I can get both the moon and the plant in a single shot. As I study the flowers, zooming in on leaf veins and petal edges, I kneel to get a shot of the underside of the blooms. The moon sneaks into my viewfinder and my brain expands, palpably. Though I don't immediately attach a word to the concept, I suddenly understand visual perspective. Later, when I try to describe the experience to a friend, she exclaims, "Oh yeah, you can put the moon where you want it."

Finally, after over a year of taking photographs and developing an understanding of how light, shadow, and reflection factor into images, I switch my camera setting to manual, where it has stayed since, demanding additional work, and causing frustration, in the form of near-constant adjustments for light and speed. But using manual settings gives me much more control over the types of photographs I take. I can expose for the gray-brown bark of a cypress tree to make it the highlight of an image while the rest of the frame is blown out or so overexposed as to create a stark white background. The painstaking process of trying to land on an appealing balance of all the variables is one of the challenges I most love about taking pictures, even though it sometimes means missing a great shot. I'm thrilled when I get what I judge to be a good photograph, but I love the striving just as much.

Walking and making photographs have become so linked for me that one without the other feels awkward. It's like car camping—just pulling into a spot, setting up camp, and roasting marshmallows—instead of backpacking, where a day of exertion earns you a solid sleep under the stars. Simply *going* to a place rather than *getting* there. For me, improving as a photographer demands a long-term commitment and lots of time for trial-and-error learning. By continually moving, I'm always in a new place with potential subjects to practice my photography skills: using mailboxes to try blurring the foreground or the background, capturing backlight on a cat's fur, swapping out lenses to better understand how focal length impacts shutter speed and depth of field. Occasionally people look at me askance, perhaps wondering why a woman in her sixties needs to take fifty photographs of their fence post or their bird feeder. When this happens, I either strike up a friendly conversation or move along, depending on the person's receptivity and my mood.

One afternoon, walking in the Davenport area northwest of Santa Cruz along the coast, I'm enthralled by a covey of forty quail feeding on seeds as they stand in an open field near a tumbledown barn. It's raining lightly and every few seconds a bird shivers the drops off its feathers, puffing out into a little ball for the effort. As the sprinkle turns to showers, the whole group runs for shelter under the eaves of the barn. More than any bird I've studied on my walks, the quail's first instinct seems to be to run rather than fly away. Even the ungainly wild turkeys I encounter in huge flocks will sometimes make a pell-mell retreat to a nearby tree branch above.

I track the running quail with my camera. Later, processing the photos, I see that I unintentionally created an effect where the birds stand out in stark contrast against a blurred background. Eager to replicate this *mistake*, I ask photographer friends about it and learn that it's called "panning." By setting the camera on a low shutter speed, such as 1/20, one twentieth of a second, you can follow a moving object in a steady, sweeping motion and blur the background while getting sharp detail on your subject. Once I get the hang of it, I ask my friend Jo to go to the historic Evergreen Cemetery near downtown Santa Cruz with me so I can pan her rising out of graves and emerging from between the bars of mausoleums like a ghost. She responds with her signature alacrity. Based on the resulting photographs, she is an excellent ghost model.

In Watsonville, I take several shots of an old abandoned house that for years has threatened to fall into ruin. I shoot from across the street, and just as I press the shutter a large flatbed truck passes by the house. Later, processing my photos, I'm delighted to find that I have created an image that gives the illusion that the house is being carried on the flatbed. This is a function of having the shutter speed set high (at 1/400 or so) and freezing the action so that the truck, though it's rolling down the road at 25 mph, looks stock-still in the image.

The house is visible from Highway 1. I've seen it dozens of times over the decades I've lived in the area. But it takes walking alongside it, glancing at its boarded windows, mossy turrets, and missing roof tiles, to fully experience it as the breathing monument it is to the area's history. As often happens when I find something of interest on my walks, I go home and lose myself in research on the history of the dwelling, the Redman–Hirahara House, and its links to the once much larger community of Japanese Americans who live in Watsonville.

I begin to understand that for me, looking through a lens breaks the world down into manageable pieces. By zeroing in on the tiniest detail, I can then step back and more fully appreciate the stunning whole. I sometimes achieve this effect when I'm walking by turning around, so that rather than having an expansive scene in view all at once, I can watch it unfold bit by bit as I step into it backward.

Translated from the Greek, *photography* means "drawing with light." The term is believed to have been coined by the British scientist Sir John Herschel in 1839, roughly eighteen years after Parisian inventor Joseph Nicéphore Niépce created what is considered to be the first photograph, an image of rooftops taken from his upstairs window using a process then called heliography. I can scarcely fathom that breathtaking moment of revelation, surrounded by his pewter plates and the mingled essence of bitumen, lavender, and petroleum, substances used to process his images.

OUT WALKING, I never feel alone with my camera in my hands.

One April morning, five years into the project, I wake up homesick for the redwoods and call in kind of . . . sort of . . . but really-not-at-all sick. Since I rarely take time off, I have a handsome accumulation of sick leave hours. But I'm a terrible liar and, making matters worse, my boss has become a friend. She is keenly aware of my obsession with being out in the world walking and will instantly put two and two together as soon as she sees that my voicemail is time-stamped at 6:00 a.m. I leave her a brief, vague message about feeling *out of sorts* and needing to take the day off, then go straight to packing up my gear and snacks for a full day's romp. The area I have in mind is in the north-easternmost part of the Santa Cruz Mountains and will require a forty-five-minute drive each way. Consulting my maps, I chart a roughly twenty-two-mile out-and-back walk and lace up my red hiking boots.

I'M ON A section of the Saratoga Toll Road Trail that starts under open sky with a view down into a vast expanse of redwoods, madrones, and firs through which a lazy dragon of morning fog meanders. Green branches quickly replace the blue overhead as the trail ducks into the woods. I've wandered only steps into the dense forest, and already I can feel my heart unclenching, my breath evening, my spine elongating. I spot a cluster of chanterelles at the base of a tree and my camera comes out of its bag.

I'm tempted to pick a few. I can just hear the gentle sizzle of a mirepoix of butter, leeks, and celery, and smell the heady aroma of cooked mushroom, but I'm new to wild mushrooms and I'm not entirely confident that these are not the false chanterelle. One of them has ribs that run almost to the stipe, but I don't have an identification chart on hand and I'm not about to find out the hard way which is which. Same with the stunning display of layered fans of turkey tail fungus stretching across a nearby log. They can make a good snack, unless you fall for their evil cousin, the false turkey tail. It won't make you sick, but it's too tough to eat. But the witches' gum or witches' butter, a bright orange jelly mushroom, dotting the same log is easily identified, so I swoop one up and chow down, not because it's particularly tasty, just because I can. Because it expands my world to do so.

I get off the trail at Beekhuis Road where I spot some massive spiderwebs. When sunlight hits a web just so, I can see a luminous display of rainbows caught in the strands. It has taken many attempts over many walks to finally perfect catching the range of color, so now when conditions are just right, I can't resist trying to capture it in a photograph. Beekhuis Road drops me back on Highway 9 and I head west. A large utility truck passes me and I watch its shadow move from one side of the vehicle to the other as it takes a curve. I watch it closely and register for the first time that shadows are caused by an object blocking the path of light. The object displaces light just as a submerged object displaces liquid, and the angle of the sun dictates the length and direction of the shadow. I have a vague recollection of noticing my shadow as a child or, more specifically, noticing that it was sometimes with me and sometimes not. Its presence seemed random, mysterious. If someone had explained that it was the sun that was pulling the strings, I might have filed it away as an interesting fact, but it would not have settled into me as it has learning through rapt observation. *Objects in the path of light displace the light, causing shadows. Objects submerged in liquid displace the liquid, causing overspill.*

I'm thinking about how these relate to my immersion in nature and beauty, and the ways these days of wandering, discovering, noticing, remembering, and expressing are fundamentally changing me. It's true: These infusions of natural beauty are displacing, maybe even replacing, my years of self-doubt and self-ridicule.

I've seen dead skunks, baby coyotes, bobcats, rabbits, foxes, and frogs on my walks along the roadsides and trails all over the county. My first reaction is always to look away, but the lure of the lens draws me closer to study the shape of claws, talons, and scales, the details you don't get to see when you're observing live animals from a respectful distance.

In Felton, north of Santa Cruz, on a long, steep walk I stop to sit along the roadside for a quick snack. When I get up to leave, I discover several feet away a nearly complete coyote skeleton with moss growing between the joints. I recoil, a split-second jolt of adrenaline stunning my bloodstream. But I settle my breath and employ my cherished lens to help me bore deeper into the simple beauty of the knobby epiphyses of the long bones, the porous insides (that admittedly always remind me of seafoam, an airy, crunchy, toffee-like confection), the spinal xylophone, and the birdcage of rib bones.

Before the walks, I hadn't understood how after moving past the reflexive wince one can appreciate the staggering beauty of the vessels we animals occupy. There's much to be gained by not looking away, and as the miles pass below my feet, the same comes to apply to looking back on my early years.

I step off the highway to stretch my calves, take a few

sips of water, and check my map. I'm within a mile of China Grade, a road that runs along Big Basin Redwoods State Park, in the mountain town of Boulder Creek, which will account for six miles of the walk, after which I'll head down Big Basin Way and retrace my steps the last eight miles back to the car. I've been keeping a steady pace, as I often do when I'm deep in thought, and after my rest I quickly fall back into the clip. I have a particular interest in China Grade. I have a list of creatures I'm keen to see on my walks, such as bobcats, foxes, mountain lions, pink meadow grasshoppers, and owls of any kind. All of which I've had the good fortune of seeing. But the tarantula, which rises to the top of the list, has remained elusive for me. I've heard that China Grade Road is one of the more likely places in the county to spot one and I have high hopes.

My stride slows when I spot a freshly eviscerated doe in the middle of the road. I scan my surroundings, half expecting to see a mountain lion and wanting to avoid getting between it and its kill. Instead, I see two sets of eyes: coyotes standing in the scrub just twenty feet away. I give them and their bloody breakfast a wide berth, but I turn back and take a few photographs of the wild canines with telltale blood-stained fur around their mouths, and of the deer's gaping chest cavity with all that was once tucked neatly inside now strewn on asphalt. I wait to feel repelled, but I don't. I zoom in, looking closer at exposed ribs, matted fur, and that carmine elixir, spilled in pools. I think gazing so frankly upon gaping wounds in the natural world has made it possible for me to more fully acknowledge and face my own emotional carnage.

I tried to have some semblance of a relationship with my mother right up until she died. From the time she left our family home when I was thirteen, until our last phone call when she told me that she intended to end her life, I was the one to initiate any interaction we had. Every few years I suggested that we get together. I tried to include her in major life events, graduations and weddings. She occasionally came. I understood that it was hard for her to trust people and that her relationships with her kids were all strained. For thirty-seven years, I wedged my foot between an invisible door and its jamb so she couldn't slam it shut. I wanted to leave a shaft of light between us in case she woke up in a darkened room regretful and lonely.

I talked to her when I first started falling in love with Ellen. I called her to share my joy when Ellen was pregnant with Miles.

"Why in the world would you do that?" she demanded, incredulous. "Kita's a teenager. You were almost free!"

It was a stabbing reminder of her conception of freedom—and motherhood.

I called her again when he was born to let her know that she had a new grandchild.

Finally, seven years into my relationship, I told her that I wanted her to meet Ellen and Miles, who was six years old at the time. We visited her in her mobile home, where she answered the door and said, "You must be Helen [to

Ellen] and I guess you're Eric [to Miles]." I clarified their names and laughed it off.

The next time I saw her was four years later, when she reluctantly agreed to come to our wedding, but not before warning me that if any of my siblings gave her a sliver of grief, she would "clobber" them. It was an empty threat. No grief was given. My mother only acknowledged the presence of those of her children who approached her directly, but no punches were thrown.

I thought I had forgiven my mother. But walking mile after mile, primarily in solitude, thinking about my life, everything is up for review. The farther I wander, the more nuanced becomes my understanding of forgiveness and the balder my self-honesty. I know what it is to authentically forgive someone; I've been on both sides of the equation. To continue to classify my *forgiveness* of Barbara as authentic was to bastardize the very concept.

I had neither forgiven nor not forgiven her, neither blamed nor excused her. I realized as my feet steered me along that I had simply exploited the idea of forgiveness, crouching in its shadows, stockpiling silent rage to avoid the work of reconciling my heart. I had crowned myself emotionally intelligent. After all, I was taking the broader view, looking not just at the individual, but at the social context within which her personality was formed. In *The Myth of Normal*, Gabor Maté notes, "Blame becomes a meaningless concept the moment one understands how suffering in a family system . . . extends back through generations. . . . The accusing finger can find no fixed target."

I largely agree. Still, I can't help envying those of my siblings who allow themselves to sum our mother up as evil or as heartless. They free themselves from her, putting the responsibility squarely where it belongs, and go on with their lives. They each have their own burden, their own emotional scars, but their anger is directed at an external target while mine festers and spreads in a fine layer on the damp underside of my skin.

My unconscious tactic, I see now, was to pity her, which made it possible to forgive her because it made her smaller than me. Pity as sleight of hand. If I'm bigger than you, you can't hurt me. If your rage stems from illness, then I feel sad for you rather than hurt by you. If you can't love your children because you weren't loved yourself, then it's not personal.

But the truth is that the single deficiency that I have hated most about my life is that I didn't have a mother who could love me. I hate the fact of it. I hate that I've wasted precious time crafting ways to keep it unnamed. I hate that my greatest pain comes down to the most pathetic, sniveling need imaginable: the need to be loved by someone who didn't and couldn't love me. I've spent a lifetime trying to wriggle out of my mother's indifference toward me like a too-tight wetsuit. It's shameful. It doesn't match with who I am. I would have been a great daughter to someone who wanted children, someone who knew how to love, or at least how to demonstrate fondness toward another human being.

I tried managing this defect by being funny, telling tales

about my mother to entertain friends. I tried to shrink it by holding it up against stories of the many people I've known, especially through my work in child welfare and as a hospital social worker, over the years whose suffering has been much greater than my own. Still, I am embarrassed that she couldn't love me and equally humiliated that I must tap out of my own fight, that I must admit defeat. I'm pinned to the mat under the weight of this loss and forced to slap the canvas in surrender.

I turn onto China Grade and wander this narrow road, a strip of rutted asphalt in an otherwise heavily wooded area. There are a number of side roads off it, but I'll have to come back another time to walk them because I don't want to add more mileage to an already long walk. It will be a late sunset, so I'm not at risk of being on the road after dark, but I am on the hook for making dinner tonight. Still, when I see the street sign for Memory Lane, I can't resist.

I pick up my pace and walk the road, snapping a photo of clean linens fluttering on an old-fashioned clothesline. I zip back down Memory Lane, stopping only to watch some grazing deer nibbling on mushrooms, then make the gradual ascent up to the top of China Grade, where I stop for a picnic of apple slices and Cotswold.

I generally prefer loops over out-and-back walks, but there is something to be said for looking at the same place from different angles. An all-day hike seems like a great idea when you wake up eager for an adventure, but eighteen miles in, I'm dragging my feet and thinking about the comfort of fresh flannel sheets. Back on Saratoga Toll Road Trail, I notice a clutch of brown spheres that I hadn't noticed earlier in the day. Curious, I lightly tap one with a twig, then jump away, startled, when a wisp of what looks like yellow smoke rises from inside of it. I lie flat on the ground to inspect it further and to capture a photo of the wisp, like a flaxen smoke signal, in motion. I deduce that I'm looking at some kind of mushroom, but identification will have to wait until I'm back in cell range.

My mother would have liked these strange fungi. She might have enjoyed looking at mushrooms with me. There's comfort in telling myself that it will never happen now because she's dead, but the truth is it would have never happened even if she was still alive. When she left us and moved out, it was for good. My older siblings saw that and protected themselves accordingly. But I was certain she'd take some deep breaths, settle in, then come around and find a way to incorporate her children back into her new life. That never fully happened.

As the years passed, I continued to explain away her absence in my life, certain that the time would come when that would change. I stifled my envy over the relationships some of my friends had with their mothers. I waited with a patience that in retrospect both embarrasses me and breaks my heart.

"WHO THE HELL do you think you are, Barbara Glass?" I say to myself under my breath, a little taken aback by the harshness of my tone. I try to remember the serenity I experienced weeks ago, after discovering mycelium, comparing my parents to fungi and plants. *She was just reaching for her own share of the sunlight*, I remind myself. But I'm unimpressed. "I wasted my time on you! Who has eight children and then walks away?" I mutter, then argue back: *Come on! She was barely an adult when she had her first baby. She was trying to get away from a terrible situation at home. She could never have started over with the baggage of all those children. Consider her trauma. Be kind.*

"Fuck kind!" I boom aloud, loud enough to send a flight of mourning doves flapping a hasty retreat.

The sun is streaming prettily through the trees. I bare my teeth at that fat ball of fire and turn my attention back to my dead mother. "You gave away my little sister to people you barely knew! How could you do that?" I'm crying now—sobbing. Though the walks have made more of a crier out of me, I've cried this heavily so infrequently that I feel as if I don't know how to do it. "She's my sister! My baby sister."

I'm yelling now. I try to stop myself. I don't like feeling out of control, but a storm is brewing in me and I seem to be but the vessel through which it's erupting. "How could you send your youngest son off to the navy? You despised the military—you just wanted to wash your hands of the curly blond boy with the tender heart who had to withstand the cruelty of childhood with you, then the cruelty of life without you. And what about Edie? She had barely turned eighteen when our father died. You couldn't have given her a corner of your living room to lay her head?"

I spew venom at her on behalf of each of her children. But I've missed one.

I slow my walking pace now, then stop and sit down on the dirt path cross-legged and put my face in my hands. "And what about me, Mom?" I whisper. "I waited all those years. I believed you'd come back. I needed a mother." I sound pathetic, petulant, and I laugh at myself through snot and tears, but it comes out entangled with a yell and a cry and sounds like an animal being strangled, which makes me laugh more . . . then cry more.

I know that capital *M* motherhood is a social construct that puts an impossible burden on women. And I'm a bit ashamed to find myself indulging the myth. When we were kids, my mother's sarcastic response to anything that hinted at criticism of her parenting was "It's always the mother's fault. Always blame the mother!" A bit ironic given her atrocious parenting, but she was not wrong.

The limits of my vocal cords have been tested, but I'm not done. I croak out, "You should have prioritized your children! You should have protected us! You should have chosen us!" I feel like a small child preparing to muster a forbidden swear word, my jutting chin creating a temporary underbite. It enervates me even as it mobilizes more shouts. "You're selfish! You're a bad mother!"

There. I've said it. I've stepped off my stubborn neutrality about her and yelled the truth that clogs my throat.

My voice is hoarse now. I come up out of the storm enough to realize that I've just had the meltdown of a lifetime and I didn't care whether anyone heard. I sit with that for a second, then feel a wave of relief that no one has heard. I'm ready to admit to myself that I am fully human, that I am not, after all, above basic human needs and emotions, but I want to adjust internally before I give myself up, turn myself in.

I sit a few more minutes to make sure the storm has subsided. Then I do something I've never done before. I turn the camera on myself and snap a photo. I'm not photogenic when I *don't* have tear tracks running through a layer of trail dirt on my cheeks. But it's not about *a photograph*; it's about seeing. I never feel alone with my camera in my hands, my constant witness to wonder and to the trepidatious outer reaches of beauty and, now, to my *own* spilled guts, served raw.

Chapter 6

Sister Status

sororal *adjective* \sə'rȯrəl\: of, relating to,
or characteristic of a sister

WHEN I RETURNED to Santa Cruz at age twenty-one af-ter my time in Sonoma County, the Peerless Stages bus dropped me off downtown and I walked the two miles to Ocean Street Extension, where I had rented a room sight unseen, carrying my backpack loaded with all my worldly possessions. My wallet was a little fatter than it had been when I'd left several months before. I still had some ille-gally replaced traveler's checks. I had enough money to pay a month's rent and my share of utilities and food while I looked for a job. I was moving into a funky old white farm-house that had a couple of outbuildings and at any given time several other residents.

The household included a few people who knew each other through a spiritual community in India and an assort-ment of others who sought affordable rent through shared housing. There were a couple and their two young daughters, a single woman and her toddler, a disparate and ever-changing assortment of young adults, long-term visitors, and various animals, including Ruby the golden retriever, Mr. Jackson the donkey, and Marilyn the goat. Mr. Jackson gave noisy, effusive greetings, and Marilyn and Ruby, with their vibrant personalities, welcomed me enthusiastically as I settled in. I was relieved to be back in my familiar Santa Cruz and thrilled to be living on a plot of land where the household grew acres of garlic and purple statice, which we shaped into long braids and drove to health food stores in an ancient blue Chevy pickup.

We shared our meals sitting on cushions on the living room floor around a circular table made from half a giant wooden cable spool, ostensibly taking turns preparing food among the adults in the house, but there was a range of experience in adulting, and cooking often ended up falling to the older women, who would rather do the work themselves than be subjected to the over- or undercooked concoctions that we younger adults were prone to making. Raw seed tacos come to mind.

On Sunday mornings, we set out blankets and beach chairs in the acre-wide garden, turned on the radio, and had brunches that lasted half the day while housemates, neighbors, and visitors came and went. People talked about books they'd read, places they'd lived or traveled, politics. Names of philosophers, authors, and historical events rolled off tongues in ways that seemed to presuppose that we were all sipping from the same general pool of knowledge. I felt like an outsider during these exchanges, but the overarching feeling of welcome and inclusion enabled me to find the courage to ask questions.

I had met Jesse through friends a few years earlier, and it was she who had invited me to rent a room in the farmhouse. Living under the same roof, our daily lives quickly became entwined. One morning a few weeks after I moved in, I stepped out onto the little upstairs balcony that ran the length of the facade of the house and unfolded a pack of cigarettes from the sleeve of my T-shirt. Jesse came out and joined me. She greeted me cheerily, saying, "Good morning, my sister." My sharp response surprised both of us: "Don't call me sister unless you mean it." Jesse took a minute to digest and responded thoughtfully, "I do mean it." I believed her, and I have believed her since.

When we wanted to go into town, we wove paths beside the San Lorenzo River, which ran along farms and agricultural fields and through a graveyard with tombs and markers dating back to the mid-1800s, or we'd beg Daniel or Angela, the "real" grown-ups, to fire up the old pickup and rumble us down the potholed road to town, about two miles away.

Thirty-five years later, I'm walking down Ocean Street Extension with a pack on my back again. This time it holds a camera and my favorite walking sandwich: sliced turkey, grated carrots, cilantro, red peppers, and sesame ginger dressing on Holy Moly bread, a sourdough batard with nuts and seeds from a shop in my neighborhood, Companion

Bakeshop. There's a walking stick attached to my bag with a carabiner because I plan to devote part of my day to exploring the river.

This area was once called Italian Gardens. In the late 1800s it was sixty acres of vineyards, gardens, and orchards. Each parcel along the water now stretches three or four acres deep from road to river and an acre or so wide, so neighbors are generously spaced. I was aware of a couple of descendants of the original Italian settlers who remained when I was here in the early '80s. One of them was our next-door neighbor, an elderly woman back then, certainly gone from the earth by now. I took seven-month-old Kita—dressed like a tiger, with a painted black nose and whiskers—trick-or-treating to her house. She welcomed us into her home, invited us to sit in her living room and chat with her, then gave us a cardboard box full of persimmons from her trees.

I stop in front of the farmhouse. It was edging toward decrepit when I lived here, and it continues to be occupied by many, as evidenced by the six or seven cars parked haphazardly out front. It looks like the once-sagging porch was repaired in the intervening forty years. I'm tempted to ask if I can go inside. I'd like to touch the rough-hewn redwood walls of the upstairs rooms, see if the little closet under the stairwell is as tiny and quaint as I remember, if the woodstove oven still warms up the big living room with the green-painted wood floor, or if there are still strawberry rows out in the back field. But I can't find the courage to knock at the door.

Instead, I linger in the dirt parking lot looking up at the balcony where an epic sororal friendship took shape decades ago. My friendship with Jesse and my two or three years in the farmhouse were a bridge between a tumultuous younger life and a more stable and ultimately fulfilling adulthood. I look at the porch through my telephoto lens and snap a picture. I don't even need to wait until I get home to my computer to know that it will be one of those shots that mean nothing to anyone but me. I don't even need to keep it or ever look at it again, but the click of the shutter has become a cue to my brain that this thing (and this one . . . and this one . . . and this one) is a part of my grand collage. I have no proof, but I swear something about this process has a powerful effect on my memory. My recall for details that I learn on my walks, and even details I learn researching after my walks, is monumentally sharper than it has been throughout my life.

Jesse looked past my shortcomings and saw something in me that she kept mirroring back to me over the years of friendship until I could finally see it myself. She saw that what I thought of as my intellectual limitations were superficial wounds that I could fully heal.

I start to walk my old routes along the road and come up against fences and overgrown flora. I can no longer wend freely between the riverbank and the graveyard. Finally, a mile down the road, I find a spot where I can wade into the San Lorenzo River. There's something about transitions and edges, stepping from asphalt to dirt, dirt to water, that attracts me. Maybe it's about pushing right up to the boundaries of a place. Trying to know every square inch of it. Owning it, in a way. Or belonging to it. It wakes me up to landscape both in concept—a new world with its own nomenclature: *sag pond, escarpment, draw*—and physically manifest as a thing whose rises and dips and rifts I can feel with my fingers and palms, under my moving feet and through my searching eyes.

At water sources, it's also about the opportunity to savor words like *confluence* and *tributary* at their source. "Confluence. Confluence. Confluence," I say just above a whisper, and to my surprise the wood duck I found along the water's edge when I scampered down the bank answers in a pitch higher than I would have expected. "Confluence," I say again, an invitation to keep the discussion going, but he's on to something else. He moves slowly, awkward on his nearly overlapping feet, balancing and counterbalancing with each step.

Once in the water, he glides with elegance befitting such a handsomely clad waterfowl. He is the Picasso triggerfish of the family Anatidae, adorned in a flamboyant array of color, bold contrasts, and graphic lines. "Who designed you?" I wonder. Whoever it was, they had to push hard through garish, matching houndstooth to plaids and polka dots to arrive at such a buoyant beauty. The duck is joined by his mate, whose equally alluring purples, greens, and blues are concentrated in trim strips along her sides, understated among a field of sand- and ivory-colored feathers. Even though they're all haute and dignity as they travel upstream and out of sight, I yearn after them.

At the end of the road, I have to crawl under a cyclone fence where I once wandered freely to get into the Masonic village Paradise Park, a planned neighborhood specifically for Masons that was started as a summer retreat by Freemasons who lived in Fresno, California, in 1924. I make my way to the office to get permission to walk each of its streets, ignoring the irony of having just trespassed to get in here to ask permission, which, in any case, is kindly granted. The park's cozy cabin-like homes are dwarfed by the massive redwoods among which they are planted. The roads are narrow, heavily shaded, and carpeted with moist forest duff. Within the park there is a covered bridge, the California Powder Works Bridge, built in 1872 and later declared a National Historic Landmark. Among the special features of the bridge are the diamond-shaped windows allowing streams of light into its otherwise dark interior. I take multiple photos through the diamond windows, trying to achieve a shot that captures both a feeling of the inside of the bridge with its trusses and timbers (and year-round fairy lights) and the swift river running between banks rich with greenery. One day I'll learn the trick of electronically stitching two images together so I can have it all. But for now I get a shot of the river framed by the window where the inside of the bridge looks all but black, and another shot where the wood and the hardware of the bridge is nicely detailed and the window is nothing but a glaring light. For the dark inside, I have to crank up my ISO, the feature that determines how long light lingers on the sensor. For the outside, I have to tone the ISO way down to avoid overexposure. I can't have both in one image unless I commit some time to learning advanced editing skills. That will have to wait.

Of the dozen covered bridges built in the 1800s that still stand in California, Santa Cruz is home to two of them. The one in Felton's Covered Bridge Park, at thirty-five feet high, likely to accommodate loaded lumber wagons, is the tallest in the United States. Santa Cruz also boasts the covered bridge with the shortest span, at the entrance to Roaring Camp & Big Trees Narrow Gauge Railroad. Though not as old as the others, it is a charming little bridge with a thirty-five-foot span over a stream and millpond. I've seen the local bridges many times throughout my years in Santa Cruz and half-heartedly registered their quaintness, but coming across them in the context of my walks, they become not only alluring spans to assist me over moving water but also opportunities to stand in quiet awe of works of engineering and architecture, as metaphorical bridges to another period of the history of a town that I've come to love madly, and as yet another layer of the treasured body of information I amass as I scour the county.

It's too early for lunch but I find a spot in a little neighborhood playground to take a break and have a sip of water and a handful of popcorn. A woman who lives in the park stops to say hello and I ask her how she likes living here. She tells me that her family has been here for three generations and they love it.

"Do you have any Masons in your lineage?" she asks. I tell her that my paternal grandfather was a Mason, my grandmother was an Eastern Star, and my father was a DeMolay, a member of a youth leadership organization with Masonic origins, before he converted to Catholicism.

"You could buy a home here if you wanted to because of your connection to the Freemasons," she tells me.

I'm not looking to move, but it dawns on me that this is yet another of the endless aspects of my father's early life that I know nothing about. One of my sisters has a tiny newspaper clipping picturing him as a teenager looking proud and dapper in his DeMolay garb. When the woman walks away, I pull out my phone and type into the search field: Can Catholics be Masons? Hundreds of articles pop up on the screen. The Masons have never had a prohibition against Catholics joining. However, Catholics are the only religious group that prohibits its members from participating in Freemasonry. A short, high-pressure sigh escapes my lips. My mind goes to the long-standing animosity between my mother and my paternal grandmother. My mother didn't grow up Catholic, I've learned as an adult, but she converted in her early twenties and demanded that my father convert too.

Seriously, Mom? I think. I'll never know for sure, but I'm led to wonder if she did it just to spite my grandmother.

In 1982, when we lived together, Jesse introduced me to a world of new foods and flavors. One day she brought pastries from a French bakery home in a paper sack with butter stains that made the bag itself a temptation. She left them on top of the refrigerator with a plan to share them with her girlfriend later that evening. I knew they were not for me but decided that just a look couldn't cause any harm. I unfolded the brown paper and moved aside the bakery tissue to reveal a treat I later learned was called pain au chocolat. The outside is a toasty, flaky pastry, dusted with confectioners' sugar, folded over an inside of airy, buttery bread with a buried treasure of melted chocolate at its core.

I thought if I took just a small peel of the bread, it could easily go unnoticed, but the sliver I'd intended pulled away in a fat strip. I replaced the thin paper over the treat, folded the bag, put it back on top of the fridge, and left the kitchen. The taste of the bittersweet chocolate mingled with the chew of the centermost bread and the flake of the outer crust haunted me to distraction, and I snuck back for another small bite . . . and another, until it only made sense to finish the first pastry. It wouldn't do to leave a half-eaten sweet in the bag. Maybe Jesse would think she'd accidentally bought only one or that the salesclerk had messed up. I resolved to leave the second one alone, and I did. For hours. But the flavors and textures wouldn't stop twirling on my taste buds and taunting from the kitchen until they were gone.

I was there when Jesse came into the kitchen late that evening to retrieve the bag. When she didn't see it where she'd left it, she reached up and felt around on top of the fridge, then got a chair and stepped up for a better look. I could feel the blush creeping up the skin of my neck and face. I was lightheaded with shame. Jesse could see that something was off with me and quickly put two and two together. She made light of the missing pastries, though I suspect she also found new hiding places for her baked goods.

Compared to my limited palate, Jesse's taste in food was wide-ranging and exotic. My preferred and most frequently consumed food was spaghetti noodles and Ragú sauce from a jar, with a thick blanket of melted cheddar on top. Jesse ate food with complex spices and sauces thick enough to obscure what was inside. Having lived in India for a time, she introduced me to curries and chutneys and dal. "No, thank you" was my reflexive response to everything she offered. "Try just one bite," she'd urge. This exchange repeated until I gave in or she gave up, usually the former. Over our years of friendship, Jesse has developed a nuanced understanding of my taste in foods. If she says, "You'll like this," I no longer question; I just taste and confirm.

I walk the length of the streets in the Masonic village, with names like Knight Templar Way, The Royal Arch, and Demolay Lane. What is now a long-standing, cohesive neighborhood was once the site of a gunpowder mill. Criss-crossing and backtracking to ensure I get every road, I cover seven miles within the small park, then head back the way I came, walking along the river.

My first time applying for a job without a social worker guiding me through the process, I was filled with dread. Even making phone calls to inquire about the application process left me shaky: I knew there had to be a *right* thing to say and feared that if I didn't say exactly that, I'd never get a job.

Jesse suggested calling 411 to get the telephone numbers of businesses I might want to submit applications to.

"But what do I say?" I asked her.

"Say, 'May I have the phone numbers for the Santa Cruz Beach Boardwalk, Marini's Candies, and Polar Bear Ice Cream?'"

I did. And the operator gave me the numbers.

Jesse helped me fill out the applications and prepared me for the interviews, which I dreaded. I landed a counter job at Polar Bear Ice Cream.

Everywhere I went, I observed people closely, trying to figure out what makes a person appear confident and intelligent. I read dictionaries, looking for big or unfamiliar words, memorized their meanings and pronunciations, and tried using them in sentences. *Soliloquy. Insouciance. Lugubrious. Vitiate. Obstreperous.* Big words are my favorite candy. I give them out like party favors, trade them like baseball cards. I first noticed the power and beauty of language as a preteen when, in the midst of actively ignoring a teacher, more from a place of utter remove than rudeness, I'd occasionally hear a word or phrase that broke through my haze and captured my interest. This is how I fell in love with the word *forte*. I liked the way it punched the air with its accentuated *e* that sounded like an *a*. I started trying to incorporate it into sentences before I even looked up its definition. I had no clue what it meant. My father tried to get me to wash some dishes and I replied, "I don't acknowledge that forte."

Anytime the opportunity to get my hands on a dictionary

presented itself, I'd fan through the pages and randomly select a word to add to my lists. My first random word selection was *coprolite*—petrified dinosaur turds. Talk about beginner's luck! I even read the dictionary's introductory pages before the actual word entries—the ones with the keys for deciphering the pronunciation and phonetic spelling of each word. The lists that explain the otherwise secret symbols for any given word's syllable count and emphasis, and particular vowel sounds, plus other secrets, like the fact that the first definition entry of a given word reflects its most common meaning.

I spent years figuring out how to fit in by observing people. Starting at age twenty-one when I lived in the farmhouse, I listened to the radio when no one else was around and repeated words aloud like a simultaneous interpreter just to practice having intelligent words cross my lips, trying to copy inflection and pace.

Having rarely experienced my opinion holding value, I wasn't used to expressing it—a reticence that Jesse slowly helped me change. If I went to see a movie, she made a point of asking me what I thought of it, peppering me with questions to which I would give one-word answers until, over time, I developed the ability to frame a point of view, put forth an argument, or paint a picture with words.

Jesse worked at Bookshop Santa Cruz. Whenever I visited her there, I headed straight to the children's section, where I felt the least intimidated. Jesse would come find me reading Maurice Sendak's *Where the Wild Things Are* or Barbara Cooney's *Miss Rumphius*. "Listen to this," she'd say, sidling up next to me and reading from a novel. She introduced me to the young adult genre and read to me one of her favorites, *A Wrinkle in Time* by Madeleine L'Engle— the story of a girl who learned she was stronger than she'd ever imagined. Just as she understood my taste in food, she came to understand what appealed to me in stories even before I had the language to describe genres.

Soon I was reading *Island of the Blue Dolphins* by Scott O'Dell. At home, Jesse would chuckle out loud while reading, then read to whoever was in earshot. She read the daily newspaper, too, and pointed out articles I might like, including human interest stories about people overcoming adversity and crime stories about heists or robberies or anything involving murder and mayhem. Reading was a chore for me, but her animation when she read aloud inspired me. I made myself read a full newspaper article now and then, just to prove that I could.

Jesse understood grammar and tried to teach me about the "parts of speech" I had missed learning in school. "I can easily help you understand," she would insist, her tone just a hair from pleading. She assured me that I already knew it, I just hadn't put labels on the parts. She could hardly get to "person, place, or thing" before I would begin slouching in my chair, eyes glazed over, rubbing my hands in my hair in agitation. My childhood block against learning and my stubborn conviction that I didn't have the capacity to understand were still rock solid even as an adult. With persistence, even rocks can wear away, and eventually I began to try.

AFTER HOURS WANDERING around Paradise Park, I head back down Ocean Street Extension, retracing my steps to my car. I approach the farmhouse lot again and stop in front of the little studio adjacent to the house that I moved into after Kita was born. It had wide, bumpy, and uneven planked floorboards, a window looking out onto fig, avocado, and persimmon trees, and a huge loft that ran the width of the studio. The loft was way too high for caring for an infant, so I put a mattress below it for myself and hung his handmade wooden cradle from the underside. My girlfriend at the time, Kita's other mother, Mardi, was a woodworker. She'd handcrafted the cradle for him.

I keep moving along the road, reluctantly leaving this old friend of a house behind. I've driven by it a thousand times over the years that Kita's been living just down the road, but I've never stopped and blown the dust off the memories of the house itself, the land, the produce, and the people and animals who occupied it all those years ago. I'm soon wrapped up in pondering a time in my life that feels at once remote and immediate, both inconsequential and essential to who I am today.

Shortly after I moved back from Sonoma, while I was still very much under construction as a human being, I experienced the first instance of what would become a living hell, what I later learned to call *intrusive thoughts*. Arriving for a medical appointment at the Santa Cruz Women's Health Collective, I stood at the reception desk to register. The woman at the desk was filling out a message slip while talking on the phone. As she hung up, she simultaneously greeted me and, with two hands, deftly added the pink note to a growing stack accumulating on a rudimentary device that consisted of a block of raw wood with a nail sticking straight up out of it.

As I went to take a seat in the waiting room, a thought flashed through me. *What if someone set the message holder on my chair and I accidentally sat down on it?* All at once, I was flooded with images of yellow spinal fluid and red blood merging into a sticky orange horror and spilling onto the chair and floor. I heard the grind of metal on marrow and saw the sharp nail tip engraving permanent marks into my bones. I imagined vessels and veins scrambled and pressed into each other, destroying their perfect, intricate map.

When my name was called, I had to steady myself to stand up and follow the nurse into the exam room.

A few minutes later, I was back outdoors, in the fresh air, shaking my head at myself and thinking, *What the hell was that all about?* During the walk from the bus stop to the farmhouse, I wondered whether I would be able to stand up if I had a nail lodged in my spine. What might the long-term impacts entail? What if the nail was rusty? I shook my head hard and sneered at myself, thinking, *What is wrong with you?*

I thought about the nail nearly nonstop for the rest of the day and slept fitfully that night. The images themselves were disturbing, but the fact that I couldn't get away from them frightened me more.

The next morning, I made it a couple of hours before violent torrents of nail-in-the-spine stories raged through me, and they continued on and off for days. I could sometimes be distracted by going out to bars to dance, hanging out with friends, or going to work, but as soon as I was alone long enough for my mind to quiet, I was deluged.

I didn't tell a soul. I was petrified that I was losing my mind. I couldn't imagine that anyone who understood what my brain was doing would want to have anything to do with me.

I managed to compartmentalize the craziness and continued to date multiple people, maintain friendships, and work for over a year without telling a single person about it. I was living in two different worlds and managing. But without warning, the images amped up and started involving not only me being tortured, but also me torturing others. I imagined myself sinking my teeth into the flesh of friends, driving knives through strangers' chests, pushing people off cliffs. I wanted out of the cage of my skin; I was frantic with terror, certain this was an indication that I would become a murderer and spend the balance of my life in prison.

I was in the passenger seat of a friend's car when she pulled up too close to the curb as she was parking, causing a crunching sound when the tire hit the concrete. I wondered how it would have sounded if someone had happened to be lying in the gutter at that moment and their head was stuck between the car and the concrete. Would it just pop and explode on impact? Would the skull break along the cranial sutures, the squiggled lines? Would it fragment into random shards like pottery? Would the blood gush like a geyser or would it just get pushed down into other parts of the body? Would the eyeballs pop out, and if so, would they become detached from their connective tissue and just roll down the gutter? Or would they dangle like those old Halloween masks with plastic eyeballs hanging from metal springs?

I became phobic about parallel parking. I hadn't yet learned to drive, but that didn't stop my brain from haunting me with image after image of me pulling up to a curb and failing to notice that someone's head was about to be pulverized, until it was too late.

Finally, I was running an errand with Jesse one day when she pulled up along the curb at our destination and I recoiled violently. I told her all about the debilitating thoughts I'd been having. I told her that I was afraid it meant that I might hurt someone. My heart raced wildly. I didn't want to be ostracized, but I could no longer bear my secret alone.

Jesse listened attentively, her face the picture of utter compassion and affection. When I'd said what I needed to say, we sat quietly, save my shuddering gasps for air. I waited to hear her thoughts and prayed that our friendship could survive this bomb.

Jesse stretched out her arm, holding her forearm right in front of my face, and said, "Here, bite my arm." I looked at her, incredulous. "Bite my arm," she repeated.

"No!" I practically yelled.

"No," she echoed. "No. You would never bite me."

I don't imagine I ever found adequate words to explain what an impact her demonstration of trust had on me. By putting her arm in front of me, she provided a reality check, and I immediately got it that the crazy images that were plaguing me were housed only inside my brain. She deftly guided me out of my jumbled, glitching mind and provided concrete evidence that there was not a maniacal murderer perched in my soul. Her quiet acceptance of my thoughts and suffering gave me the courage to seek help and try to understand what was going on with me. Jesse wasn't a therapist at the time, but in the years ahead she would earn her master's and become a licensed marriage and family counselor. If her support during this frightening time is any measure, and I'm positive that it is, she is a good one.

I had heard of obsessive-compulsive disorder, or OCD, before, but I thought it was all about washing your hands too much, avoiding stepping on cracks, counting obsessively, and double-checking to make sure you really had turned off the stove. When the therapist I went to see used the term to describe what I'd been experiencing, I was perplexed. She explained that the actions I'd heard about, some of which I had even practiced myself, were the "compulsive" aspects of the disorder; what I was struggling with now was the "obsessive" side.

The obsessions were sufficiently disruptive that my therapist, Jocelyn, discussed medication as an option, if the skills she wanted to teach me were not effective. At the time, antipsychotics were the main drugs being used to treat OCD, and the risk of tardive dyskinesia—a disorder that results in involuntary, repetitive movements, especially around the face, and can be permanent—was significant.

Jocelyn taught me about using breathing exercises to relax and calm my mind, visualizing myself recovering, talking directly to the obsessions ("You can't control me!"), immersing myself in the thoughts until they ran out of steam, ignoring them, or imagining that I wrapped them in a box and flung them out into space.

The relief that came with having a name for the nightmare my thoughts had become was lifesaving. Seeing words in print that echoed my experience brought profound comfort. I wish I could say that I immediately thought back to my mother's seeming excitement when she was diagnosed with bipolar disorder, but that connection came many years later—during a walk, in fact.

Throughout this project I've had to fight off negative internal comments about the wisdom of digging around in memories. There've been times when I hear myself say, "Don't dwell in the past. Don't air your dirty laundry. Why retraumatize yourself?" But as I mosey down a bucolic side street and come across a handsome treehouse, a rope swing, stalking cats and gossipy chickens, I don't feel traumatized by or obsessed with the past. Instead, I feel profound clarity about my life. Compassion for myself, both now and as a child. Self-forgiveness for my imperfections. Peace, acceptance, even satisfaction with my contradicting parts. And a fuller understanding as to why I was brimming with fear and rage as a young adult, leading to some challenging confrontations.

ONE EARLY EVENING, Jesse, her girlfriend, Ace, and I walked downtown, through the graveyard and along the river, to hang out on Pacific Avenue, the main shopping strip in town. A young man roughly our age, early to mid-twenties, came out of a club with a group of friends. Out of the blue, he walked right up to me with a big smile on his face, looked me in the eye, and grabbed my crotch. He was only a few inches taller than I was, but easily forty pounds heavier. I lunged at him, yelling in his face. He stepped away from me in a kind of taunting backward skip, laughing and showing off for his friends. When he saw that I wasn't backing down, he turned and walked away quickly. I followed him. My friends stayed with me. I caught up to him easily and grabbed the back of his jacket, yanking it one way, then the other, until he stumbled to the ground. He managed to escape my grip and crab-walked, still on all fours, backward, with a look of utter bewilderment, until he regained his balance, stood up, and fled on two feet. His friends stayed behind as I chased him. He had seemed initially to think I was his prey, but after I chased him and dragged him to the ground, he'd become my prey—until we stepped into the park.

I pursued him over the footbridge on River Street into the darkening park, where he managed to get several strides ahead of me. Then, in a single motion, he stopped and turned toward me. The balance of power shifted again. Now, visible only in silhouette, he reached for something in his shoe (to this day I don't know what).

I scanned the area for a weapon of my own, spotted a

beer bottle on the ground, and smashed it against a cement curb—simultaneously shattering the glass and the pressurized silence. I moved slowly and deliberately in his direction, gripping the jagged remains of the beer bottle by the neck in my raised hand, at the mercy of my own rage. Jesse and Ace had managed to catch up and stood behind me, panting after the long, unexpected sprint covering several blocks.

Appealing to any semblance of reason remaining in me, Jesse whispered with measured calm: "We're out of our depth. Walk backward toward me . . . slowly." I was able to hear her voice, as I always have, through the din of my racing thoughts and wild heartbeat, and I stepped back from the scene. The man turned and walked away from us across the park as the three of us retreated over the bridge.

It wasn't the first time I'd knocked a grown man flat on his ass, nor would it be the last. Jesse was also with me when one night a broad-shouldered man, much older than us, shuffled drunkenly out of a bar on Cedar Street and slurred a lewd comment in our direction. I marched all 115 pounds of myself up to him and shoved him hard, with my open hands against his chest. He landed on the parking lot asphalt and stayed there, flummoxed, while I let out a diatribe inches from his face about respecting women and not being an asshole, then kicked him in the side for good measure before running away, poor Jesse keeping up.

I put myself in danger repeatedly, using offenses against me—whether they were lewd comments, homophobic remarks, or physical confrontations—as opportunities to unleash and focus my fury. The element of surprise was my superpower, and I wielded it like a battle-ax.

Decades later, as I make my way back to the top of Ocean Street Extension to wrap up the day's walk, I wander through Santa Cruz Memorial Park graveyard and think back to that period when rage percolated just below the surface, and I feel a wave of relief that over the years I have managed to set it aside. I find a cement curbstone wide enough to double as a bench and sit down for a picnic lunch. I've been captivated by graveyards since I first moved to Santa Cruz. Michele and I went out exploring on my nineteenth birthday and found one on Capitola Road Extension. We found a suitcase full of silverware sitting on a gravestone and, later, in a graveyard on the upper west side, a treehouse in a dirt lot beyond the headstones. We ascribed great mystery and meaning to both and made up stories to go with the finds.

It was a few months later, while Michele was visiting her family in Europe, that she talked me through the process of going to the post office to get a passport so I could join her at her grandmother's home in Vienna. Being a person who needed a passport was like a rite of passage. I felt a little self-important telling the post office clerk that I needed a passport application. She just distractedly pointed me toward a different window, where another clerk pointed to a wire rack of forms from which I should select the document I needed.

I was working as a cook in a preschool at that time. A funny job for someone whose primary nutrition derived from Top Ramen or Golden Grain spaghetti with a jar of sauce. The first time I made chicken stock following a recipe step-by-step, one of the teachers told me I should run the soup through a colander to filter out any chicken bones or twigs from the herbs. She didn't mention that I should put a stockpot under the colander. Those chickens gave their lives up for nothing. The soup stock went through the strainer and right down the drain.

The same teacher helped me fill out my passport application. Once I got my passport, Michele mailed me an airline ticket. The day before I left for my international journey, I found a small cardboard box on the doorstep of the place I was living, left by the teacher. In it was a chapter book written for children ages nine through twelve by Finnish author Tove Jansson called *Moominland Midwinter*, a roll of Maria biscuits, and some of my favorite candies: Good & Plenty and Jujubes. It was like a mom in a box. In the good way. I was elated.

After staying with Michele's grandmother for a week, we spent two weeks hitchhiking on the autobahn in Germany and living off stolen baguettes, spreadable cheese, green peppers, and raw garlic in France. We slept on the steps of the train station in Venice, until six in the morning when big dudes in black vests with "Polizia" emblazoned across their backs gave us and the dozens of other young travelers sprawled out there a gentle nudge with their big black boots and told us to disappear.

Everyone would creep back around midnight and the police would leave us alone until early the next morning, before most of the tourists and travelers came out in droves.

Somewhere in Italy, we spent a night in a graveyard, cocooned in sleeping bags under a plastic tube tent for which we had no stakes or lines, so it just fell over us like a tarp. Another night, after hitching a ride in the cab of a semi, we slept in a random grove of trees alongside an industrial area.

I'm sitting on the curbstone, thinking about my nineteen-year-old self in 1980, before then having only once crossed a state line and once been on an airplane, boarding a plane alone to travel six thousand miles. I still have the cardstock map of the world that was handed to me as I boarded the plane. Over the all-day flight from San Francisco to Iceland, then on to Vienna, I indicated the route with a continuous line of tiny arrows, and I'd occasionally ask the flight attendant what part of the world we were flying over to make more marks on my map.

I had rarely heard a language other than English or seen the currency of another country. To this day I can barely get my mind around time zones. Back then, it hurt my brain to even try. I arrived in Austria bewildered. Michele met me as I got off the flight and was with me nearly every moment for the next fifteen days as we traveled by train through the Swiss Alps and borrowed her cousin's tiny old Citroën car and drove through picturesque mountain passes, from which an occasional church spire rose.

In true lesbian fashion, Michele and I became close friends within months of our breakup. On my twenty-second birthday, she and Jesse and my new girlfriend, Allison, who had moved into the farmhouse with me within weeks of our first date, surprised me with an elaborate treasure hunt that started in the farmhouse kitchen and led me through this graveyard and into town for a series of surprises, including joining Allison at the restaurant where she was working as a dishwasher. In the years since, Allison, who has remained a dear friend, went from dishwashing to rug cleaning to law school, became the mother of triplets to whom Jesse and I are godmothers, and is now a United States magistrate judge.

At home after the walk, I go in search of the clues from that long-ago treasure hunt, hoping I kept them. I pull accordion files and plastic storage bins down from the garage shelves and start going through what I've kept over the last decades. After many false starts, I open a large white envelope that has remained in my possession for over forty years, with my name penned across the front. Inside I find eleven strips of worn paper from a yellow legal pad. The first clue starts, "The first step you take from this room leads you to a giant tomb . . ." The last reads "At the top of the mall you'll find a space with more words than any other place. Often you go and often you look now we will help you to pick out a . . ."

Chapter 7.

Belonging

---

terebrating *verb* \\'terəbrāting\\: boring;
perforating

T HE TWENTY-NINE-MILE STRETCH of California's Highway 1 that runs through Santa Cruz County is but a single bead on an expansive coastal necklace, but it's the longest continuous road within the county. Known along its reaches as Cabrillo Highway, Shoreline Highway, and Pacific Coast Highway, "One" is the longest state route in California, hugging 660 miles of the state's 840-mile coastline, from the town of Leggett in Mendocino County to Capistrano Beach in Orange County.

Today I am walking south along the shoulder of the highway in the direction of Davenport, a tiny town built around the workings of a now-defunct cement plant. With the ocean below me on my right and a sandstone bluff face rising directly across the two-lane highway, I slow my steps and listen. Among the sounds of occasional passing vehicles, the distant squeaky-toy call of oystercatchers, and the push-pull thrum of waves, I hear the faintest tinkle, like a gentle rain against metal: small rocks and pebbles journeying down the wall face. The descending scree shapes into triangles at the toe of the slope, forming a row of larger-than-life hourglasses. It is gripping proof of the passage of time, the inevitability of change, told in clinks and slides of ancient sandstone.

When I amble alone, I experience something that I've come to think of as *delicious loneliness*, a place just past the pleasantness of solitude, where I lean out of my comfort zone, teetering at the cliff's edge toward isolation. I linger there, flirting with the edges of despair, then I step back and remind myself that, later, I will sit down to dinner with my wife and sons and revel in the comfort and familiarity of family.

The rising sun angles its light over the cliffs in dramatic streams, making the beach blush bronze-pink. The tide pulls back like a cuff of luxurious sheets and blankets turned down to reveal a bed of rocks and pools ripe for exploration. I use every limb to maneuver as carefully as I can down a sloped wall of large rocks from the highway to the beach below, mindful to keep my excitement in check until my feet have landed squarely on the shoreline.

At the shore there's life everywhere: Sand crabs burrow frantically for cover, starfish cling to rocks, some bunched up like a fist over a mussel shell, drawing out the delicacy, others as tiny as the pad of my finger. Among a tightly packed patch of spongy anemones, I find a pile of neon-green eggs with visibly discernible larval fish inside. In the cavity of a small beach rock, a bright red speck catches my eye. Looking through my camera's macro lens, I see dozens of minuscule arachnids, red velvet mites. I pick up one of the thousands of beach rocks spread along the shore and run my thumb over the uniform divots that pock its surface, rounded holes where piddocks, small terebrating clams, once bored into the rock for a dwelling place, using a reinforced portion of their otherwise fragile shell to drill into the stone. Over time the creatures die and their shells degrade, leaving behind smooth, round holes to be repurposed as homes to red velvet mites, sea snails, anemones, urchins, and limpets. I set this cool, unoccupied stone back onto the sand, then move along the shoreline pondering my own divots and hollows and bored-out holes.

Today I'm dressed in my favorite eleven-dollar Costco sweatpants, socks adorned with frogs and toadstools that cost twice as much, a black Wilder Ranch State Park T-shirt, and gaudily colored hiking shoes that I bought for the heavy lugs that boost my confidence when I am trying to balance myself as I climb over rocks. These are my adventure clothes. My second skin. I wear the whole mismatched ensemble in private defiance of a time when my clothes were a source of ostracization and shame.

In sixth grade, Mrs. Cross called me up to the front of the class and, with all the students looking at me, said, "Miss Glass, if there is a problem with bathing and laundry at home, I'll be happy to discuss it with your parents." She did nothing to try to curb my classmates' spiteful laughter. Red-faced, I sank into my chair. Looking down at my hands, I noticed that my fingernails were caked with dirt, so I retracted my fingers into fists, trying to disappear my grime. I never gave any thought to my hygiene until moments like this, when I was reminded that I stuck out among the other kids. At twelve, I didn't feel comfortable trying to tell Mrs. Cross that I didn't have the tools at home to trim my nails, and I had no language to explain, or understand myself, that the lack of consistent hygiene was normalized at home. I didn't understand that children need modeling and reminders to develop habits successfully, or that my siblings and I were living in filth.

Our pathetic hygiene could go unchecked for weeks, but when our mother decided it was time to clean up, whether because of a family outbreak of scabies or lice, or some occasion that she decided required that we be presentable, she asserted her daunting will to achieve it. If it was time for our ears to be cleaned, for example, anything short of utter submission resulted in her tackling us, using her considerable heft to pin us to the floor. Digging her knee into our sides, she wrestled a metal bobby pin from her hair and used it to clean our ears, admonishing through clenched jaw, "You move a fraction of an inch and so help me God, I will puncture your eardrum!"

The hairbrush was the worst. She demanded that we each assume a station sitting on the floor at her feet, one after the next, while she sat on the couch, her thighs pressing into our shoulders and clamping us in place as she tried over and over, with increasing agitation, to pull the brush through our hair, the palm of one hand pushing our heads away while she battled through the tangled mats, tearing out clumps of hair as she went. Once she got the idea in her mind, anyone within sight was trapped. If she could hold Debbie, who was tall and strong and six years older than I, within the vise of her knees, there was no chance of escape for me. If any of us waiting so much as fidgeted, she'd point the hairbrush at the offender and announce firmly, "Don't go anywhere, you're next!" The sound of ripping hair added layers to our collective sensory torment. If we complained or moved, she turned the brush over in her hand and used the back side to smack our skulls with enough force that it sometimes raised bumps on our heads. The time she hit Cathy over the head so hard that she broke the cheap acrylic hairbrush became part of family legend, a story she was as likely to tell with pride as we were to recount with horror.

Though our two-story house on Ogden Drive in Fremont—with its reverse floor plan so the kitchen and living room were upstairs and most of the bedrooms were downstairs—looked much like all the other houses in the neighborhood, I knew from a young age that my family was different. When we moved into this house when I was six, Cathy, the third born, Edie, the fifth, and I, the sixth, all slept in one big bed, with baby Margaret, the eighth, at the foot of the bed in a crib, though she often ended up in the big bed in the tangle of sisters. Debbie, the second born, slept in a windowless room that had been designed for storage. Kevin, the fourth, and John, the seventh, shared a room at the other end of the family room. To get to their room, we had to pass through a very short hallway that held a gas heater, its safety cover missing so the open pilot flame stood exposed, a glowing sentinel, day and night. I used to hold pieces of paper in it until they caught fire, then run to the bathroom to put them out in the toilet. Years later, when I started smoking, I did the same in lieu of matches, as I'd seen the older kids do.

The upstairs belonged to the adults. We kids mainly went up for food and to watch television. Downstairs, we were pretty much on our own.

Jerry was kicked out of the house at age seventeen, ostensibly for getting into a physical fight with my mother while defending Kevin, then thirteen, from one of her attacks. The moment he cleared out and moved in with a friend, my mother took her belongings out of the room she'd shared with my father and moved her boyfriend, a young man only a couple of years older than Jerry, into the house, where they took over Jerry's former bedroom. Not long after, my father moved one of his girlfriends in with us, then promptly painted his bedroom royal purple.

To this day, I don't know if my parents were formally separated at that point or were simply what I would now call polyamorous. It was never discussed. It was none of our business.

My bedroom, shared with an ever-shifting combination of sisters, faced Ogden Drive. When Margaret grew out of her crib, a set of basic metal bunk beds were installed in the room. When Debbie moved out of the house, Cathy moved into the windowless room, Edie took over one side of the girls' room, and Margaret and I shared the bunk beds on the other side of the room. Each time an older sibling moved out, rooms shuffled again. Somehow, Edie and I were the only siblings who were never a part of the moves. We both occupied the girls' room throughout all our childhood years there. For much of my childhood, there were no curtains in the girls' room, which left me feeling exposed to the world. I always had half an eye scanning that street-facing window, plagued by the fear that someone might be watching me. I had a habit of sleeping in the same clothes I'd worn all day, sometimes even shoes, so I could get up and run if I needed to. I never wanted the house door locked at night. I wanted to be able to get out quickly without any obstructions. Only as an adult did it strike me as sad that I was more frightened about not being able to get out of the house than about having a stranger come into the house.

I continued to pee in my bed well past the typical age to avoid having to walk through the house to the bathroom. The urine soaked into the bed night after night so that the mattress was perpetually damp. The resulting stench that clung to my clothes earned me the nickname Pampers at school.

As I transitioned from elementary to junior high school, kids started calling me Scuzzy, which morphed to the Scuz.

I think it was when I was ten or eleven years old that my mother, who had been souring on the idea of parenting for some time, gave up on it entirely. The first time I heard her lamenting from behind her bedroom door through heaving sobs, "I never wanted children!" was around the time her boyfriend moved in with us. I've learned as an adult that during the same period, my mother received an award from our local diocese hailing her as Catholic Mother of the Year. This tells me that once there was a time when life was steadier, at least outwardly, that my parents had been able to project the appearance of steadiness to their church community.

When Margaret was born in 1968, all of us girls helped take care of her, but it was Edie, eight years old when Margaret was born, who prevailed as the clear favorite. Edie became something of a second mother for the first ten years of Margaret's life. My eldest sisters, Cathy and Debbie, changed and fed Margaret when she woke up during the night. Cloth diapers were left to soak in the toilet and often forgotten. If we needed to pee, we hauled the heavy, waterlogged cotton out of the toilet, stuck it in the sink, used the toilet, then put it back when we were done until someone got around to running the dirty diapers through the wash.

I helped with Margaret during the day, but at eight and nine years old it was a challenge for me to muster the hand strength needed to get the diaper pins with their plastic duck clasps through the multiple layers of cotton.

If we needed to pee and didn't want the hassle of dealing with the diapers, we would just pee in the bathtub or in the sink. When someone took the initiative to run a bath, they left the water in the tub, and anyone else who wanted a bath just sank into the same water. Depending on where you landed in the line, you might step into distinctly gray and tepid water in a bathtub so thick with scum you could scrape messages into it with your fingernail.

Every now and then, one of our parents would take an interest in what was going on downstairs, but for the most part, we kids went unmonitored. No one asked if we had homework to do, unless one of my parents received a call from the school. No one told us to go to bed or suggested that we take a bath, or brush our teeth, or comb our hair. Bedding went unwashed until it took on a graphite sheen. Spent light bulbs were left unchanged for long periods. There were no rules governing whether kids could have their boyfriends or girlfriends stay overnight. We were free to smoke cigarettes or joints and often used the floor to put them out, so that the linoleum squares around the downstairs family room were pocked with burn marks. I didn't try my first cigarette, a mentholated Eve with a pretty ring of flowers around the filter, until I was fourteen, but Cathy smoked openly at home from age twelve, and Edie and Debbie were close behind. By the time we were full-fledged teenagers, most of us smoked a pack or two a day.

There was a patch of drywall missing from the bathroom wall next to the toilet, exposing the studs. In lieu of a garbage can, we tossed all manner of trash into that hole, adding new layers of stench to the ammonia of the abandoned diapers. Thinking about it now, I cringe to think what later owners of the house found if they ever remodeled and tore down that wall.

The curly cord of the sand-colored phone mounted on

the wall downstairs was so stretched out that I could move halfway across the family room with the receiver at my ear or walk into the backyard and shut the sliding glass door against the cord if I had top-secret information to discuss with my best friend, Melinda. Next to the phone was an impressive collection of boogers, picked by the various kids while talking on the phone and wiped on the wall without a second thought. A similar masterpiece embellished the edge of the bathtub.

Melinda and I regularly met at the corner of Davis Street and Bidwell Drive, the halfway point between our homes, where we sat on the curb and talked for hours. When we went back home, we called each other and talked some more. As we chatted on the phone one day, I looked at that wall and, for the first time, fully registered the booger collection. It had always been there, growing in breadth and raised dimension, but it never struck me as unusual. I finally clocked it and felt physically ill. I saw my life, for a moment, from an outsider's perspective. I started paying more attention, and over time, I began to see that there were some serious problems in our home. And I didn't know how to talk about my changing perception of my family, or to whom.

One day, coming home from fourth grade, I found my mother passed out on the couch upstairs in the living room, likely from depression or Valium, a medication that she, and thousands of mothers throughout the country, had developed a taste for.

When I headed downstairs to look for Margaret, a rank smell assaulted me from the family room, where I found her asleep on the cold, grimy floor, her little face smeared with crusty snot, her arms and legs tucked up under her for warmth. She had the knuckle of her forefinger in her mouth, her middle finger hooked over her nose, and her thumb pressed into the underside of her chin, her quirky little equivalent to thumb-sucking. She'd often tell us, with her knuckle obscuring her speech, "I thuck my thumb," which all her siblings found adorable, just as we adored everything she said or did. She had nothing on but a wet and heavily soiled diaper, which drew a halo of buzzing horseflies. I stood looking down at her and thought to myself, *This is not right.*

I went back upstairs and tried to shake my mother awake. She wouldn't budge. I woke Margaret up, and as the older kids arrived home, we changed her diaper, gave her a bath, and got her dressed.

We had a washing machine and dryer and massive cardboard boxes of All detergent with the tops torn off and the powder in rock-hard clumps. Occasionally someone would do laundry, but clothes were invariably forgotten in the washer until the stench of mildew signaled their location. Eventually someone would move them to the dryer, but the smell, especially after walking to school in the rain, remained in the fabric, now dotted with the gray petechiae of mildew.

There was a full-size outdoor garbage can next to the

washing machine, meant to be used as a supersize laundry hamper, but the mound of clothes in it quickly overflowed the can to the point where you couldn't see it beneath the pile. When the heap got especially large, you had to climb over it to reach the bathroom beyond. The more we tramped over the clothes, the more compacted they became, until many items of clothing transformed into a near-solid heap. Before school every morning I would rifle through the pile to try to find something to wear, peeling pieces of profoundly wrinkled and likely ripe-smelling clothing away from the rest. It was just the smell of our lives, so we didn't especially notice it unless someone pointed it out. If you couldn't find underwear or socks, you might get lucky and find a pair of tights: two for one. There were holes in the knees and heels, but pants could cover the knee holes and shoes the heel holes. Ownership of clothing was fluid. It was the same with toothbrushes when one could be found.

Occasionally, without warning, my father stormed downstairs, the veins in his neck protruding and his face crimson with rage at the mess. He made a startling sound by folding his thick leather belt in two, creating an O shape of the leather, then aggressively yanking each end with a resounding snap, made more powerful by the fact that each of us had felt the sting of that belt on our bare flesh. Once he had our attention, he hung the belt over a doorknob, where it stayed as a silent threat, and roared, "This place is clean in an hour!" He was much less prone to rage than our mother, but in such moments when he was angry, there was nothing we could do but comply.

Every kid at home at that moment the leather belt sounded its warning jumped into action. We made dustpans out of random items like part of a cereal box or an old *Highlights* magazine. We moved everything on the floor into a huge heap in the middle of the room: stray clothing, coat hangers, shoes, stuffed animals, dirty dishes. We'd put the larger items into the rooms they belonged in and keep working our way down the pile, tossing out food wrappers, massive wads of spit-out bubble gum, and piles of cat feces ignored and left to dry up until stepping barefoot on a pile was as painful as stepping on a Lego block. Finally, down to the smallest debris—sunflower seed shells, cigarette butts, and dirt—we'd sweep the rest under the orange-and-white-vinyl couch or into one of the bedrooms. I don't know if the downstairs floor was ever mopped in the years I lived on Ogden Drive.

One afternoon after school in seventh grade, I came home and drew a bath of fresh, warm water and luxuriated in being the first one to sink into the tub. My older sisters, all in high school—except Debbie, who had dropped out, left home, and had her daughter Shasta—had started paying attention to their looks and taking better care of themselves. I was trying to do the same. I ducked under the water and moved my head, admiring my underwater hair as it swayed in slow motion. Auburn tones were more pronounced when my hair was wet, and my volume rivaled

Miss Clairol's. I was homely on land—"uncomely" as our neighbor Mrs. Rogers once called me, not cruelly, just descriptively—but underwater I was an ethereal beauty. I mermaided from one end of the tub to the other, then popped up to check the window directly above the bathtub. All clear. This was something I did at intervals, without thought. I always had an acute awareness of my surroundings.

A few moments later, I double-checked the window again and met the eyes of my sister Edie's boyfriend, staring at me. I jumped out of the tub, ran to my room, and got dressed.

A few weeks earlier, I had awoken with a start in the middle of the night to find him standing next to my top bunk with his hand under my shirt, rubbing my chest. His long greasy hair was barely visible in the near darkness, but I knew instantly who it was. He pressed his other hand over my mouth and silently cautioned me to be quiet. Once I indicated with a nod that I would comply, he took his hand away from my mouth and lightly ran his fingers along the waistband of my pants, whispering in a soft and reassuring voice, "I'm not going to hurt you. I just want to make sure you're a virgin. And I think you are. Good girl." He left our side of the room and I heard him get back into bed with my sleeping sister.

I climbed down onto the bottom bunk and hid behind six-year-old Margaret, feeling like a terrible big sister but promising myself that I would protect her if he came back. Breathing as shallowly and quietly as I could, I lay there awake, my eyes stretched wide open, trying to see into the dark. Moments passed before I heard him stirring, then his bare feet on the linoleum as he came back and looked for me. Not finding me in my bed, he slowly crouched down and saw me cowering behind Margaret. He pointed up, indicating he wanted me to get back on my bunk. I shook my head and he retreated back to Edie's side of the room.

Between the nighttime incident and now the spying, I realized I needed help. I hastily pulled on the dirty clothes I'd worn before my bath, and with dripping hair I ran upstairs to find Edie, who was watching TV in the living room. Her boyfriend had made it to her first and was sitting next to her on the couch. I found the courage to say, "He was just spying on me in the bathroom." I braced for her to defend him or, worse, make light of my problem, as my parents tended to do. He was only a couple of years older than me, after all. With my teeth I stanched a quiver in my lower lip. Edie stared at him, waiting for a reply. He said, "I wasn't spying. I've been sitting right here."

Edie countered, "You just showed up here panting like you'd run up the stairs."

He stammered, grasping for a defense. Edie stood up and demanded that he leave. He attempted to argue, but she stood her ground. I never saw him again. Edie made sure of that.

Edie was a tough cookie. She could burp the entire alphabet and ignite her farts into bursts of blue flame, or so she claimed. She smoked like a chimney and swore like a sailor and could blow little clouds of concentric smoke rings. She could be ferociously mean like a rabid raccoon, all sharp teeth and claws, but her maternal instinct was every bit as ferocious, and the youngest three—John, Margaret, and I—all benefited. It wasn't the same as having an involved parent—she was only eighteen months older than me—but she showed me again and again what it felt like to have someone stand up for me, make hard choices in favor of my well-being, and accept me wholeheartedly.

The day Edie kicked her boyfriend out, my paternal grandmother, who hated my mother and, by extension, her children, made a rare appearance at our house for dinner. We didn't especially care for her either, though we looked forward to hearing her British accent, especially when she asked for tomato juice to go with her drink. She had an impressive collection of Wild Turkey bourbon decanters shaped like actual turkeys, and she drank them down quickly so she could expand her collection. Her disdain for my mother was apparently rooted in the fact that when my parents married, my mother had insisted that my father convert to Catholicism.

That night my father prepared a meal he called "chicken divan"—or as we snidely called it behind his back, "chicken divine"—trying to impress his mother, a futile task. My grandmother lamented that no one had placed serviettes on the table—as if anyone knew what they were. My father sheepishly admitted there were no napkins in the house. I saw an opportunity to save my father from humiliation and to shine in my grandmother's eyes. I jumped up and ran to the hallway cabinet where I had seen a huge lavender box of fancy napkins. I pulled the box from its shelf and zipped back to the dining room, proudly announcing, "We do have napkins!" My father grimaced and the older siblings laughed uproariously. I was perplexed. Not only had I delivered a jumbo box of napkins, but they were special, sanitary (it said so right on the box), which I thought my grandmother would appreciate. Instead, her already pinched countenance took on new severity as she stared down her sharp nose.

Before I put the box back on the shelf, I opened it. I'd been curious since I first noticed it in the cupboard how a sanitary napkin differed from a regular paper napkin. I took one out and immediately understood my mistake.

IT HAD NEVER crossed my mind to tell my mother that I'd started my period, just as it had never occurred to me to tell her about Edie's boyfriend and others creeping into our room at night. I had no idea how to have a conversation with her of any kind. Now it seemed like a luxury to have menstrual supplies right at home. I resolved to come back when no one was around and steal several pads to start a stash of my own.

AS I WALK, I'm so distracted by my musings that I only vaguely notice that there's a giant rock at the water's edge. As I draw close to it, the rock seems to suddenly rear up, displaying an enormous proboscis. Pushing itself up from the sand on flippers, it seems nearly as tall as me. A typical male elephant seal is fourteen feet long and weighs four thousand pounds. I take several quick backward steps to put distance between me and what is obviously an enormous male elephant seal. I scan the beach to make sure he doesn't have company and then give him a wide berth until I reach a point where I can collect myself and observe from a safe distance. I watch as he lowers himself back onto the sand and snuffles for a few minutes, then I carry on walking.

Besides the massive pinniped, the seagulls and oyster-catchers, and the awe-inspiring array of tide pool creatures, I'm alone on what is now, courtesy of the ebb tide, a long and widening stretch of beach. The sheen of the water that has not yet been absorbed into the newly exposed sand reflects cliffs and clouds and V's of pelicans mirrored in its surface in a fruit-salad palette of mandarin, raspberry, and plum. I walk suspended between the two worlds, the sky overhead but also at my feet, half expecting to feel a shift in gravity.

I notice strange markings in the sand, miniature criss-crossing freeways of tiny lines and dots. Before I make a conscious decision to do so, I'm on my hands and knees investigating them with the magnifying glass I pull out of my jacket pocket. A small crab tiptoes out of a snicket in the rocks and into a pool, leaving behind an identical section of freeway, solving my mystery. I follow the trails, crawling alongside them, gawking and laughing aloud when a snail track leaves an avant-garde labyrinth in loops and spirals or a crab track takes a sharp right turn. I take photos of the tracks and imagine lining up a series of photos of various tracks so they look like one continuous trail around the circumference of my office.

I sit back in the wet sand, awkwardly human among the inhabitants of a usually submerged world, yet I feel utterly at home. I feel fully alive here, where particulate spindrift circulates through my lungs, blurring the imagined boundary between self and nature and diluting everything from petty worries to harsh memories, rendering them soluble, resolvable. Feeling the textures of fine grit and grain under my palms, I sink my hands farther into the sand, into a granular museum of ancient history in fragmented seashells, feldspar, and quartz, and I allow myself to blend into it. To belong to it.

I felt as if I belonged to my family when we sang together. When we lined up youngest to oldest at the sliding glass door on Easter morning, giddy to be released into the backyard to collect the Easter eggs we'd dyed a few nights before and plastic eggs full of foil-wrapped chocolates. When Christmastime smelled like oranges with cloves pressed into their peels and gingerbread and we woke up to find a tube sock beside our beds stuffed with tangerines, candy canes, chocolate bells, and little toys: sliding number puzzles, clickers shaped like insects, and wood animals strung on elastic on a wood base you could press to make the animal fall apart, then let it go and watch it snap back to its original form.

I don't know if our family life fell apart somewhere along the way or if it had never been right for any of us. I don't recall exactly when we became essentially two separate households, the upstairs and the downstairs, overlapping primarily at dinnertime, a daily ritual that endured intact up until I moved out when I was fifteen, one of the few touchstones that remained dependable in the midst of chaos.

My older siblings can recount a time when our mother cooked and baked and made some of our clothes, and when I listen to them talk about that time, little snippets of my own memory surface. I recall fruits shaped from marzipan that my mother used to make: a tiny red apple topped with a single clove to serve as a stem, or a bright yellow banana. They had that kind of excruciating beauty that tortures the heart even in memory because you can't quite own it, even if you eat it.

I have an image of my mother kneeling in the driveway in front of the first house I remember living in, with a hose and a bucket, rinsing out diapers and scrubbing them against an old wooden washboard before bringing them to the back of the house to run them through a wringer washer, which she operated with a crank.

From age twenty with the birth of her first child to age thirty with her seventh, my mother had three children in cloth diapers at any given time. The four eldest remember that she interacted much more frequently with them than with her younger children, but they also admit that her violent outbursts were worse. As she disengaged and shifted her attention away from being a mother, while there was less attention devoted to us younger children, there was also less physical violence directed at us than what they'd endured. They have memories of my parents fighting, which shocked me, since I can't remember any type of interaction between them at all.

There's no question that my mother was a difficult person. No one who knew her well would say otherwise. She herself wouldn't say otherwise. She was a survivor of a harrowing childhood with neglectful caregivers, poor nutrition, and exposure to physical and sexual violence. She was hurt and angry and trusted no one. To me, as a young child, she was simply my mother. I couldn't see her or separate her from my home or my life any more than I could see or separate myself. With time and distance it's become clear to me that as someone who never experienced a feeling of true belonging in her own family, she had no idea how to instill a sense of belonging in her children. The same was true for my father.

Both of my parents came to their relationship with histories they wanted to forget. They rarely talked about their own childhoods and they both did their best to leave the past behind. My mother went so far as to raise us with the belief that both of her parents were dead and that she had no siblings. So it was a surprise when I was twelve and a man we were told to call Uncle Bob came to our house. Bob had been in prison for the first dozen years of my life for something having to do with either a sex crime or homophobia or both, depending on who told the story. From whispered conversations among the adults and the sibling rumor mill, I pieced together that he had solicited the services of a male prostitute whom he assumed to be of age, but upon being arrested learned that the young sailor he'd engaged was not.

Whatever the case, an uncle—our mother's brother—appeared out of thin air. We liked him. He worked at the old Tower movie theater in Oakland and sometimes he took us to see scary movies like *Tales from the Crypt* and *Night of the Living Dead*, until the theater changed hands in the mid-'70s and became the Pussycat, part of an adult theater chain. Uncle Bob remained a solid employee of the Pussycat for most of his remaining years. When he died, he left what money he had to us, his nieces and nephews, a few hundred dollars each. It was with this gift that I bought my first *real* camera.

As a young adult in the late '70s, Kevin, the fourth born, tried to sort out the gaping abyss of our family lineage. He'd barely started before he came back to us with the news that our maternal grandfather had been living in Santa Cruz and Monterey Counties throughout our childhoods, less than a two-hour drive from our home. We immediately set about arranging to meet him, to our mother's great dismay.

My sister Cathy had offered to host him at her house and all of us went there to meet him. At the time, I was nineteen, and my girlfriend, Michele, came with me. When he met us, my grandfather unsubtly looked down her shirt, then sat next to me and announced, "Your girlfriend's not wearing a bra." It was the only time I ever saw him and I felt no need to see him again. He died a few years later.

THE BEACH BEGINS to narrow. The rising tide is erasing some of the sea creatures' tracks. It dawns on me that I should check the time; I've covered less than a mile of my all-day hike and I've already completely lost myself in tide pools, sea caves, and memories. I'm astonished to find that over three hours have passed since I crabbed my way over the boulders and down to the beach. I shake my phone like an old Etch A Sketch, trying to clear the screen and reset the clock. I'll need to stay in motion for the rest of the day if I want to reach the town church by four, so I scurry back up the rocks and continue down the road.

After two miles on the narrow shoulder, a left turn from the highway puts me at the northern entrance of Swanton Road, a seven-mile pass named for Fred Swanton, the builder of the famous Santa Cruz Beach Boardwalk. The road will lead me to Swanton Berry Farm, where I'll have my pick of delicious treats to buy: chocolate-dipped strawberries, a variety of freshly picked berries, and baked goods.

This expansive neighborhood has a distinct personality formed by the rural balance of human presence and wilderness, the rich history of coastal farming, and the density of plant life. I can't always catch it through a car window, or even by bicycle, but walking through it, I can sense the shifts in place. There are visual cues in the blend of flora and fauna, the farm equipment, the tiny old schoolhouse, but there are also things unseen. The way air shapes itself along the contours of the hills or the way the cotton-batting fog hangs low over the ground, glancing weeds and wild-flowers with dew. History leaves breadcrumbs on the land-scape, markers unseen by untrained eyes, but sensed and felt nonetheless.

There's a pond near the southernmost end of the road. I see a man with binoculars standing along the edge and I step off the road, closer to the water, to see what he's spot-ted. It's a single white swan. A swan on Swanton. Clinging to the reeds along the edge of the water are dozens of blue damselflies. Barn swallows dart and skim the surface. Adorably ugly baby coots, heads ablaze with yellow and red feathers, paddle double time to keep up with their mothers. Telephone wires sag under the weight of hundreds of red-winged blackbirds, until they lift off in a unified cloud, a valentine of bright red shoulders.

Swanton Road is surrounded by one hundred square miles of heavily forested wilderness. Bobcats can be seen regularly. I spot one in an open field and watch it from a distance, my 300mm telephoto lens a poor excuse for bin-oculars. The bobcat sits stock-still, staring intently at the ground at what I imagine must be a gopher in a hole, and I follow suit, sitting in the dirt to observe. I sit for several moments before deciding it's time to carry on. Just as I make a move to leave, the cat jumps straight up from his spot, all fours well off the ground, and pounces. Swing and a miss. He goes back to his statue pose and I do the same, set on capturing a shot of the next pounce. The pounce that never comes. At least not until I turn to go again, which he seems to take as a cue. Up he shoots, this time capturing his prey and digging into his breakfast.

I stop at a self-serve produce stand along the side of the road and drop a couple of dollars in the box in exchange for some greens. Throughout the project, I've discovered that there are tiny stands all over the county. I never pass one by. Mostly I choose an apple or two, but if apples aren't on offer, I'll buy a bell pepper or an onion. Anything I can fit in my camera bag.

A man driving by in an old pickup stops and asks, "Did you get any of the pears?" I shake my head and say, "Shucks, must have missed them." With a smile he says, "I'll restock them this afternoon and set a few aside for you."

Since I'm out walking, he likely assumes that I live nearby. Later in the day, after Ellen picks me up and takes me back to my car, I drive along Swanton Road and, sure enough, sitting on the shelf with all the other produce is a brown paper bag with the word *reserved* scrawled in pencil and three delicious pears inside.

I cross little bridges over the creeks that run under the road, each step bringing me closer to the berry farm, a fixture for Santa Cruzans and anyone who regularly drives along this section of coast on Highway 1. In 1978, it became the first certified organic strawberry farm in California. Twenty years later, it was the first organic farm to sign a contract with the United Farm Workers.

Stepping through the screen door into the main building, I find myself in the familiar open-beam farmhouse. I've been here many times over the years. On bright blue wooden picnic tables there are glass jars full of freshly picked calla lilies. More flowers hang upside down, drying in bunches from the rafters. There's always a chess set at the ready. I don't play, but the board conveys an old-fashioned invitation to stay awhile, which warms like a woodstove fire.

In the refrigerator case, there's raspberry lemonade dispensed from a spigoted jug and a choice of decadent desserts: strawberry shortcake or blackberry cobbler, each with a generous serving of whipped cream as thick as butter. The dense and not-too-sweet shortbread absorbs the berry juice, creating riots of flavor and texture, an irresistible treat post-exertion. I choose the cobbler and sit at a picnic table outside in the salty breeze, gazing out at the ocean, watching birds of prey swoop and dive over the berry rows. I see red-shouldered hawks, white-tailed kites, harriers, kestrels.

The dessert energizes me sufficiently to fuel the remaining two miles, which will land me in the tiny town of Davenport. The cement plant, originally called the Santa Cruz Portland Cement Company, operated from 1906 until it closed in 2010. It covers one hundred acres. The industrial structures blemish an otherwise stunning stretch of coastal beauty, and its ghost-town allure creates a challenging job for the security guards who remain posted outside its gates. I know of at least two young men who have snuck onto the grounds over the years and made a sport of scaling the tallest structures on creaking metal staircases and dodging security guards. There was a time when one could get into the buildings through a system of underground pipes and tunnels extending below the freeway and onto the beach. I go in search of the legendary tunnels, walking the train tracks, a no-longer-functioning section of the Santa Cruz & Monterey Bay Railway. I locate a couple of the pipes and wander into one of them, wading through craggy rocks and knee-deep water. I can get several yards before meeting a metal grid. I try another and another, then finally concede that, just as my kids have told me, the pipes are no longer passable.

As I backtrack along Cement Plant Road, my heart quickens to see that the main gates into the facility are wide open. Looking down the driveway, I see an alluring collage of rusting metal staircases, boarded windows, chutes, and platforms. I romp toward the gate like a Girl Scout in pursuit of an adventure badge. I don't believe an eight-year-old finding the entrance to Willy Wonka's chocolate factory standing open could have been any more excited.

I make it about ten paces before my jaunt is interrupted by a guard. She must have been sitting out of sight in the little security cabin when I arrived. "The plant is closed," she says, not unkindly.

"But the gate's open," I say defensively, immediately embarrassed by my petulant tone.

"The gates are open for authorized vehicles," she explains. Her face is soft with understanding. She gets the draw.

As I turn to leave, a gray fox trots between the guard

and me, a breakfast of small unrecognizable mammal held gingerly in its jaws, and saunters unbothered through the open gate.

"I see them here regularly," she tells me. "It gets me every time." Before I can concur, a second fox zips through, trying to catch up to the one carrying the food. The guard and I exchange fresh smiles, no longer trapped in our flimsy cop/criminal dichotomy. I bid her a shy goodbye.

The fox sightings stay with me as I follow the frontage road back onto the highway, absorbed in the mingled scent ribbons of ocean, strawberries ripening on their runners, and truck exhaust. I allow myself to be hypnotized by an endless sea of top-heavy artichoke plants, nodding their dusky-green heads in agreement with the breeze. Aerial photographs of the agricultural fields illustrate luscious patchwork quilts in blocks of greens and browns, but on the ground I see the finer details: the raised dirt mounds that prevent water from pooling around low-lying strawberry plants, the sturdy stalks from which brussels sprouts emerge, and the delicate purple pom-poms that remind me that artichokes are but edible thistles.

The walks fortify my heart, lining it like a nest festooned in tiny abalone shells, beach rocks, and veined flower petals. I shelter beneath canopies of thousand-year-old redwoods or burrow in ancient sands while I build a chamber big enough to hold it all—the heartache and the joy and all their convoluted overlays—and I cradle there, suspended in the feeling that the very stars have reconstellated to make a space for me.

I've been stunned by the many ways this project has affected me, considering that I embarked on it with the simplest of goals: getting exercise and lightening my emotionally weighty work life with infusions of beauty. But I begin to see that the desire to get out and walk was also driven by an unrecognized need to absorb enough beauty to soften the blow of telling myself my story and anchoring a sense of belonging in this world.

Chapter 8

Love and History

---

dehisce *verb* \də'his\: to split along a
natural line

SOME ROADS, such as Humbug Lane, Milky Way, and Fiddlesticks Drive, I can't wait to walk based on their names alone. Love Creek Road. Who could resist? And true to the title, the road and the creek for which it's named entwine, crossing over and flowing alongside each other and all but merging at points.

But love is complicated, and so is history. The road, as it turns out, was named for a man who ran a sawmill along the creek, Captain Harry Love. He also led the California Rangers, the first statewide law enforcement agency in the Bear Flag Republic. Before settling in the Santa Cruz Mountains, he was believed to have captured and beheaded Joaquin Murrieta, a miner turned "bandit" who came to be known as the Robin Hood of the West or the Mexican Robin Hood.

Murrieta came to an area of California, then known as

Alta California, about 150 miles northeast of what is now Santa Cruz County, in 1849, from his native Sonora, Mexico. He came to join his older brother to mine for gold one year before California became the thirty-first state in the union. He and his family were subjected to racist laws that allowed for legal discrimination, such as seizing of their claims, and the Foreign Miners' Tax Act, which took effect in 1850, imposing a monthly tax on non–US citizens to mine in the state. The rape of his wife and the death by hanging of his brother after being falsely accused of stealing a donkey are said to have been the catalysts that turned Murrieta to life as a bandit. He and his fellow bandits sought revenge and reputedly killed over a dozen Anglo-American Chinese miners and settlers. The California Rangers were authorized by the California State Legislature in 1853, spurred specifically by the drive to capture Murrieta.

There is a road in Newark, California, two miles from my childhood home, named Joaquin Murieta Avenue. For some, he was a folk hero, a socially minded bandit; others saw him as a criminal who deserved his death. Many did not believe the severed head preserved in a jar of whiskey that Harry Love presented to the authorities was, as he claimed, that of Murrieta. They thought that he had escaped the authorities and lived long after 1853, the year of his alleged capture.

To start my Love Creek walk, I park just off Highway 9 in Ben Lomond. I know this area of the Santa Cruz Mountains because Jerry bought a home and orchard in an adjoining neighborhood several years ago and I visit him often. But in all my time in the county, I have never taken the right turn off the highway that leads to the little neighborhood of Glen Arbor. I park and get walking, using my paper map as a guide to wander all the side streets I can along the slightly bigger artery that will eventually meet with Love Creek Road.

I've started out early enough that just moments into the walk I am witness to the pensive questions that great horned owls pose to each other in the crepuscular window between their bedtime and the early stirrings of their human neighbors. I can't see them, but the call-and-response between two leafy treetops, one on either side of the road, is unmistakable.

I stop and eavesdrop and hold myself back from adding my own two cents to the conversation. My input is superfluous, I know.

For being part of a mountain community, the neighborhood is fairly flat, but I find a side street that gives me a little elevation, and before I reach its peak I spot the moon hanging between the branches of a Monterey cypress, a protected tree that is considered rare. It's only found naturally along the coast of central California, primarily at Cypress Point in Pebble Beach and at Point Lobos State Natural Reserve. The moon and cypress tree, I decide on the spot, will be the photo for Tipping Way.

I wander from one street to the next, slowly making my way to Love Creek Road. In a dirt turnout, I see a painted wooden crate, an oversize toy box stuffed with toy animals and figurines amassed on top of it. There are low tree stumps set out in a semicircle, defining a space and preventing vehicles from entering. Each stump is heaped with more toys and trinkets. A hand-lettered sign reads SOMEWHERE HERE LIE MY TWO GRANDSONS TREVOR 7 & KELLY 5. PLEASE DO NOT DUMP ANY TRASH.

The stuffed animals are waterlogged. Jigsaw puzzle pieces have expanded with moisture, the picture layer peeling away. The scene causes knots in my stomach. Is this a creative rant? Public art? I can't make sense of it. *Of course there aren't children buried in our mountains*, I think. Yet the feeling in my gut doesn't square with this being an art exhibit.

I walk along the road, but then wander back, disturbed. I want to understand.

There are two side roads indicated on my map very close to this turnout. I turn my attention to locating them, pacing up and down Love Creek. I find chained-off areas where there might once have been roads, but I don't see any way to access them by vehicle or even on foot.

As I search, a postal carrier drives by. I flag her down and show her my map, indicating the roads I'm trying to find.

"Those roads were wiped out by a landslide in 1982 that killed over twenty people," she tells me. I have some recollection of the ravaging rainstorms that year that caused the San Lorenzo River to overflow its banks. There were stories of horses being swept into the currents and futilely trying to find footing. She points to the toy box. "That's a memorial for two children who died that day. Their bodies were never recovered." She goes on her way and I continue down the road, shaking my head at the fragility of life and the randomness of nature.

Since I first came to Santa Cruz in 1979, I've sensed that there's a certain hardiness required for mountain living. The mountain areas experience more than their share of fires, floods, landslides, falling trees, and crumbling roads. But walking this road, seeing these toys left out for the ghosts of someone's grandchildren, the full weight of the harshness in the midst of this natural beauty hits home.

I continue down Love Creek until I reach a locked gate across the road. I turn to walk away, but as I do a woman drives up and rolls down her window. I ask her permission to walk the rest of the road and she kindly obliges. She tells me to keep my eyes open for a wooden plaque, a memorial to the two souls who were lost when a pregnant woman's boyfriend murdered her and dumped her body along Love Creek Road in 2006. She knew the woman who discovered the body several days later.

So many cultures and religions sense and acknowledge the liminal, the sacred, the tenuous place between life and death. They hold a place for their dead, a day or a week, an altar or a shrine, fire or flags, coins for the ferrymen. Right here beside the marker for the woman and her baby, I say the names of my dead and bow to the place where they live on to the cadence of my own transitory metronome.

I think about the ways that grief and loss have shaped me and the ways we are all shaped by our losses. I ponder some of the ways that loss touched each of my sons' early lives and marvel at the magnitude of being the person who breaks the news to a child that life is temporary. Something that we all must learn again and again. But I say a silent prayer that all the love in their lives will smooth their paths.

In the mid-'80s, Jesse and I were sitting at my kitchen table talking about a friend whose mother had recently died. We were so engaged in our conversation that we hadn't noticed that Kita, age three at the time, was listening intently. "Moms die?" he asked, a stricken look clouding his little face.

I looked to Jesse for help, but her expression communicated that she felt as uncertain about the right answer as I did. It was on me.

"Everybody dies, at some point," I said, searching for the tone to inform honestly without frightening him. "But I'm not going to die for a long, long time, and neither is Mardi." This seemed to settle the matter for the time being.

Several weeks later, Kita and I were visiting with Jesse once again, and I guess he was beginning to understand the concept of replacement. "It's good to have two moms!" he exclaimed to Jesse. I beamed, eager to hear how the discussion would unfold.

"I think so too. What do you think is good about it?" Jesse asked.

"Well, if one dies, you still have another one," he chirped pragmatically.

My friend Jo used to go dumpster diving at the University of California, Santa Cruz, at the end of the school year when students were moving out of the dorms and throwing away tons of perfectly good stuff to avoid having to lug it onto the next step of their journey. One year she found a full Habitrail, an elaborate hamster cage, then went out and bought a mouse to live in it and gave it to Kita, then a kindergartner, who was over the moon with his new pet, whom he named Squeaky.

The mouse became a part of our daily lives. I helped Kita clean the cage every couple of weeks. Once, after putting Squeaky back in his plastic home, I suggested we let him have some fresh air before bringing the cage back in. We forgot about Squeaky outside, however, and I found him the next afternoon, baked in the sun.

I wanted to hide the evidence and tell Kita that Squeaky fell in love with another mouse and went off to start a mouse family. I wanted to promise that we could go visit once they were all settled in. I felt horrible that I'd been so careless with a living creature and with my son's heart.

I had to break the news to Kita when I picked him up from school that afternoon. It was the first and only time I have witnessed projectile tears.

We buried him in our postage-stamp backyard. As we did, Kita stood near the tiny burial site and tearfully asked, "Can mouses dig?"

I wasn't sure what I was supposed to say, but I gave him what I sensed was the needed answer. "Yes."

"Good," he replied. "So he can dig out if he wakes up."

I bought Kita a goldfish in hopes of easing the pain of the mouse death. Bubble Eyes lived happily on the window-sill briefly, but then it, too, went belly-up. So I bought another fish, which he ardently named Livelong. Livelong lived two days.

I started considering another mouse or maybe an upgrade to a hamster, but Jesse gently suggested that I give Kita a moment to experience the loss of one animal before piling on a new one. In my defense, I was a young parent still learning how to manage grief myself.

Almost twenty years later, Miles, born sixteen years after his older brother, asked me about death at around the same age. I had just read him a bedtime story and we continued to sit in the rocking chair as he drew closer to sleep but then took a U-turn back to the conscious world.

"What means *dead*?" he asked earnestly.

I'd fallen out of practice at answering such questions and I was stumped all over again.

"Well, people usually live long, full lives, but when they get really old their bodies start to slow down, sometimes they get sick, and some parts of their bodies stop working and . . ." I'd lost him.

"So, it's just like turning off the lights," he summarized, neatly wrapping up the discussion.

"Yeah, it's like that," I hesitantly confirmed as he climbed up onto his stars-and-moons-themed bed. "Kind of like that."

When Miles was five, we took him to pick a puppy from a litter of yellow Labs, and we brought Izzie home in a laundry basket. Miles became deeply attached to his dog, and Ellen and I would whisper to Izzie, "Please stick around at least through high school." She obliged and graced our lives until Miles went off to college. She lived a good life, full of walks and biscuits. A perpetual puppy, she loved her toys to the very end and always brought one with her to greet us at the door. She died just weeks after we became aware of the COVID pandemic, while we were still dazed by the sudden changes in our world and adjusting to constant hand sanitizing, washing our groceries before bringing them into the house, and watching the news with increasing horror. The vet put her down in the front yard and we were all masked as we said our goodbyes.

A fallen maple leaf catches my eye and momentarily pulls my attention out into the light of day. The brown center in the five-point shape of the leaf is echoed in an outline of bright yellow. Only the outer edges of the leaf are green. I pick it up and twirl the stem between my thumb and forefinger as I reach back into the past, trying to recall my own early experiences with loss.

When I was five, there was Sleepy, one of many cats in our home I'd claimed as my own. One day I went outside to put something in the metal garbage can on the side of the house and found Sleepy under the lid. He wouldn't move. I told my mother.

She said, "Of course he's not moving, he's dead!" She was sentimental about animals, but not about carcasses.

I told her that Sleepy's eyes were open, so he couldn't be dead.

She gave a snort of exasperation and returned to what she'd been doing without saying anything else.

I put a quarter in the garbage can with Sleepy, which

seemed a fitting sacrifice for the gravity of the situation. Something to ease the transition from garbage to heaven. Later, it dawned on me that Sleepy probably wouldn't have any use for a quarter in heaven, so before the garbageman came I went back and took it off his stiffening body and slipped it into my pocket.

It's not just pets that come to mind, however, when I think of my earliest losses. I also remember breakfast cereal. I was in kindergarten the first time I lost my mother. I was home from school, sick. She made me a bowl of cereal, mixing powdered milk with cold water and pouring it over the bright circles as I lay on the orange-and-white-vinyl couch with a blanket over me. I was an only child for the moment; I was a specific person, not just part of a brood. I wanted the attention, but I was too sick to eat, my insides shaking and churning.

I watched the cereal grow soggy over the course of the morning. I tried several times to drink the rainbow mush it had dissolved into, desperate to take advantage of my mother's gesture, but I couldn't stomach it. To this day, I can smell the cereal's fruity goodness and see the colorful dyes slowly dissolving in swirling patterns as I moved the milk with my spoon.

When my mother checked on me and figured out I wasn't going to eat the cereal, she poured it down the sink. I cried a little, then a lot, then some more. I bawled and wailed, refusing to accept the fact that I couldn't get that bowl of Froot Loops back, that it couldn't somehow be preserved for me, or time set back.

I tried bowl after bowl of Froot Loops after that, but they never hit the spot like that one could have if only I'd had the stomach for it.

My mother was perplexed and noticeably irritated by my outburst. She disappeared into another room and I lay on the sticky couch heartbroken over the missed chance until my brothers and sisters started filing in from school.

It's impossible to know now how much new meaning I've ascribed to what was likely simply a five-year-old tantrum. But it lives in me still as a flood of grief that I had pushed a meaningful connection to my mother out of reach.

I've been only vaguely aware of the maple leaf in my hand, but I look at it now and see that it's spinning with my thoughts like a whirligig. I've been walking so slowly since I came across the toy chest that the six or seven miles since I left my car have felt like nothing. I keep the same pace until I reach the end of Love Creek, then, after a rummage through my bag for an apple, I turn around and head back in the direction of Glen Arbor. I stop along the creek at the wooden memorial to the pregnant woman and her unborn baby and stand near the sign.

I've heard a friend who worked for hospice say, "Every loss needs a thousand tellings." It's a kind and simple way of telling the person who has suffered a loss that it is okay to talk and talk and talk about what happened and how destroyed or relieved or vindicated they feel. Some deaths are conducive to a thousand tellings. Some are left unspoken, lodged between realms like a stopper in the throat.

THE EXPECTATION THAT each of us Glass children would leave home on or before our eighteenth birthday was made explicit to Debbie, my eldest sister, and she was out of the house on schedule. Having dropped out of high school in the 1970s, her job prospects were limited. But she moved to Southern California to look for work. Within the year, she was pregnant and she and her boyfriend moved to Oregon. I was excited to be an aunty at only twelve years old. When Debbie named the baby Shasta, we were a little surprised. Our only reference was Shasta cola. "It hasta be Shasta" went the TV jingle, so naturally we chanted the slogan to the baby. We didn't know about Mount Shasta back then.

We wanted to spend as much time as we could with the baby, but because Debbie and her boyfriend had moved away, our visits with Shasta were limited to occasional weekend visits and holidays. As she got older, Shasta had a favorite word: *moon*, which she pronounced "moo-in." Anything round qualified. Even at the age of two she knew how much she charmed us. Holding up a cookie or pointing at a doorknob, she'd declare, "Moon! My moon!"

I reached to hold her tiny hand as we walked down the street to visit a neighbor; the precious burden of being momentarily responsible for her safety was breathtaking.

At Thanksgiving when Shasta was a year old there were brandied pears on the table. She gorged herself on the fruit until Debbie had to push them out of her reach. Shasta wiggled and craned out of Debbie's arms and onto the table, crawling over mashed potatoes and around green beans like a tiny athlete in an obstacle course to get some more. We cheered her on. Someone snapped a black-and-white photo: little Shasta on all fours reaching for the pears, wearing nothing but rubber pants over a diaper. It was the kind of photo a parent wants to hold on to forever, to inflict playful humiliation by showing future dates or grandchildren.

My siblings and I had noticed a pattern in our birth order: boy girl girl, boy girl girl, boy girl . . . and we were thrilled when Shasta kept the pattern going . . . as did our first nephew, Cathy's eldest son, Christopher. Though they were cousins and not siblings, some of us felt too young to be aunts and uncle (Margaret, John, Edie, and I were ages five, eleven, thirteen, and twelve, respectively), and we thought of them as an extension of our own generation. Shortly after the Thanksgiving of brandied pears, Debbie and her boyfriend split up and she started a new relationship with a man named Johnathan. She continued to live in Oregon, and she brought him home with her when she visited us. Until we got a phone call that Shasta was in the hospital with extensive second- and third-degree burns.

We used the dining room as a central command each time Debbie called with updates about Shasta's condition. Sitting vigil, I skipped school and waited for news; the not-knowing was unbearable. Then we began to get reports. Her tiny body couldn't overcome the shock of the burns. Her heart failed. When word finally came that Shasta had died, my ears buzzed a high-pitched alarm. She was gone. Little moon baby. Gone.

At a loss as to what to do with myself, I sat on the front

porch step and wrote a poem. It was rhymey and singsongy in the way of a young person who was not practiced at writing. *She's part of the flowers and part of the trees and part of the wind that's making that breeze . . .* I desperately wanted to shape words big enough to hold my sister, who was only twenty-one at the time, in all her grief. I tried to imagine her pain, but my fourteen-year-old brain couldn't stretch that far. I worked the rhymes over and over, frustrated that they couldn't touch the magnitude of my emotion. I shook my fist at God, demanding the right words. They never came.

Years later, reconnecting as adults, I learned that Debbie, to this day, keeps the poem in her wallet, occasionally tracing the fading words with new lines of graphite. It's one of the only things related to Shasta that Debbie was able to keep. Johnathan had destroyed everything else.

There was an investigation into Shasta's death, but no charges were filed. Suspicions loomed in each of us, haunting the gaping silence, but over time denial prevailed—a kind of denial upon which outsiders can readily cast aspersions. A kind of denial that cannot be understood or even imagined without the lived experience.

My parents had copies of the investigation and autopsy reports. Each of us read them over and over, trying to understand what had happened, hoping there was something in them that all of us had missed. Something to point away from the conclusion that Johnathan had lost his mind and poured a pot of boiling water over his girlfriend's daughter. My tiny, wispy-haired niece.

When Debbie's second child, Johnathan Jr., was born a few years later, it took only a single photo to confirm for his California relatives that he was blessed with "Glass ears," as we refer to a genetic trait of ears that stick out. I only saw his elfin face in photos. I never got to hold his little hand or hear the sound of his voice.

Shortly after my nephew was born, we learned that Johnathan Sr. was abusing our sister and had been abusing her all along, which reawakened the old suspicion that he had caused Shasta's death. We were gravely concerned for Debbie and baby Johnathan's safety. My sister Edie went to visit Debbie in Oregon and witnessed the abuse first-hand when Johnathan aimed a loaded gun at Debbie because she didn't get up and wash the dishes when he'd told her to.

A few months later he beat her up badly, leaving her with broken ribs and loosened teeth. Debbie fled for her life. While she sought medical attention, Johnathan went to the preschool and picked up Johnathan Jr. He told Debbie that he had obtained full custody of him through the court and left town with their son. She confirmed that no such custody order had been made and she tried in vain to track them down. Debbie never saw her boy again.

Several months after Johnathan Sr. left with her son, in 1982, Debbie, who had moved back to California, got a phone call informing her that she could go to Southern California to pick up the ashes of her four-year-old son, unless she preferred to have them shipped. This is how she learned that Johnathan had been living with Johnathan Jr. in Los Angeles and that when Johnathan's mother had gone to his house to try to check on her grandson, he shot and killed her in the doorway of his home, then went into the garage where he'd been keeping little Johnathan locked up and shot and killed him, then shot and killed himself.

When my mother learned about the murder-suicide, she went to Debbie's house, where she found her under the kitchen table terrorized, inconsolable, and emotionally broken. At age twenty-one, I got a phone call from my sister Cathy, the same sister who had called me four years earlier to inform me that my father had died, letting me know that my nephew, his father, and his paternal grandmother had all died.

After a long, horrifying road through grief and shame, Debbie dredged herself up from despair, and over the decades has made a life for herself with activism against gun violence at its heart.

I eat my apple absently as I stare at the water moving along the creek like blood through veins. My mind peels away from thoughts of loss and pain. I wonder how the water can just keep moving. It is mysterious. Mystical. Miraculous. Here is one of those moments when my aversion to technology is easily beaten out by desire for ready information. I type into the search engine, "How can rivers just move on their own?" and up comes an answer: "Over time, the downward force of moving water and rocks can carve into bedrock, creating valleys and canyons. It is the basic principle of gravity that allows rivers to constantly flow from the mountains to the sea, as long as there is a continuous source of water."

So all rivers and streams and creeks are heading downhill toward the ocean? I suspect this is one of those givens that *everyone* already knows. A line from a song that Ellen sang as a Girl Scout and taught me in our first few months together comes to mind: "Silently go the rivers to the sea, and the barges too go silently." Water goes down. Rain goes down. Tears go down. I close my eyes against gravity trying to pull them to trickle down my cheeks as I marvel over the motion of water and allow the full weight of the loss of my niece and nephew—and the devastating lessons their murders transmitted to our young brains about the depths of human depravity—to finally register. Not merely in my brain, where they've been trapped for decades, but in my body. I learn what it is to literally fall to one's knees; my half-eaten apple drops from my hand and my eyes dehisce a torrent, like a gaping wound freshly reopened.

I think about Debbie having to manage unimaginably complex and overwhelming grief at such a young age. I think of every member of my family. Of my baby sister Margaret hearing open discussions of infanticide by boiling water when she was only seven, during the same year that her mother, my mother, left the family, never to return.

It's easier, somehow, to think about it through the perspective of someone else, someone more vulnerable than I. That slight remove protects me, insulates me like the layer of water in a wetsuit that warms up between skin and neoprene and defends against deep chill. I have this abiding if illogical belief that I was old enough at the times of my niece's, nephew's, and father's deaths and my mother leaving to not be so affected by them.

Because Margaret was so young—seven when our mother left and when Shasta died, ten when our father died and she was suddenly moved to a new home, fourteen when Johnathan died—I think of her as entirely innocent, different from me. I am seven years older than she is. *Was John any less innocent at age thirteen?* I ask myself, and answer without hesitation. *Of course not!* I realize as I start walking again that a sliver of me still believes that I was partially at fault for my mother leaving and for my father's death.

A few years after Shasta died, my father died. I saw him in a thousand faces and, each time, did a double take. I sensed his ghost lurking around corners or streaming by the window as I stood at the kitchen sink. In vivid dreams, I'd find him alive, milling around the gravestones in a cemetery. There were things I wanted to say, but I was sobbing in relief to see him again, so I couldn't form words. And when my dream sobs wrenched me awake to find that it was not true, that he was still dead, my soul was wounded all over again.

I used to wear a tattered Irish cap that he had worn as a young man, and his brown-and-orange argyle sweater of itchy wool that was too big for me. A few months after he died, I accidentally left it in a grocery cart, and when I realized this, I ran several blocks back to reclaim it, but it was gone. I never saw the sweater again.

At seventeen, my grief over my father was uncomplicated. I loved him, and now he was gone. As I began to learn, bit by bit, over the years, about the various ways he harmed some of my siblings, and began to acknowledge and understand some of the ways he hurt me, it became more challenging to simply love and miss him. My instinct was to throw away the few photos I had of him and close off my memory of him, wholesale. But it is something of an art, learning to embrace aspects of him while banishing others, a delicate and nerve-racking surgery—a tiny slip of the scalpel and I could slice into my own organs.

A FEW HOURS after he died, while we were still all milling around aimlessly, the woman he was engaged to marry, Laura, came to the house, shocked and shaken, having just left my father's body at the hospital in Santa Cruz. "He promised to buy me a waterbed and now I'll never have one," she sobbed to me.

While Laura grieved for her dream bed, our mother, who had been informed by someone—maybe one of my siblings, maybe a neighbor—that her children, three of whom were still under eighteen, were suddenly fatherless, came from Berkeley, all business, to monitor emotions and dispense Valium tablets. She marched up to me with a Valium and a cup of water and for no discernible reason instructed, "Don't get hysterical. Take this!" I declined, reminding her that I'd stopped taking Valium after I over-dosed on it in junior high.

"Take it!" she insisted.

I took the pill.

Our mother also insisted that Margaret, the ten-year-old, take a Valium. For years after, Margaret believed that if a loved one dies, one must take drugs to calm their nerves.

A couple of weeks later, when we received a cardboard box of my father's ashes, my father's fiancée went with us to spread them at Point Reyes Beach, about ninety miles north of Fremont, one of his favorite places. She brought Cornish game hens for lunch. None of us knew what those were, but they looked like baby-size chickens and I wasn't about to eat them. We traveled in two vehicles. Four of the sisters in one car, and the brothers, Laura, and me in the other. Somewhere along the way, we all gathered at a gas station to fill up and discuss directions. The two carloads ended up in a heated argument over directions to the beach that quickly devolved into yelling, spitting, and a physical confrontation between a jumble of siblings, until everyone piled back into the cars and headed for Point Reyes.

A while later the car I was in arrived at a beach. Not the beach we had intended, but we didn't know it at the time. We stayed in the vehicle to avoid standing in the sand-strewn wind as we waited for the rest of my siblings to show up. After a few minutes, my older brothers decided we should go about the business of pouring the ashes into the ocean without them. We climbed up a craggy outcrop, and my older brothers gave me the task of emptying the box.

They held my jacket so I could lean as far out as possible, to avoid the ashes blowing back into our faces.

When I imagined my father's ashes, I thought they'd look something like what you would find at the bottom of a fireplace. I expected them to be gray in color. Instead, they were bone-colored and porous. Rather than fine ash, my father was chunks. I steadied myself as best I could and leaned out to pour the bone-rocks that were once my father into the frigid Pacific below.

In the spirit of this day of feeling suspended between realms, I continue to walk slowly. The content of my thoughts is weighty but the dappled light through a mix of familiar evergreens lightens me. At the confluence of two creeks, Love and Fritch, I head up Fritch Creek Road with my second apple of the day in hand and take in the pleasure of moss-covered trees and huge ferns overhanging a rutted road. There's a cabin-like feel to some of the houses along here. I quietly hum a song we sang as children, "Little Cabin in the Woods." It's the story of a rabbit seeking refuge from a hunter. The cabin dweller invites the rabbit in to sit by the fire and reassures him, "Safely you'll abide."

Some of the deaths that shaped me did not involve direct personal losses, but nonetheless significantly affected communities I was involved with and compounded my sense that there was scant safety to be found in the world. When I went into foster care in the Bay Area, I attended another of what was becoming a succession of continuation high schools.

In one class, an art workshop, a fellow student offered to give me a tattoo using a straight pin with thread wrapped tightly around it right up to the portion of the tip he needed exposed to deliver ink into my skin. He dipped the pin, his makeshift tattoo needle, into a little angular bottle of ink again and again as he meticulously transferred the image I had drawn for him on paper, a double women's symbol, onto my shoulder. I followed the teacher with my eyes, hoping my classmate would work fast so we wouldn't get caught. The student noticed and reassured me, "Don't worry. He doesn't care. I've done lots of these." Before long, the teacher ambled over to us and observed the process with interest, commenting on the student's steady hand before moving on to another group of kids.

In another class, I told my teacher I wasn't feeling well and that I was going to go home. She offered to drive me if I could wait until the end of the school day. We stopped by her house, where she picked up a hot water bottle for me to hold against my cramps, then she drove me home. Rather than just dropping me off, she followed me into the house and sat down beside me on my bed. She leaned over and kissed me, full on. I had been involved with older women at that point, but I wasn't remotely attracted to her and tried to communicate this to her by physically moving away from her. I didn't want to hurt her feelings. I liked her.

She invited me to her house sometimes and always made sure I had five dollars in my pocket for "cigarettes and incidentals," and she rigged a fake report card for me, with B's and C's I hadn't earned, in case I needed a passing record in the future. As my teacher she felt like something of an ally, but there was also an unsettling string attached.

While I was in school she would occasionally circle back to see if I'd changed my mind about becoming more than friends. Once while I was visiting her home, she tried to get me into bed with her while her partner was in the house, preparing their dinner.

Rather than go outside for a cigarette break, as we were free to do at any point in the school day, I'd sit on the radiator next to an open window in her classroom and light up. She'd wander over and whisper urgently, her eyes darting to the door, where the principal occasionally showed up unannounced, "You can't smoke in the classroom." I'd turn and level my gaze on her, posing a wordless challenge. I figured out that I could get away with anything with her. I had power over her both because she wanted a romantic relationship with me and because she could lose her job if anyone learned that she was actively pursuing me.

Then, at seventeen, I was transferred to my fifth and final high school, Opportunity II in San Francisco. One morning, between classes, as I walked down a hallway, I heard the sound of a girl crying and found one of my classmates sitting on a table in a conference room turned cafeteria.

"Are you OK?" I asked.

She could barely form the words to tell me that her mother had died. Moments later, I learned that another classmate's best friend had also died.

As I walked through the halls and stairwell, teachers

were crying and convening in small groups, discussing the details of a terrible tragedy. I caught snippets over the ensuing days, but not enough to understand the context. "... Peoples Temple ... her little brothers ... Guyana ..." The name Jim Jones was spoken repeatedly.

Jim Jones, I learned many years later, was a preacher. He founded the Peoples Temple in the 1950s in Indiana and moved his following to California in the 1960s. By the mid-1970s, his headquarters and many of his followers, largely African American families drawn to his promotion of racial integration and equality, had moved to San Francisco.

He reached out to Opportunity II High School administration to discuss enrolling teenagers from his community. In 1976, about 120 teens from Peoples Temple attended Opportunity II. In 1977, the majority of them, with their families, followed Jones to a commune he established in the jungle in Guyana, called Jonestown. By the time I attended Opportunity II in 1978, only a handful of Peoples Temple kids were still enrolled; most had moved to Guyana.

That November, while I was a student at Opportunity, Jim Jones led those living with him at Jonestown in a mass murder–suicide by poison. The students who had a family member or close friend who died at Jonestown were encouraged to take some time off from school.

In 2018, authors Judy Bebelaar and Ron Cabral, both of whom worked at Opportunity II High, wrote the book *And Then They Were Gone: Teenagers of Peoples Temple from High School to Jonestown.*

It was surreal reading from the perspective of an adult,

to learn about a historical event that I brushed up against as a teenager more than forty years earlier. In addition to reading about the tragedy itself, I was fascinated to learn about the philosophy of the school, a public alternative school with progressive politics that was initially led democratically by the teachers, most of whom were influenced by new teaching practices of the '60s and '70s that put students at the center of their own learning. I wish I could go back now. I'd be ready for it, as I wasn't then.

On November 27, 1978, only nine days after Jonestown, while the classrooms still had the sucked air of a ghost town, I heard an anguished shout from one of the teachers and followed the sound. That's how I learned that San Francisco Mayor George Moscone and Supervisor Harvey Milk, a gay activist, had been shot and killed by former city supervisor Dan White. The principal, Yvonne, gave us the opportunity to take off the rest of the school day and go to City Hall for a vigil. I went to the vigil and stayed into the evening.

Six months after the murders, Dan White was found guilty of voluntary manslaughter rather than first-degree murder. The lenient finding was predicated on what came to be called the "Twinkie defense," a reference to Dan White's lawyers' claim that a diet of junk food, combined with depression, were indicators of his poor state of mind at the time of the murders.

Already strained relationships between the San Francisco Police Department and the city's gay community flared when the SFPD, along with the San Francisco Fire

Department, raised funds to support Dan White and printed "Free Dan White" T-shirts.

The night of the verdict, May 21, 1978, a few months after my eighteenth birthday, a march started in the Castro, a gay neighborhood within the larger Eureka Valley neighborhood of San Francsico, with hundreds of enraged gay people and supporters chanting, "Out of the bars and into the streets." It gathered momentum as it moved toward City Hall. One police car was vandalized and set on fire, then another and another.

I had been in the Castro with the crowds and I walked the streets chanting, but I'd already headed home before violence erupted. The firefighters had their T-shirt and we had ours, a graphic of a burning police car with the words "No Apologies!" along with the date and place of what came to be known as the White Night Riots, May 21, 1979, San Francisco. Mine was a sleeveless purple tank top. I wore it until it was threadbare.

There's a road I was hoping to reach today because it made me smile when I saw it on the map: Elsie Mae Drive. Early in my relationship with Ellen, my friend Jo started calling her Ellie Mae, and it has stuck all these years. Walking it would add an additional six miles. I consider it, but as I return to the base of Fritch Creek Road I decide to walk the couple of miles back to my car, then call it a day. I'll save Elsie Mae for a morning when I have a fresh heart that hasn't been squeezed through an emotional wringer.

I'm ridiculously pleased with myself when I find a perfect spot in the dirt to sit where I'm framed in ferns and can rest my back against a rocky mud wall. I pull out my lunch of baguette with salami, paper-thin lemon slices, and Swiss, and an absurdly delicious orange. Long walks and picnics bring even the simplest flavors to new heights. When I'm finished, the reverse trip, from sitting on the ground to standing, is cumbersome, but I make quick work of it and set out in the general direction of the car.

I amble on as an image of my mother-in-law, Susan, plays at the edges of my mind. From the instant I met her to the last time I saw her, she was a force of love in my life. Sitting at her kitchen table breaking the ends off snaps, also known as green beans, while she stood at the counter preparing dinner and telling me about the latest book she'd read infused me with a feeling of belonging. Once when she was visiting us in Santa Cruz, we passed each other in the hallway as I was bringing food out to grill in the backyard and she was preparing to set the table. She stopped me, put her hands on either side of my face, and said, "You are like another daughter to me."

When she was in her mid-sixties, Susan was diagnosed with Alzheimer's. She managed to live independently in her home for several years but eventually she moved into an assisted-living facility. After an unrelated surgery, her health and cognition quickly declined, and she died the day after her seventy-third birthday. Ellen tried to get back to Virginia in time to be at her side, but her mother died before her plane landed. Ellen's grief was instant, deep, and lasting. I've always envied people who have close relationships with their parents, but here I saw the cost of wholesome love. It is well worth the fee, of course, but, man alive, it exacts a toll.

Six months after Ellen's mother's passing, when my own mother died, I felt nothing. In the days following her death, in the middle of the night, I would awaken to a wet face: effortless and unwanted tears, interesting only for the physiological curiosity that they were. It was as if some irritatingly deep-rooted mammalian response to maternal loss spoke louder than any felt emotion.

She had told me a few weeks earlier that she planned to end her life around Hallowmas, a historical pagan holiday, but I hesitated too long before making the trip to see her and I missed the chance. She had threatened suicide over the years and had made several attempts, so part of me didn't believe there was any urgency. I didn't know this was *the* time. Or maybe I did. But there was a brawl brewing in my gut between vestigial filial piety and long-repressed simmering resentment.

As kids, my siblings and I occasionally were divvied up to go stay with various neighbors or family friends. We were told that our mother was having surgery. Years later, I learned that we were farmed out so our father could deal with the fallout of my mother's suicide attempts. I imagine we were only away from home for several days all told, but when we saw each other in the schoolyard, we ran and clung to each other as if we had been apart for years. After one such hospitalization, my mother convinced Debbie her suicide attempt was a direct result of Debbie having hit her in the face, breaking her glasses. The fact that she'd hit her in self-defense as my mother physically attacked her had no bearing on my mother's peevish resentment.

I visited my mother in the hospital months before her death. She told me calmly that she had made a recent suicide attempt by swallowing a large quantity of pennyroyal, a highly toxic herb in the mint family that causes kidney and liver failure and eventually death. My mother told me that a friend of hers had admonished her for not "doing it right," and convinced her to get her affairs in order and say her goodbyes, including to her children. She told me that she agreed with her friend and intended to write a goodbye letter to each of us before she ended her life. She assured me that her next attempt would be her last.

As I waited for her promised goodbye letter, I imagined what it would be like to read something that would bring some sense of closure to this turbulent relationship. I hoped for something to help me understand how she felt about us, her children, and how she perceived her role in our lives.

When I came home, I told Ellen that I was waiting for a letter from my mother. She cautioned me to stay realistic about what my mother might have the capacity to say. I assured her that my expectations were in check.

Over the next few days, I would slip into daydreams of reading her heartfelt letter. I wondered what type of paper it would be on, whether she would sign her name in ink, how many pages it would take for her to say goodbye to the eight children she'd brought into the world. Every day was an eternity of waiting. I lost track of the idea of keeping my expectations in check and tried to imagine the weight of the fat envelope I'd convinced myself was forthcoming.

I imagined myself hopping into my car and racing to her house to say goodbye in person before she died. The healing had already commenced in my mind, the in-the-nick-of-time relief of finally hearing what I needed to hear from her. And I felt relieved for her, too, finally being unburdened of the guilt I always imagined she must have harbored.

On October 25, 2011, she sent an email message to my brother:

> Kevin, would you forward this to your siblings, please? I don't have anyone else's email address.

In turn, Kevin forwarded her letter to the rest of us, with the introduction:

> Hi All, Below is an email from your mother.
>
> —Kevin

> To the Glass Menagerie,
>
> I want to tell each of you that, whatever mistakes have been made in the past, I am sorry for any pain or problem my choices have caused you . . . I know that none of us have had the easiest of relationships. Now, with more

maturity, I would still make many of the same choices, but differently, much differently. Whatever hurt we have caused each other, let there be forgiveness and compassion all around. I wish health, happiness and a full life to each of you and the children who follow you . . .

L'chaim!
—mom

Two days later we learned from a social media post that our mother died on October 26, 2011, the day after she sent her goodbye letter to her children:

> This is Wade. Barbara's husband. Barbara had a seizure yesterday and slipped into a coma. It was her wish that no steps were to be taken to extend her life and she died quietly with no signs of distress. I want you all to know that your presence in her life was a blessing.

Her social media page was flooded with comments from friends, former colleagues from her days of teaching English at a parochial school, and students expounding on her wisdom, intelligence, and community-mindedness. Posts saying things like "stable pillar" and "most memorable teacher" and "Your influence will never be diminished" were written by people I'd never heard of.

The sentiments of her children in the ensuing weeks, on social media and in emails to each other, had a wildly different tone:

First, the people you wrote to are the Glass FAMILY, Jerry, Debbie, Cathy, Kevin, Edie, Angel, John and Maggie are humans, we are not some wild herd of animals that you and Fred collected over the years, albeit you two certainly did your damnedest to treat us as such . . .

Ummm. . . . can I just be the first to say FUCK YOU . . .

For all of my siblings, those who gave up hope early on and those who held out to the last breath, we all did what we needed to get through. The one thing I think we can cling to, the one bit of constancy in the madness we have been put through, is the love we have for each other.

I understand from Uncle Bob (our mother's brother) that you had a crappy life, you were abused and a lot of stuff happened to you, and in front of you. On the other hand, I also know 8 men and women who had a lot of crappy things happen to them as children and all of them have been able to become loving mature adults . . . all with emotional problems, all pretty scarred up from having two parents who obviously did not want us, or used us as play toys, but still loving and caring.

It amazes me how so many people saw Barbara Glass in a different light. I read these posts about what a wonderful inspiration she was and all I could think is who the hell are they all talking about? It bothers me that she touched so many people in so many ways. The only way I remember her touching my life was with a slap or a closed fist. She touched my life with her brutal words, which are buried in the depths of my soul. Though her death may hurt some, for me it is a time of celebration and not for the same reason others may be celebrating

her passing. If I were a Christian I would hope that she
was burning in hell.

Her friends held a memorial service. Only two of her
children—Debbie, the second born, and I—attended.

My mother's presence and support during the most challenging days of Debbie's life had healed a rift between them.
Of all of us, Debbie is the child who managed to have a
meaningful connection with my mother that lasted until
our mother died.

ABOUT THIRTY YEARS EARLIER, in the late 1980s, my mother
and her partner were married in a pagan custom called
handfasting. My parents had finally divorced in 1976, a
couple of years after my mother left. She started practicing
paganism shortly after she moved out of our family house.
Only a few of her children were invited to the wedding.
Cathy and I attended the ceremony. When I arrived with
my son, Kita, her grandson, I asked my mother where we
should sit. She replied, "Anywhere but the first two rows.
Those are reserved for family."

I stood looking at her, dumbfounded, waiting for more
information. She explained that the rows were for her coven
members and some members of her partner Wade's family.
My sister Cathy and I sat off to the side with our dressed-up
children, far enough back that we wouldn't be mistaken for
family. We knew no one else at the wedding and she made
no effort to introduce us.

WHEN SHE DIED, I was out of sorts for days. The fact that I felt none of the emotions I thought a person who'd lost their mother should feel scraped against my self-image, values, and beliefs. I didn't want to be a person who wouldn't shed a tear over the death of her own mother. And with equal conviction, I stubbornly refused to waste my salt.

At her memorial service, I read a eulogy I had written without invitation, intoning the full name of each of her children. I don't know how her remains were handled or whether there is a place I could go and sit beside them—her husband never told any of us and none of us ever asked. I know how I could find out, but because I was not included in any discussion about it, my silly pride won't allow it.

WEEKS AFTER SHE DIED, I sat on our back porch with Ellen and our friend Susan. I mentioned my mother and as if in response, a hummingbird flew up to me and hovered at eye level for a few seconds.

I am not doing the hummingbird thing with you, Barbara, I thought, and the tiny bird flew away

When my sister Debbie and I were at the service, from among a disparate cast of characters of Catholic school-teachers, druids, and witches emerged a crone in flowy clothes and overlapping layers of tarnished silver goddess jewelry. She floated up to us with her whiskered face and milky eyes. I had to stare toward the floor to resist the overwhelming urge to roll my eyes and guffaw. What could this crazy old bat have to say to us?

She leaned in close and whispered, her voice somber and serious, "Throughout my own mother's funeral, one song kept playing through my head." We waited for a lecture but an impish grin wedged the corner of her mouth into a broad, radiant smile as she blurted out, "'Ding-Dong! The Witch Is Dead.'"

Debbie and I snort-laughed in response.

"Listen, though," she added, anchored now in personal authority. "Our stories change. What manifests as heartache, anger, and resentment now may morph to compassion and understanding, maybe even love, with time."

WHEN I THINK of my mother now, I work that woman's words like a sourdough starter, feeding them regularly to keep them alive and growing. Her indifference has been formalized by death and any hope of a relationship has been ineffaceably extinguished. But I still test myself sometimes by asking, "Did I love her? Did she love me?" No matter how hard I try, I can never land on an authentic yes. I want to be a person of compassion, and I want to be someone who can unequivocally say, "Yes, of course I loved my mother, of course she loved me." So I leave a window open to let hope flutter the gauzy liminal curtain and let air circulate between and around us, just in case. Just, exhaustively, forbearingly, pathetically, in case.

Chapter 9

Why Tom Jones Couldn't Wear High Heels

saporous *adjective* \ˈsapərəs\: of, relating
to, or capable of exciting the sensation
of taste: having flavor

NEITHER OF MY PARENTS was a great cook, but each of them strived in their way to ensure that we had a balanced meal each night as defined by the times—some type of protein, a vegetable, and a starch. I ate nearly all the vegetables with gusto, earning the right to decline any of them I didn't care for—lima beans and brussels sprouts— to the envy of my siblings. Knowing that I cringed at the very idea of eating animals from an early age, my brothers and sisters took their revenge by clucking and lowing under their breath whenever chicken or beef was served and making fart noises when we had rump roast. But I wasn't completely vegetarian: I didn't think twice about biting into fried bologna slathered in mustard, or a hot dog. As far as

I was concerned, they were barely traceable to anything resembling an animal.

There was always enough food for a first serving of dinner, but anything left in the big pot sitting in the middle of the table went to the first ones to empty their plates. The race was on to get a shot at it. All of us developed a lifelong habit of eating quickly. John, the seventh born, cleverly strategized by being upstairs early and getting a spot near the head of the table, as close to the pot as he could get. Most of us walked away from the table still hungry.

For breakfast and lunch, we were on our own. Any food in the refrigerator was available on a first-come-first-served basis, but once it was gone, we were out of luck until the next grocery run, which depended on our mother's mood. Many days she couldn't manage to leave the couch. The combination of serious depression and being the mother of eight children left her chronically weary—exhausted both physically and emotionally.

Most food that didn't require refrigeration my mother stored in a locked kitchen cabinet or in the locked full-size freezer that stood prominently in the family room downstairs. She doled out the food when the mood struck her, which didn't follow any pattern that my siblings and I could ever discern. No amount of pleading, even for a piece of fruit, could sway her. She bought bunches of bananas, bags of Red Delicious apples, ten-pound sacks of potatoes, and canned peaches, apricots, and fruit cocktail packed in syrup with the occasional prize of a maraschino cherry—and locked them away where none of us could access them.

Often she forgot about the stowed food, and there were many times when there were shelves full of black bananas, stale crackers, and shriveling apples. It made my stomach churn—not so much the appearance of the spoiled food, but the memory of how irresistible it had looked fresh from the store, and how much I'd wanted to ask if I could have one piece of fruit. But I resisted to spare myself the humiliation.

Decades later, it occurs to me that something else was going on. It's true, I hated to appear needy. I still do. But even more, I wanted to neutralize my mother's power over me. I had no way of controlling her behavior, but I could release the steam from the pressure cooker she created by not engaging, by not giving her something to lord over me. No matter how hungry I was or how much I wanted one of the oranges or some of the Mother's taffy cookies that she locked in the cupboard, I turned my yearnings inward and swallowed them.

This is not a small realization. I'm pulling on a thread that can help me unravel deep-rooted habits that were born of need but have not served me well over the years. Needing from others can deepen bonds. There can be profound tenderness in asking for something, in requesting help, in saying what you need and crafting thoughtful, balanced interdependence.

Eventually, my older brothers and sisters figured out how to temporarily remove the cabinet door from its hinges and we could take food from the cupboard sparingly when our mother was out of the house. We did our best to eat just enough to avoid detection, a tricky proposition when several of us descended on the food at once.

When groceries ran low, a frequent occurrence with so many mouths to feed, some of my older siblings took the initiative and went to the store themselves to buy or steal food. Favorites were corn chips with canned bean dip and a salty snack called Bugles for their horn shape that could fit over small fingers to make what I called "witch hands."

In the letter my mother sent to me in 1988, she describes the role food played in her own childhood. "I don't remember ever having enough to eat as a child," she wrote, "which probably accounts for my passion for cooking and my obesity. I suffered from diseases caused by malnutrition . . . the first time I ever saw a dentist he pulled four teeth. I was 12 years old."

My parents used powdered milk and mixed in lots of oatmeal when cooking ground beef, two food-stretching practices from their Depression-era childhoods. Still, they sometimes splurged on such delicacies as vacuum-packed Columbus salami and Cotswold, a delicious English cheese with chives and onions. Jerry remembers times our parents covered the dinner table with newspapers and feasted on whole crabs. And we all remember the platters of deep-fried tacos my father occasionally made, which were everyone's favorite.

I don't remember the crabs, but there were times—such as holidays—when food was more plentiful and my mother would cut up vegetables and make sour cream dip with fresh dill or even bake an apple crisp.

Unlike my mother's childhood experiences, we weren't at risk of serious health issues related to malnutrition. Millions of people around the world can live on one meal a day. Some diet trends even recommend it. But children need fuel for all the energy they burn. So each of us found ways to supplement our diets. I used to visit neighbors around lunchtime and hope their parents would offer me a sandwich. Some of the moms even gave a gaggle of kids a full-size bag of potato chips to go with the peanut butter sandwiches. I always suggested that we play a game of seeing who could stuff the most potato chips in their mouth, which gave me a chance to devour fistfuls of chips without standing out.

Melinda and I made a fort out of an abandoned cellar in the middle of a field of tumbleweeds a couple of blocks from our homes. The house that once stood there had long since been razed. Steps led into a big, open concrete room with a floor of mud and plant detritus and nothing but the vault of sky and a huge overhanging loquat tree for a ceiling. We weren't the first to make a fort of the basement. There was a makeshift table of plywood on plastic milk crates, some discarded wobbly kitchen chairs, and a waterlogged couch with missing cushions. We'd sit on the concrete steps and peel and eat one loquat—a small golden fruit with big shiny brown seeds—after another. The fruit isn't typically harvested in large quantities because it's thin-peeled and soft and best eaten right off the tree. It's one of those fruits that are taken for granted, like the sapid red arbutus berry that grows on strawberry madrones, often seen only as part of a landscape and left to fall to the ground and rot.

In contrast to my mother's control over our food, when I was around eleven, my father, who was either oblivious to the fact that his kids had chronically rumbling stomachs or was powerless to intervene, decided to start giving us an allowance. Margaret got a quarter or, as she called it at age four, "a big nickel with a bird on the back." John and I each got a dollar and Edie got two. I didn't compare notes with the older kids, but I imagine they got more. The minute I got my dollar, I'd make a beeline for the Quik Stop about a half mile from the house, where I'd buy a bagful of penny candies—Tootsie Pops, Kits taffy chews, hot-dog-shaped bubble gum—and ten-cent candy bars—Snickers, Almond Joy, Rocky Road, and Abba-Zaba—along with Bub's Daddy, long ropes of grape-, green-apple-, and watermelon-flavored bubble gum dusted in confectioners' sugar. I could scarcely make it a block holding the bulging sack before I sat down on a curb and set about eating one piece of candy after the next. There was no savoring, just greedy consumption. As much as I tried, I could never manage to spit out the gum after chewing it, so I ate it, just like the rest of the candy.

Week after week I made myself so sick that it was hard to walk home. I had to double my arms, hands to elbows, and press them hard into my stomach to keep my insides from contorting as I walked home half hunched. When I finally managed to get there, I'd crawl into bed, dizzy and shaky, and fall into a deep sleep from which I woke feeling not much better.

In addition to any food I could get my hands on, I ate weird things as a child.

In kindergarten and first grade, when I wasn't using the tongue depressors the teachers handed out to apply paste to our art projects, I used them as spoons to help myself to a mouthful of paste. It had a minty smell but to my frustration the taste didn't match. I tried glue, but it was entirely unsatisfying.

Throughout elementary school, on my walks home I was always on the lookout for tar trucks, a piece of equipment that was left at sites where roads were being repaved. Somehow the tar was kept hot, ready to be spread like frosting over old, rutted asphalt with tools that looked like industrial-strength push brooms with metal plates in place of bristles. When the road workers weren't looking, I pried off cooling wads of tar oozing down the sides of the contraption and popped them in my mouth to chew like gum. There was no chance of blowing a bubble, and you can't save it for later unless you like to eat obsidian, but I used to take it out of my mouth and work off fingernail-size bits to swallow. It wasn't particularly tasty, kind of chemical-y, but somehow it fed a craving. It astonishes me that I wasn't poisoned—or worse.

My teeth recall the delicate crunch of the crème brûlée of gastropods, the sublime slime of the garden snail, before my brain does. It's also likely that I don't actually remember at all but simply heard the story repeatedly of me as a small child pulling a snail off a fence and eating it. Being the sixth born of eight children, there was always a witness.

Still, I have the faintest recollection of the taste, which aligns with the nondescript brown-gray color of this domiciled slug. Earthy.

My brother Jerry swears that he also witnessed my eating a fresh, wriggling caterpillar. I refuse to believe him. I try to convince him he's mixing it up with the snail, but he is adamant. I suspect that bugs are easier to eat than, say, a full bag of sunflower seeds, shells and all, in a single sitting. I stole that from the corner liquor store but ultimately, I had to pay. Or rather my intestines did: They are less hardy than sunflower seed shells are pokey.

My dad used to say that he would eat "anything that stands still and some things that crawl slowly." I guess we had this in common. Just ask Tom Jones.

I called my Barbie "Tom Jones" and made her sing all the songs that I—incorrectly, as it turned out—attributed to the Welsh baritone singer. I'd heard his name often when I was growing up in the 1960s, but I didn't know which songs were his, so my Tom Jones sang "Mr. Bojangles" and "Feelin' Groovy" and "Leaving on a Jet Plane." Tom Jones went naked and could never keep her shoes on. This was my fault. I ate her toes. The texture of the flexible rubber between my teeth was irresistible. It was the perfect balance of give and resistance, and the easy snap of the tiny, barely differentiated toes was incomparable. I learned early that if I bit farther up into the leg, my teeth would eventually strike the metal used to facilitate the limbs' bendability, and it hit a nerve in me, like aluminum foil touching a metal filling, so I stuck with the toes.

In my thirties as a graduate student in social work, I was introduced to the *Diagnostic and Statistical Manual* (DSM) published by the American Psychiatric Association, which offers "a common language and standard criteria for the classification of mental disorders." We students were urged to resist the temptation to hold ourselves or others up against the diagnostic criteria, and we were reminded that all aspects of human behavior run along a continuum. The truth is, it's impossible to review the contents without finding yourself and your family members burrowed between the covers.

I came across a condition called pica in which otherwise healthy people eat nonnutritive, nonfood items including glue, paper, or, in severe cases, even glass. Pica is categorized in the DSM-5 as a "persistent disturbance of eating." It struck a chord, but I didn't give it much thought.

In grade school, the sectioned plastic trays from the free-lunch line had compartments for ground beef and gravy on reconstituted mashed potatoes or spaghetti, with "orange smiles," wedges of orange with the peel still on. Even as a child, I wondered why it was necessary to separate the lines when the meals looked precisely the same as those the paying kids got. Melinda and I amused ourselves by putting the wedges of citrus in our mouths and closing our lips around them, then smiling big bright orange smiles. Sometimes one of my older sisters would pack a lunch for me at home. Edie once put a peanut butter and jelly sandwich in a brown paper lunch bag and lovingly wrote my name across the front in blue crayon, accidentally rearranging the letters so that "Angel" read as "Anleg." To this day, some fifty-five years later, my siblings still occasionally call me Anleg.

After eating my own food at lunch, I ate whatever leftovers other kids would give me: Hostess Ding Dongs, Dolly Madison cupcakes with a perfect ribbon of icing across the top that came two to a pack, or fruit pies in a crinkly wrapper with a thick outer layer of cracked sugar glaze. I was baffled that a person could part with such treats. There was zero chance that one would have lasted until I got to school, let alone that I would ever consider giving it away.

In elementary school, eating an entire banana—fruit, stem, and peel—earned me temporary fame in the form of the nickname "Garbage Disposal," a title that had also been bestowed on my brother Kevin in the same cafeteria years before. Kids challenged me to eat their apple cores, hard-boiled egg shells, and orange peels, and I happily obliged. But my odd eating habits weren't enough to sustain the brief popularity. Neither banana peels nor eggshells were among the foods I craved. I ate them strictly for the entertainment value. If I hadn't had a chronic low rumble of hunger, I suspect I never would have learned that banana peels and eggshells are both awful to eat.

I'M WALKING ALONG Pleasant Valley Road as I take stock of my relationship to food. I try not to pick favorites among my byways, but if pressed, both Camp Joy, a little road tucked into a crook of the San Lorenzo River, and Pleasant Valley, this alluring country road between Day Valley and

Corralitos, would certainly be in the running. Pleasant Valley is occupied by olive and apple orchards, peacocks, persimmon trees, horses, productive farmers and gardeners. I walk along, appreciating the lush scenery, and munch on an apple I bought a couple of days ago from a self-serve fruit stand on Camp Joy Road. The apple is squatty with a brown top and striped green and red, and I'm kicking myself for not paying closer attention to the name. It's got to be one of best apples I've ever tasted.

It is still predawn dark as I walk along Pleasant Valley Road, absentmindedly gnawing on the stem. I have the ambitious goal of reaching Avocado Road, thirteen miles away, and getting back to my car before evening falls. I'd never heard of Avocado Road until I mapped the walk, but it's become a beacon. The sun is only considering rising, like a night-light with a towel thrown over it and a faint halo of illumination escaping. History meets me at the corner of Pleasant Valley and Hames Roads in the shape of the outline of a dark barn against a dark sky. As I wander by vineyards, orchards, and farm stands, I feel as if I've traveled back in time.

I float the length of Pleasant Valley Road in a one-sided inquiry: Where *am* I? The Italian countryside? Is this really the same Santa Cruz where I've lived for the past forty years? How can it be that I've never set foot on this road? That I've never even heard of it? Throughout the walking project, I've found myself similarly incredulous again and again as I discover new restaurants, markets, farms, even an egg ranch. I can no longer imagine a version of myself that could tolerate not knowing the contours of my community to the fullest degree.

I pass an olive orchard on my left with a sign announcing local extra-virgin olive oil. Olive oil! Here in Santa Cruz! I cross my fingers that I'll find an open gate on my way back down the road and go home with a bottle of local oil.

On the other side of the road, just past the olive trees, I spot another small self-serve fruit stand. The sun is beginning to show signs of rising but it's a bit early to traipse onto someone's property to select fruits and vegetables. Another stop to make on my way back down the road. I move along with a gait that can scarcely restrain a skip.

I find a side street: Hauer Apple Way, lined with apple trees. I appreciate that there's a fence so I don't have to grapple with temptation. But farther up the road I'm tested when I find a small stand of easily accessible trees. I edge close and take a good look at the apples hanging from them and even snap some photographs, but I curb my ardor and mind my manners as I continue down the road. There's a home of simple beauty with dormered windows set just off the road. I eye it with envy. Ellen and I have a beautiful home and a comfortable life, but envy is a habit with deep roots. I remind myself that I don't need to own a thing for it to belong to me. The pleasure of seeing things of evocative beauty and the sensations and memories that spring from them are mine to keep and use to design my own internal landscape. I'm a kind of inverse decorator crab, the crustacean that embellishes its shell with bits of seaweed, anemones, and sea sponges. Some have even been spotted scuttling along the seafloor selecting and adhering jellyfish to their setae, the bristle-hairs that run along their bodies like built-in Velcro. I do something similar. I have been known to attach decorations from my walks to my internal setae: the tulip tree flower on Dellview Avenue, the Fuyu persimmon a woman picked and handed to me over her garden fence on Fanning Grade, the apples on Lavender Hill a man gave to me when I stopped to admire his pet rooster, Doug. With each walk my shell is more richly festooned.

I reach the end of the road and turn around. On my way back I spot an extravagantly tree-lined walkway that leads to an estate that my dormered home from earlier appears to be simply the garage to. On the way back down Pleasant Valley, I stop at the outdoor produce stand tucked between the owner's art studio and a massive avocado tree that produces purple avocados. I spot wooden crates full of apples. A handwritten tag on one of them tells me I'm looking at Hauer apples.

I fill a paper lunch bag to the brim, drop cash in the slot of a mailbox nailed to the studio doorframe, and continue on my way. I reach into the bag for an apple, shine it against my T-shirt, then sink my teeth into its crisp surface. The Hauer looks like a green apple that changed its mind and went red. Its surface is freckled with white spots. It tastes otherworldly delicious, sweet and juicy and fresh, but also like unexpectedly discovering an orchard on a street named for an apple and like steeping in a project that heals a fractured heart.

I rearrange my camera bag to accommodate my new stash of *Malus pumila* and return to the road and my thoughts. A telltale sign that my mother had been shopping was the leftover cup from a lemon chiffon milkshake that sat on our car's passenger seat. Whenever it was me who found it, I always snapped off the plastic lid and used the striped straw to vacuum up any remaining sweet, tart drops. It was just enough to spark a mad desire for more.

On a walk five months into the project, I discovered a flavor that came close to replicating those lemon chiffon shakes at Marianne's Ice Cream, a classic shop that has sat at the corner of Ocean and Hubbard Streets in Santa Cruz since 1947. I stopped in and ordered a lemon custard cone, then walked down Hubbard, a two-block road off busy Ocean Street—the thoroughfare driven by tourists to get from Highway 17 to the Santa Cruz Beach Boardwalk—and branched off into the surrounding neighborhood comprised of single-story homes with space for a small yard or garden. I lapped up the generous scoop on a cake cone. The ice cream was gone too soon, as ice cream always is, but a memory crept back from childhood, of stopping at an ice cream store after visiting the boardwalk with my father and several of my siblings when I was around nine years old.

We unfolded from our cramped places in our father's red Volkswagen van like clowns from a circus car, pushing and shoving to win a place in line behind the already gathered customers. With sandy bare feet and in cutoff shorts we eagerly awaited our turn. The older kids craned to read the flavor choices on the wall behind the high counter while young ones chirped, "I want chocolate chip!" or "I want the rainbow one," then changed our minds again and again until we reached the head of the line.

I realized as I walked along Hubbard Street that the visit of my memory must have been to Marianne's.

The store is on the main road that leads from the boardwalk straight to the only freeway entrance we would have used to get home to Fremont.

Eating at Marianne's many times over the course of the more than four decades that I've lived in Santa Cruz, I never consciously registered that the place held a fond childhood memory for me. Suddenly the establishment, with its whimsical ice-cream-eating-cow wallpaper, its hand-lettered wooden signs for each flavor, and its cheerful red exterior with candy-cane-striped awnings, takes on a new depth of meaning as a direct thread between my childhood and my adulthood.

Now I'm so entrenched in my creamy, lemony daydream that I've barely registered that Pleasant Valley Road has given way to Freedom Boulevard. I notice a vulture eyeing me from atop a utility pole as I pass crops and greenhouses on either side of the road. Freedom Boulevard leads into the small town of Freedom, then into Watsonville, the second largest of the four incorporated cities within the county. Walking along the edges of the fields, I see groups of farmworkers starting their day dressed in hats and long sleeves against what will be long hours of direct sun exposure, bundling or boxing produce alongside farm machinery. I remember as a kid seeing signs in store windows exclaiming ¡UVAS NO! or NO GRAPES! The 1965 grape strike and boycott was started in Delano, California, by Filipino farmworkers under the leadership of Larry Itliong, and it influenced further actions, including lettuce and strawberry boycotts, resolved only in 1970 when union contracts promised better pay and working conditions, including health care and equipment to safeguard against toxic pesticides.

Farmworkers were mistreated by police and farm owners during the strike and boycott; many were subjected to violence. Cesar Chavez, along with community activist Dolores Huerta, established the National Farm Workers Association, which later came to be called the United Farm Workers of America. Chavez's legacy underwent significant reappraisal in 2026 when allegations of sexual misconduct, including sexual abuse of children, were raised. My mother was passionate about the UFW's cause and used it as an opportunity to talk to us about social justice, "poor people's rights," and the peace movement. My siblings and I each had a handful of "¡Uvas No!" buttons bearing an image of a stylized black bird with open wings, the United Farm Workers emblem, which we wore with pride alongside our neon-and-black peace-sign buttons.

I skirt the fields, trying to fathom the efforts and the

sacrifices made by farmworkers and their families in the fight for better pay and conditions during that period, even while working long, grueling days, while sixty-five miles away, as a clueless little girl in Fremont, I puzzled over the sudden importance of grapes and got my first glimpses of my mother's passion for justice.

When she talked about injustice, racism, poverty, animal cruelty, and the many issues about which she felt passionate, her face changed: She would thrust out her lower jaw, purse her lips, snap her shoulders back, and puff out her chest. Social justice mattered to her, but her commitment to the plight of others whose needs she stood ready to fight for didn't translate fluidly into her more personal relationships. She had strong values about equity, dignity, and respect, but her aversion to close relationships was even stronger, so these values didn't extend to those with whom she shared a roof, ancestry, or DNA.

FOR A RELATIVELY small county, Santa Cruz is spoiled with choices when it comes to good things to eat. I find a spot along the roadside to sit down for a few bites of my lunch: a chicken-and-eggplant sandwich from my favorite Italian deli, Zoccoli's, that I've stowed in my camera bag. I warmed it up before I left in the wee hours and double wrapped it in foil to try to preserve some heat. Now I sit on a curb savoring the melded flavors of sauteed onion, roasted red pepper, and Italian spices settled between portions of perfectly grilled eggplant and tender chicken, with provolone cheese melted so fully into the crannies of the francese roll that cheese and bread are as one.

When I covered the streets of Capitola, the smallest of the incorporated Santa Cruz cities, about six miles south of Santa Cruz, my go-tos included the mouthwatering corn quesadillas, blistered brown in corn oil, with legendary salsa from plastic squeeze bottles from Tacos Moreno on Capitola Road, and ficelle sandwiches wrapped in wax paper with blue harlequin diamonds from Gayle's Bakery & Rosticceria on Bay Avenue. In Watsonville, I picked up ice-cold cans of Coke and carne asada from taco trucks or, downtown, steak tortas on cloud-soft bread at El Frijolito on Alexander Street.

I turn left to follow Airport Boulevard briefly before making another left up Green Valley and another still up Amesti Road. I hit what looks like an abrupt dead end but quickly discover a walking path that will get me through this section that is closed to vehicles. I realize that I've been here before. Many years ago I was called out to this area for an after-hours child abuse investigation. Amesti Road appeared on my paper map to be the quickest route to the address where dispatch requested I meet sheriff's deputies. I'd been so dead asleep when dispatch called that I almost hung up because I couldn't make sense of what the caller was saying, but as I went to put the phone down I realized that I was holding the receiver upside down and talking directly into the earpiece. This was the era of landlines.

After stopping by the office to assess whether the family

had any previous child welfare involvement, I took off for what should have been a thirty-minute drive. I was on the highway headed south before I realized that I was in a county car that wasn't equipped with a car seat, so I doubled back and picked one up in case I needed it. I got off at the airport exit and drove through neighborhoods and agricultural fields in the dark and drizzle, finding my way to Amesti Road. I followed the road until it abruptly stopped well before the map indicated it should. I turned the car around and headed back to retrace my route and hit another dead end. This made no sense because I'd just come from that direction. I drove back and forth along the road slowly, trying to see if I'd missed a turn or accidentally gone down a long driveway, but I couldn't find my way back the way I'd come.

I did my best to ignore the volcano of emotions rumbling in my gut. The pressure of having a family and law enforcement officers waiting for over an hour. The fear of being lost and stuck in unfamiliar terrain in the middle of the night while drizzle turned to downpour. The humiliation of having to ask for help. I tried calling dispatch on my office-issued mobile phone that looked like a giant police radio but the first calls failed. After a few tries, I managed to get a connection, and the dispatcher stayed on the line with me consulting her map while I wrangled my emotions and got myself rerouted to the scene, which by the time I arrived was wrapped up. The deputies had determined that there was an adult willing and able to protect the children in the home, and the family came up with a safety plan that involved the parent about whom the concerns had been raised staying somewhere else for the time being. The four school-age kids were safe for the night, so child welfare could follow up during business hours the following day. I was no longer needed. Only several days later did I learn that the reason I couldn't find my way was that a landslide had taken out sections of the road and seemingly hemmed me in. Without the dispatcher guiding me through what felt like a maze of private driveways and small roads, I have no idea how long I would have been driving around looking for a way out.

I rummage through my camera bag for another Hauer, my new favorite apple. I'm fickle, though—my loyalty has changed from the Camp Joy apple to the Hauer in the course of a morning and I may change again before the moon rises. As I make my way through the now overgrown path that traces the scars left by the landslide and emerge onto the road, a memory that has been shyly hovering unfolds in living color.

Walking to school one day when I was around ten or eleven, I found a hidden lunch bag behind a hedge on the side yard of a neighbor's house. In the bag was a generous handful of potato chips, a shiny red apple, and a peanut butter and jelly sandwich. I sat down and ate it on the spot, then continued on my way to school. The next day, I hopped over the low fence along the small strip of yard and made my way behind the hedge. To my surprise, there was another lunch bag, with the same snacks. Again I sat down and ate it. I stopped and ate the contents of the bag every morning, sitting behind the bush, out of sight of passersby.

It never occurred to me to wonder who'd left it or why it was there. Decades later, walking along this road, I gasp aloud. "Oh my God. I wonder if someone left that food specifically for me." I'm flooded with questions. Who left the lunches there? How did I know to look in that spot? Had someone dropped a hint? As a child, it hadn't seemed weird at all to discover a complete lunch all prepared and waiting. It was just a dependable little supplementary meal. But looking back at it for the first time through the lens of adulthood, I sense a bigger picture: Someone was looking out for me.

I continue to think about the lunch bags as Amesti Road ushers me right onto Browns Valley Road and I'm momentarily distracted by the bucolic beauty of big, open farmland, plowed fields, and orchards. I realize I've significantly underestimated the time it would take me to walk the distance of a full marathon, drive back home, and have dinner ready for Ellen and Miles when they get home at five thirty. Ellen will have worked a long day and Miles will be sandwiched between his school day and a night of homework. But I'm so close to Avocado Road, and it's only a mile and a half out and back. I pick up my pace. But when I arrive, I see that Avocado is a gated road. Before I have a chance to so much as pout, a woman pulls up to let herself in the gate and I ask her if she would mind if I walk on her road. "Feel free," she replies, no questions asked.

I speed-walk down this beautiful road, stopping only to admire an enchanting fairy-tale cottage of a house in a clearing. I'd imagined an avocado orchard when I saw the street name on the map, and now, zipping along at a fourteen-minute mile, I scan the area. Finally, near the end of the road, I spot an avocado tree and stop to soak it in and snap a photo. There's a kind of simple, wholesome joy that comes over me finding an avocado tree on Avocado Road. I felt the same tickle of happiness when I found a feather on Feather Lane and when I cast a hand-puppet shadow in the late afternoon light on Shadow Court. But none of these can touch the ebullience of standing at the corner of Ice Cream Grade and Candy Lane with the bag of Skittles and chewy Life Savers I stowed in my camera bag in anticipation of the occasion.

I'm fourteen miles in with twelve miles to go and I'm walking as fast as my exhausted legs will carry me and rebuking myself for being too damn zealous. I run the math in my head again: If I can keep up a fast, steady pace all the way back to my car, I could conceivably walk in the door by six and have dinner ready by seven thirty. On the late side, but not entirely neglectful.

There's no sidewalk on this stretch of Browns Valley so I walk along the shoulder, which gets uncomfortably narrow at points.

I jump when I hear a vehicle honk at me and turn my head to see that it's Scott, the father of a school pal of Miles's. Ellen and I have become friends with him and his wife over the course of many track-and-field meets and basketball games. I laugh aloud and I can see through his windshield as he finds a safe place to pull over that he's laughing too. He travels all over the county for his work designing and building swimming pools, and this is the fourth time during my walking project that he's seen me trudging in remote areas and stopped to offer me a lift. This time, I happily accept.

He goes a couple of miles out of his way to deliver me to my car. I thank him profusely and marvel at my lucky stars as he drives away. He's just saved me a few hours.

No one is home when I get there. I preheat the oven, drizzle olive oil, lemon zest, and coarse salt in a roasting pan, and use it to slather chicken, onions, garlic, cherry tomatoes, carrots, and red potatoes. I throw in a haphazard array of spices, toss the whole mess in the oven, set the timer for sixty minutes, and hope for the best. On a whim, before closing the oven door, I toss in a couple of the apples from my camera bag.

I put away my gear and get on the computer to research pica and Hauer Pippin apples. I check the most recent *Diagnostic and Statistical Manual* and learn that in addition to the various conditions with which pica typically correlates, such as autism and pregnancy, there are environmental factors that can lead to the disorder, namely neglect and lack of supervision. I don't go so far as to self-diagnose, but there is a tug of curiosity, a part of me that wants to fit my flaws and foibles into tidy packets that can be easily organized and stored on a shelf or discarded, as needed.

I do a quick search to see if I can figure out the name of the Camp Joy apple, but I find more than thirty varieties that start with *m* and none rings a bell.

As for the Hauer Pippin apple, I learn that while it's

also grown and harvested in Canada, Northern Virginia, and the state of Washington, the original seedling, thought to be a hybrid of the Cox's Orange Pippin and the Yellow Bellflower, was discovered in 1890 in Santa Cruz County.

Miles and Ellen come in the front door, and from my office I can hear them in the kitchen reveling in the scents of dinner wafting from the oven and commenting on how hungry they are.

Chapter 10

Helpers

grace note *noun* \\'grās 'nōt\\: a small
addition to make something more
beautiful or interesting

IN LATE SEPTEMBER of 2016, the third year of the project, I
have a period of two weeks when a combination of work,
sporting events, and social obligations prevents me from
getting to walk at all. As a result, I am like a fractious horse
pawing at the dirt. I take a day off work and wrangle my
heavy sky-blue old-lady bike onto the rack on my car before I give Miles a ride to school in Scotts Valley. After his
last class he'll have basketball practice, so I park in a lot
adjacent to the school with an agreement that I'll meet him
back at the car at five thirty.

I give him the briefest side-shoulder hug, the only acceptable kind for high school drop-off and only if you're quick
on the draw. I start taking my bike off the car but realize
that I haven't thought through my plan. I'd decided to bring
the bike along so I can cover more distance, knowing that

the return trip will be much quicker on wheels. But if I take the bike with me from here, I'll have to walk it one way and ride it back the other. So I resecure the straps, drive the car to my intended end point, lock the bike to a tree, then drive back to the school and start my walk. I have nine hours to travel twenty-four miles—twelve on foot and twelve on bike. I have time for photos and quick breaks, but none of my typical extensive lollygagging.

I grab my gear, lock the car, and almost instantly melt into the motion of walking. My feet are wrung sponges drinking in the asphalt like still, humble water straight from the coldest, freshest spring. I admonish myself for going full speed, but anything less and I feel as if I'll implode. Walking has become as essential to me as food, and I'm ravenous. Pacing myself will have to wait until I've shaved the edge off this hunger.

I've fashioned a walk that takes roughly the shape of a V on my map, heading west back toward the ocean for about five miles, then making a sharp (at least on the map) left, angling back up into the hills for six miles before turning right on a side street that will lead me in a vague spiral, giving the last stretch of my twelve-mile walk a curly flourish before I retrieve my bike and pedal my way back to meet Miles at the car.

To morning commuters using Granite Creek Road to reach Highway 17, I might look like a woman in a hurry. I am anything but. My muscles all collude for a fast pace, but my psyche is motionless, like the moment a downpour stops, not gradually but all at once, and everything, every sense and the very earth, rings fresh, awake, and attentive. It's like the air is breathing me.

I've walked through many neighborhoods within the county where wealth is on prominent display. A swimming pool surrounded by sand so you feel as if you're at the beach; another not confined by a fenced yard but set out in the open among sprawling acreage with nearby trees to climb. Massive houses with intricately carved corbels, elaborate stained glass, private tennis courts, adult-size wooden swings hung from solid arbors by thick, braided ropes, overlooking pastures, vineyards, orchards, and the entire bay, open-air stone entryways furnished like outdoor living rooms. The jumble of emotions that accompanies witnessing such riches is so consistent from one occasion to the next that it deserves its own word.

It's not simply *envy*. *Covetousness* slants in the right direction but it lacks the necessary nuance. What is the word for when you present yourself as nonmaterialistic but you know the drool is glistening on your lips AND you have more than plenty at this point in your life, but you still have slivers under your fingernails from a time when you didn't, yet you can't dip too far into the self-pity pool because you grew up in a two-story house and your father was consistently employed and maybe you only ever had one pair of shoes at a time but you always had *a* pair of shoes AND your career has been largely devoted to people who struggle mightily to enjoy the simplest comforts while other people have garages that could comfortably house a family AND while you're rooting into righteousness about the inequity of it all you must admit that you are not lining up to offer your garage? What's the word for that?

There is a particular house I'd like to see on this walk. Melinda pointed it out to me when we were teenagers and I'd come to Santa Cruz to visit her at the boarding school she'd been sent to because of a tangle of behavioral and learning issues. We had been constant companions and her absence left a void in my life. The house was the home and vineyards of the Smothers Brothers. We didn't know then who they were exactly, but we knew they'd been on TV and that was famous enough for us. I have only a vague recollection of a driveway framed by trees and ivy that she pointed out as we rode in the back of a friend's car.

A song from childhood called "Helping" has been playing through my mind lately. Margaret had a record album called *Free to Be . . . You and Me.* It was the brainchild of Marlo Thomas, who wanted to send a message to children of the 1970s about breaking out of traditional gender roles. It had songs but also poems and skits. At twelve I believed I was way too old for its childish stories, even though I secretly loved every one of them, so I used the guise of entertaining five-year-old Margaret to listen to it over and over until Margaret and I both knew every song and story by heart.

The "Helping" song was written by author Shel Silverstein and, I learned later, performed by Tom Smothers. Those names meant nothing to us as school-age kids, but hearing them now, with a little more knowledge of the various musicians and actors on the album, I more fully appreciate what a monumental piece of work the album was in its time.

I hum the tune and our neighbor Mrs. Sutherland comes to mind. I was nine or ten the first time she invited me for tea in her home, around the corner from where we lived. With her husband dead and her children grown, her two-story house felt empty. When I arrived, she brought me into her kitchen, where I stood on one leg like a stork, with the flat of my raised foot resting along the inside of my opposite knee, so that my legs made the number four. It was my natural stance as a kid unless someone pointed it out and I would rearrange myself onto two feet like a human. She prepared a tray of fragile cups and little pots of sugar and honey, which I learned was her daily practice. She poured milk into her tea, then started pouring it into mine.

"I don't want none," I told her. "I hate milk."

She offered alternative language. "None for me, thank you. I don't care for milk."

I was game for trying, but the new locution felt like marbles in my mouth.

If she invited me to tea at 4 p.m., as she did about half a dozen times, and I showed up late, she answered the door, greeted me kindly, then suggested another time, when I could arrive promptly. Once, when she encouraged me to wear cleaner clothes, I found a dress among the mountain of our family's dirty laundry—gray with a white collar and a little carousel embroidered in red thread. It was made for someone smaller than me, but I could put it on without ripping it. I wore it to tea. She told me to go home and change, then bring the dress back to her. While we had our tea and biscuits, she laundered and ironed the dress and returned it to me for the next visit.

A few days later I stood at her door in the clean gray dress (and bare feet), very close to the prescribed time. She smiled broadly and told me I looked like "a proper little girl." I wanted to be a proper little girl. I wanted to be a girl with a locket or a charm bracelet or little cotton underpants with matching undershirts.

As I remember, a thought enters my head: Mrs. Sutherland's house was directly across the street from the lunch bags with peanut butter sandwiches that I found behind the hedge on my way to school every morning. *Could it have been her?* I remember that after greedily consuming them, I would crumple up the bag into a ball and toss it behind the bushes, only to find the bag gone and a fresh one taking its place every school day. Did I find the lunches there for weeks? Months? I don't remember.

My last memory of seeing Mrs. Sutherland is of her opening the door to me the day I stood on the concrete step in front of her house in my gray dress. Maybe she didn't invite me back after that day, or maybe she did and the memory has just faded. Maybe I was a lost cause and she gave up on me, or maybe she died and no one ever told me. I wasn't mindful of her absence in my life. I enjoyed being with her and always accepted her invitations, but like most kids, I didn't have the agency to initiate interactions with adults. She was a small part of my world. Her invitations to tea were a grace note that I only fully register in hindsight.

She found a way to reach out to me and offer concrete help without calling out that she suspected something was amiss in my family, as I imagine was the case. She was gracious and caring, and she used her manners to teach me how to present myself in a way that would help me navigate the world more smoothly and successfully.

Information and education about child abuse, particularly in its more subtle forms, was scant in the early 1970s. Child Protective Services, as we know it now, both in California and around the country, was very much in its formative stages. All states had child welfare agencies and there were some professionals who had been identified as mandated reporters, but interventions tended to be geared toward serious physical injuries—kids who had been burned with cigarettes, for example, or had broken bones, or were covered in readily visible bruises. It would be some time before mandated reporters consistently made referrals, and longer still before it became more common for neighbors, friends, and extended family members to contact child welfare agencies with concerns about children they knew. Though that didn't stop some people from finding small ways to intervene and send important messages to children they were worried about.

Mrs. Lombardi lived directly across the street from us. Her daughters, Heather and Carol, were close in age to me. They sometimes invited me to attend church with them. They were Christian, but not Catholic—a distinction that meant nothing to me but seemed important to them. I didn't know any of the songs at first, which made me feel I was somehow betraying the God in my church, but impassioned rounds of "The King of glory comes, the nation rejoices. Open the gates before him, lift up your voices" quickly became part of my repertoire.

Mrs. Lombardi was a Girl Scout leader, and she talked to my mother about signing me up to be in her troop with her daughters and told her that there were scholarship funds available for any activities that had associated costs. Many of my siblings had been involved with Scouts over the years and my mother readily agreed to let me join.

One afternoon I went over to play with Heather and Carol. We were running around the sparse, tidy living room and Mrs. Lombardi called out from the kitchen, "If you're going to run, go outside!" We stopped for a while, then one of the girls started a game of tag. I chased after her and knocked into a small round table upon which a glass terrarium full of gravel and leafy plants perched. I had admired it on previous visits; it was a delicate orb of glass containing a little world within a world, with a tiny ceramic bridge set among the plants that, by scale, made them look like trees. The terrarium fell and exploded loudly on the tile floor, shattering into a million slivers. Mrs. Lombardi ran in from the kitchen and I cowered with both arms raised in front of my face, ready for a blow. Mrs. Lombardi stopped in her tracks and said cheerily, "It's not a problem at all. It can easily be replaced."

I felt frozen to my spot. I could feel my face going bright red. Mrs. Lombardi got a broom and a box and asked if I would hold the box while she swept the glass into it, which

I agreed to with relief at having something to do. Afterward, she made a motion like brushing off her hands and said in a reassuring tone, "That's all done."

When I left the house, Mrs. Lombardi walked me out. Standing in her driveway, she said, "Angel, I want you to know that I am here if you ever need to talk about anything at all."

I nodded and started to walk away, and she added, "It is never OK for anyone to hurt you, do you know that?" I nodded again, though I wasn't sure that I did know. I never did tell her about anything happening at home, but her words stuck with me.

I return my attention to walking and move along with a quiet mind for a bit, grateful for a slight breeze. Knowing that I wouldn't be passing by any stores or restaurants for most of the day, I'd packed a good lunch and plenty of snacks. I reach into a side pocket of my bag and bring out a square of dark chocolate. I'm not ready for a sit-down break yet, so I take little bites as I go. There's a clearing along the side of the road and I notice motion out of the corner of my eye. I turn my head to see what I first assume is a puppy but quickly realize is a coyote pup. I've only seen a couple of young ones during my walks, usually in the late afternoon or early evening.

I happily note that my camera is already fitted with its telephoto lens, and I use it to get a closer look. I can see the fuzz outlining his ears and the white fur under his chin. He looks behind him, and following his gaze, I can see, partially obscured by tall weeds, another pup. I've never seen more than one at a time and my heart skips a beat. I get so excited when I see wildlife that it's hard to hold my camera perfectly still and even harder to remember to check my settings before snapping away. So I often end up with photos where it's very clear that I've spotted a mammal of some type, but sometimes, as in this case, they appear more like apparitions than coyotes. The first pup turns his head toward the second and they romp back into the thicket from which they emerged. I stand in the same spot after they've gone, cherishing the moment.

This is fun, I think. *A day of gratitude.* I feel like Mrs. Sutherland and Mrs. Lombardi are at my side as friendly ghosts. Mrs. Sutherland seemed old to me when I knew her, but I realize with a little twinge that when I knew her she was likely close to the age I am now.

Then I recall poor Mrs. Pfizer, who was clearly trying to help me but severely blundered her attempt. I was a sophomore at the first continuation school I attended. I had a surly attitude; as one of the teachers there told me, "Your looks could curdle milk." I wore throughout the day a huge olive-green hunting jacket with a bright orange liner and a faux-fur collar zipped to my chin, regardless of weather. I remember my brother Kevin wearing it for a while before I claimed it. I refused to take it off even to play volleyball, the only physical activity at a school comprised of two portable classroom trailers and a portable office arranged in a U shape around a makeshift volleyball court with a single net.

One day I was called into the counselor's office to talk

to Mrs. Pfizer, who was not only the school's counselor but also its principal. Mrs. Pfizer sat on the other side of a wide desk and asked me why I came to school dressed in the same clothes every day. Before I could respond, she suggested I take off the jacket since it was hot in her office. I refused. I wasn't hiding anything; the jacket had just become a kind of second skin. She gave it a couple more tries, with tones that ranged from coaxing to demanding to practically pleading, but I was not peeling my skin off in the principal's office, counselor or no.

Mrs. Pfizer looked me in the eye and asked, "Are you in love with your father?"

Maybe concepts like rapport building and not confusing sexual abuse with "being in love" hadn't taken hold in the education system by the mid-'70s, but I was dumbfounded. She looked a little surprised herself at what she had just asked.

"No!" I said, recoiling. The interview was over. I stood up and walked out of her office.

I suppose she got an answer she could report back to whoever had assigned her the task of talking to me. I never again heard from her or anyone else on the subjects of my jacket or my father, and I never learned what prompted her to ask.

Maybe one of the teachers thought I was using the coat to hide injuries. Maybe a friend or neighbor had concerns and reached out to the school. Maybe one of my siblings had disclosed something to someone about their own abuse.

I chalked it up to Mrs. Pfizer being off-kilter, and anytime it entered my mind over the years, I'd dismiss it with a roll of my eyes. Until this walk.

She was trying to help, I realize now. Not skillfully. Not tactfully. Quite horrendously, in fact. But she tried. She had made an effort, however bungling, to reach me.

I whisper a thank-you and let Mrs. Pfizer join my band of helpful, or at least well-intentioned, ghosts.

If I had known at that time what I learned several years later, that two of my siblings had been seriously sexually abused by my father, Mrs. Pfizer's seemingly bizarre question probably wouldn't have caught me so off guard. Of course, sexual abuse of any type is serious, but my father's behaviors ran along a continuum from sexually laced humor that would have been innocuous among consenting adults—such as asking one of my older sisters if he could "squeeze Mickey's ear" when she wore her Mickey Mouse T-shirt—but was plainly wrong with children; to boundaryless but not overtly sexual affection, like back massages where he'd have me lie on the floor on my stomach, then straddle me in a kneeling position, running his hands up and down my back under my shirt in a way that made my skin crawl; to outright sexual assault of at least two of his children that caused significant, long-lasting suffering.

Working in child welfare, I have had experience in the art of trying to help children and families. I was operating with more education, training, and support than I imagine poor Mrs. Pfizer had been provided, but helping people in situations where there is abuse or neglect is complicated and difficult, no matter how prepared you are.

During the first several months after graduating from the social work program at San Francisco State and taking a job as a child abuse investigator in a nearby county, I was assigned to meet with a four-year-old girl I'll call Ivy. She had been interviewed several times about allegations of sexual abuse and it was determined that she was not to be interviewed again. There were concerns that she might have been coached by adults in her family not to talk to social workers. During the current investigation she'd told the forensic interviewer, "If I talk to 'sokel' workers, I have to stay at foster care forever." Ivy was on the young side to be formally interviewed in the first place, and since it had caused clear distress for her to participate, the last interview had been cut short.

In California, each party in child welfare cases involved with the dependency court system has an attorney. In Ivy's situation, attorneys for both her parents and her had requested that Ivy not be interviewed further. My supervisor suggested that I simply meet with Ivy at her foster home to check in with her and her foster mother about how she was doing in care.

During my first visit, Ivy's foster mother introduced us and we chatted for a couple of minutes about cats and the fact that moths, as she had just learned, are drawn to light. Ivy picked up a crayon and started "writing" in loops and squiggles. Ivy's focus on her writing was particularly intense. She appeared to tune me out completely and I thought I could see a range of emotions playing across her face as she hunched over her work at a child-size table. She appeared to be truly putting her thoughts on paper, never mind that it wasn't decipherable. After several minutes she put the crayon down, put her hands on top of the stack of papers on the table in front of her, and announced, "I'm done." Then she informed me, "It's about what happened."

Oh shit, I thought, thrown off by this unexpected turn. *I can't interview her, but if she's going to spontaneously disclose information, I'm not going to just ignore it.*

The foster mother, who was sitting on a nearby couch, and I exchanged a quick glance.

"It's about what happened," I echoed back, hoping that if she wanted to talk, she would do so without much involvement from me. A direct, unprompted quote from her about her experience could be helpful in ensuring that she'd get the help she needed if she had, in fact, been abused. But she replied simply, "Yep."

I wavered as to whether to pursue it any further. If I started asking questions, it could easily have been construed as an interview, which didn't square with what had been determined was best for Ivy or with my agreement with my supervisor to steer clear of asking questions for the time being.

Ivy looked at me expectantly and I decided to make one more comment. "You can read it to me, if you'd like," I said.

She responded instantaneously and incredulously, "I'm only four, I can't read!"

I wanted to rearrange my words, maybe say, "You can *tell* me what you wrote." But these were not nuances a four-year-old was likely to appreciate.

I was relatively green in social work, but with several months in the field and a year's internship behind me, I knew the basics of child interviewing skills, such as building rapport, asking open-ended questions, using developmentally appropriate language, establishing competency by determining whether a child can differentiate between truth and lie, and gaining an understanding of the child's perspective. But I had the words of my supervisor in my mind, admonishing me not to conduct an interview, though neither of us had accounted for the fact the child might initiate a discussion, and I was well-enough versed in child development to know that repeated inquiries by relative strangers could compound any trauma Ivy was already experiencing. I was operating under the rigid timelines of California's child welfare system, with the next court hearing nipping at my heels, where I would need to demonstrate the need for continued out-of-home care or recommend Ivy be returned home to her parents.

In the end, I said something along the lines of "Ivy, I'm worried that a grown-up might be hurting you or touching you in a way that isn't OK, and I want to help make sure you stay safe."

Ivy walked to the corner of the room, turned her back to me, and said, "Yeah, right. It's too late for that."

During more than twenty years of working in the field, I have heard countless troubling details about abuse and neglect. But those words from a four-year-old child, spoken in a deflated tone, flattened me.

I recommended that Ivy remain in out-of-home care while we continued to assess her needs and investigate, though I knew the judge wouldn't be able to follow the recommendation. Put bluntly, I was passing the buck. To my dismay, despite my efforts and those of the other social workers who'd met with Ivy and law enforcement's investigations of possible sexual abuse, there was not enough evidence for my recommendation to stick. Ivy was returned to her parents only briefly before she came back into the system with physical injuries that conclusively demonstrated sexual abuse. Ultimately, a relative who didn't live with Ivy's family was arrested and convicted. Ivy went to live with the same foster family while her parents had counseling and took part in parenting classes in hopes that she would once again be returned to their care. When I went to visit her at her foster family's home, she told me, "When I was at the 'hosible' I thought my heart was bleeding from sadness."

Looking back, I'm not sure how I continued in this line of work. Trying to help a small child and not being able to do so was emotionally ruinous. I reviewed Ivy's case with a coworker, my supervisor, and my manager, all of us trying to figure out what I might have done differently. They kindly pointed out what I had done well, reminded me that such a big decision as returning a child to her home under Ivy's circumstances is not balanced on a single attempt at intervention, and gave me the feedback I was looking for: I shouldn't have told Ivy that I wanted to help her.

I'd introduced concepts like someone trying to hurt her when she hadn't indicated that herself, which in court could be considered "leading." I'd implied that I could likely help her when I had no way of knowing at that point whether our intervention would be helpful. On the other hand, I was reminded by my manager that people who try to help children and families in crisis can get so caught up in crafting the right language, complying with laws, regulations, best practices, and covering our asses that we fail to deliver the right messages to the children we're trying to help. She recognized that I was trying to deliver a supportive message to Ivy.

I turn my thoughts back to Mrs. Pfizer. What was she thinking I might say as she braced for my answer about how exactly I loved my father? Had she discussed her concerns about me with her supervisor? Did she have more questions for me before I fled her office? Had she experienced something in her childhood that left her alert to signs in others? Or had she read that kids who won't take their jackets off were probably victims of sexual abuse?

IF MRS. PFIZER is to be invited to what is becoming a regular parade in my mind, then most certainly Maxine, Gertrude, and Melvin should be included as well. This trio briefly graced my life a few months after my interview with Mrs. Pfizer. The stay at Kaiser Hospital in Richmond after I threatened to my counselor that I would commit suicide was only supposed to last seventy-two hours, but my father must have agreed to allow them to keep me lon-ger. I don't believe a fifteen-year-old would be held in an adult facility beyond twenty-four hours today, but apparently it was an acceptable practice in the '70s.

It's hard to keep track of time in a timeless place. For the first two days I was there, there was a girl my age, Arlene. After she left, it was just a lot of old people and a middle-aged woman who had broken her arm while trying to engage intimately with her horse, or so other patients told me. I steered clear of her. She scared me.

I didn't mind the hospital at all; it was clean, there was a routine to follow, and sometimes we went out in the community in the Kaiser van for pizza. I would have sooner died than be seen at Pizza Hut with half a dozen old crazy people in Fremont. But Richmond seemed a world away and this was my new, if very temporary, life.

On the ward, there was a dispenser with apple, orange, and cranberry juice, which you could help yourself to anytime. There was a vending machine with diagonally cut sandwiches in plastic containers. They were dry, on their way to stale, but they came with little packets of mayonnaise and mustard. I liked getting my lunch out of the machine until I got a sandwich with a large snarl of hair in it. After that I stuck mostly to oyster crackers and juice.

Maxine, Gertrude, and Melvin were a unit. They were truly old. Probably in their seventies. They spoke to each other like grumpy longtime spouses, bickering and snapping at each other constantly. They lavished me with attention and fell over themselves to tell me how much they cherished my company. They were instant family, in that way of people who are thrown into an unusual circumstance together. They told me I should be a model. I knew that they all needed glasses, but I humored them, even using the psych ward hallway as a runway, premiering the smart look of a hospital gown with sweatpants underneath. There was nothing surly about me on the psych ward.

We sat together in occupational therapy, working on projects like vinyl lanyard keychains and decorative weavings called God's Eyes where we wove lengths of colored yarn between two or three crossed sticks. I've always thought of them as craft projects for occupational therapy or Sunday school. But I learned recently that Ojos de Dios have cultural and spiritual significance in Peru, New Mexico, and Mexico. Maxine, Gertrude, and Melvin all marveled at everything I made. They asked me for help with their projects even when they clearly didn't need it.

I didn't want to leave the ward, but after several days, my time was up. The day shift nurse let me know that I'd be leaving the following morning. I tried acting crazy that night to see if I could fool them into keeping me longer. I slept with the gooseneck lamp that was attached to the wall above the bed bent as close as I could get it so it shone directly on my face in the otherwise dark room. Probably because of my age, I had a room to myself next to the nurse's station. I called the nurse in repeatedly to tell her that my sheets were breathing or that I'd just seen a cat ghost. Apparently acting was not my strong suit. The next morning, I had to stuff my belongings into a bag and shove off. I left my art projects behind for the trio, who received them as if they were priceless objects.

I've been walking for a few hours and hunger is creeping in, so I keep my eyes peeled for a spot where I can sit comfortably and enjoy my food. I look down the road and I'm surprised to see a bright red telephone booth, the kind I've seen in photographs of London, at the side of the road, replete with a gold crown emblem. Its presence is made all the starker by the morning fog still entangled in the trees, the charcoal gray of the single-lane road, and the ground carpet of crunchy brown scrub oak leaves. I feel a sudden need to make a call, but not to a place with an area code or a name. A crazy notion grabs me: I want to call Mrs. Sutherland. I resist the urge to step into the booth. Instead I snap a photo, which will no doubt be the one I choose to represent Rider Ridge Road.

Mrs. Sutherland, Mrs. Lombardi, Mrs. Pfizer, and the psych ward trio are joined by others who helped me in my younger years.

When I lived with Sue, my foster mother in San Francisco, at seventeen, I came and went at will. I had no interest in asking permission of anyone, but by waiting until Sue was asleep, I avoided having to navigate expectations. I'd take buses to hang out with friends and strangers in front of the Greyhound station or go around the corner and stand in front of the amusingly named Terminal Drugs store dressed in men's vests and ties from the Goodwill and smoke Tiparillo cigars.

Whenever I was on a bus, I always sat in the middle of

the bench seat at the rear, the best vantage point from which to see everyone who boarded. I used to wear a double-bladed dagger hanging from my belt in a leather sheath, something I can't imagine would be tolerated on public transportation today. If I felt remotely threatened, I would take out my knife and carefully use it to clean my fingernails. I would not have had a clue how to use it against an attacker, but it made me feel safe. I was hedging my bets.

I have a black-and-white photograph of Em, my girl-friend at the time, and me dressed in our vests and ties. She's wearing a brimmed hat on top of her springy curls. I believed we were beyond tough, all but untouchable, and I was convinced that I was passing as male, which I was con-fident made it perfectly safe for me to travel by bus alone at all hours of the night across San Francisco.

Looking at the photograph some forty years later, I practically guffaw. We were both dimpled and fresh-faced. We would never have been construed as men from any an-gle, at least by the standards of the time. I was wisp slight and sharp featured, practically elfin. My rough veneer, which felt impenetrable from the inside, was about as for-tified, I see now, as a drawbridge built of toothpicks, a cas-tle door of sheet ice.

Walking back to Sue's house in the dark from the bus stop one night, I heard a mew in a hedge. The sound led me to a tiny calico kitten, not old enough to be away from its mother. I crouched down and brushed dirt and leaves off its unbearably soft fur and carried it home. I gave it some milk and put it on a pillow beside me for the night. In the morning, I was nervous, unsure how to find out if I could keep it without appearing attached. Asking directly for something I wanted felt like setting a trap for myself. I didn't want to use the word *kitten*; it sounded weak and needy. Instead, I found Sue at the kitchen sink and in a flat tone, communicating only a fact, I said, "I found a little cat." Sue, probably sensing what I was facing, instantly told me that I could keep it if no one came to claim it. I felt like I was taking care of him by occasionally feeding him. I let him cuddle into my bed at night. In retrospect, I'm sure Sue did the lion's share of caring for him.

I named him Kintar. He lived a long life at Sue's house. He gave me one of the few typical experiences I had during the transition from childhood to adulthood: getting a pet, taking care of it as best you can with an adult's help, then leaving it with your parents when you move out.

I had friends around the city, mostly current and former foster kids and "runaways," who rented rooms in old flats with high ceilings, crown molding, and clawfoot bathtubs. The bold-patterned floor tiles in kitchens and bathrooms recalled old-fashioned soda shops, a whisper of another, more opulent era obscured by precarious stacks of milk crates and wood pallets serving as makeshift beds, book-shelves, and dressers. The houses, once home to wealthy families, were now subdivided, and divided again, with multiple individuals crowding in to make rent more man-ageable. Windowless walk-in closets served as small bed-rooms.

Everyone I knew at the time used Bee & Flower soap from China, which smelled of sandalwood and came packaged in brown floral-print paper with a shiny gold seal, embossed with a bee. The spice scent of that soap and the powerful voice of Patti Smith blaring from portable record players were common threads from one flat to the next. I had a girlfriend in one of the flats who subsisted on a diet of Mystic Mint cookies and pink lemonade. When I stayed with her, that was my diet too. The apples Sue brought home, in addition to communicating affection, provided reprieve from the gastronomic calamity of sweet cookies washed down with sour lemonade.

Jocelyn, a therapist I saw in my mid-twenties, comes to mind next. She charged me next to nothing for my sessions, allowed me to bring baby Kita when I couldn't find childcare, and was incredibly kind, warm, and supportive, which for some reason irritated the hell out of me. I was chronically late to appointments, I was sarcastic toward her, and sometimes I made personal barbs. We lived in a relatively small community that was made even smaller by the fact that we were both gay. I had a welter of pent-up emotions about counselors and educators who'd blurred professional boundaries with me during my high school years by becoming personal friends or sexual partners. I'd told Jocelyn about several such relationships in a lighthearted way, skimming over the emotions they prompted in me. I knew that she and her girlfriend had recently broken up, and during one session I said, "I heard you got dumped." I could see a flash of woundedness in her face, but she recovered quickly.

"It makes sense that you've needed to poke at me," she said, "to make sure I won't fall over or disappear or break the contract of what it means to be your therapist. That's part of what can happen in therapy. But you have an even more important task here. You need to decide if you want to do the work. And at some point, it can't just be about pushing me away or using humor to deflect your emotions."

She paused, giving me a minute to let that sink in. Then she added, "Your trust has been tested, going all the way back to the first people you should have been able to trust implicitly, your parents."

I hated the simplicity of these words. They made me feel like a victim. But I wanted her to see that I didn't want her to kick me out, so I nodded.

"The fault for how you were treated lies with your parents and other people who made the world unsafe for you, but the responsibility for how you deal with the fallout and move forward lies squarely with you," she continued.

These words were not simple. She had my undivided attention. Healing doesn't come wrapped in ribbons, she was telling me. You can't just passively sit and wait for it to be delivered. It's not a gift. It's a hard-earned reward. I was used to life happening to me; it was time for me to learn how to guide my life where I wanted it to go. Joceyln tamed a beast with a single, cleanly executed boundary.

She talked to me about the role of a therapist, and committed to working with me within the ethical parameters that a good therapist abides by, and asked me to think about whether I wanted to work with her. "Don't answer me today," she said. "Let's schedule an appointment for next week and talk more about this then."

I didn't need to wait for the appointment, but I followed her direction and waited to tell her that I did want her help and that I was willing to do the work. I knew that I needed therapy and I didn't want to be fired.

The work, it turns out, is as heavy and as layered as the ancient sedimentary rock walls that I marvel at on my walks along the shoreline, and sometimes it feels just as old. It started with my learning a basic language for talking about emotions, finding my voice to express myself about them, and learning to take care of myself emotionally and physically. It ranged from simple tasks—such as learning to pay my bills on time so that I wouldn't lose my housing—to honing the skills to manage my continued intrusive thoughts and sorting out my complicated personal relationships. I got back on track with my weekly appointments with Jocelyn and tried to stay on my best behavior.

The helpers joining me on my walk expand to include my current-day people Ellen, Kita, and Miles, and my close friends, siblings, nieces and nephews, and godchildren, who all fall into step. Ellen's family are all here. Neighbors. Coworkers. Exes. My old friends Kate and Jennifer, who bought me a washer and dryer when they saw me struggling as a single parent, adding a bit of practical relief to my daily grind and an even bigger dose of love and support when I was hanging on by my fingertips. Everyone I can think of who's brightened my days, lent me a hand, sat with me through seemingly hopeless moments, or graciously allowed me to help them.

Whenever I find a face-up penny on the ground, I pick it up and put it in my pocket. If it's tails up, I turn it over for the next person. If I see a lucky penny today, I will leave it where it rests. I don't want to be greedy. My pockets are full. Threads would snap under the weight.

I sail the last few miles back to the school on my bike, my heart so full and happy it could pop corn. I promise myself that I'll stretch before getting in the car, but when I reach it, hoist the bike onto the rack, and throw my gear in the back seat, the allure of a cushioned seat trumps (I hesitate here, but it's a perfectly good lowercase word that's been in use since the early sixteenth century) the good practice of stretching, and I barely shut the door before I recline the driver's seat, bunch up my windbreaker as a pillow, shut my eyes, and drift off contentedly. That's how Miles finds me and startles me awake with a *tap-tap* on the car window. We tell each other a bit about our days, or perhaps more accurately, I grill him for any bit of information he'll impart and I tell him about the highlights of my walk.

He hasn't said much directly to me about what he thinks of my wanderings, but the mother of one of his friends told me that she's overheard him bragging about me and my project more than once. For my birthday, he gave me a coupon good for a long walk with him. I'd been requesting for months that he join me on one of my walks. I held on to the coupon like a charm until I cashed it in for a walk on Cadillac Drive in Scotts Valley, along with our yellow Lab, Izzie.

I cherish the photograph I selected for Cadillac Drive. In the foreground, in shadow, is an out-of-focus yellow traffic sign with a zigzagging black arrow indicating a winding road and the words DRIVE SLOWLY, while in the distance Miles can be seen in sharper focus running ahead with Izzie. Miles's right shoulder, the red leash, and the back of his beloved dog are all saturated in sunlight. The forest is implied by a dark background but barely decipherable as specific trees.

The first time I saw the photograph, I loved it as a token of a thoughtful birthday gift from my teenage son. Now I love it as that kind of torture-joy of nostalgia. It's almost as if I played a trick on my future self when I shot the image; the sign says go slow but he's running ahead. The ageless story of parenting, of life.

Chapter 11

Moving In

epigenome *noun* \,epəjēnōm\:
the complement of chemical compounds
that modify the expression and function
of the genome

O N A FOREST hike in the small unincorporated town of
Aptos, I find a series of ropes leading up a long, steep
hillside, wrapped from tree to tree. I pick up the first knotted length and try its strength with a firm tug before hoist-
ing myself upward, hand over hand. Each attempt to find
footing grows increasingly strategic as the grade steepens
and the ground transitions from firmly packed mud to a
loose loamy mulch where I land my foot only briefly to
avoid slipping, then pull the rope taut as I quickly take the
next step. I'm relying on my upper body to bear much of
my weight. With all my walking, I've come to expect much
of my feet and legs, bandaging blisters, binding the fascia
of my feet in neoprene to try to fend off another bout of
plantar fasciitis, a constant need to stretch my overworked

calves, but my arm muscles get off too easy. Now they complain under the strain.

When I reach the top, I practically lunge the last few feet to ground that I can stand on unaided. I take a long draw of fresh forest air and breathe out an exhilarated whoop.

I've come upon similarly unexpected ropes leading down bluff sides or into ravines, just when I've thought there was no way to lower myself down or pull myself up. These climbing ropes, knotted to create handholds and anchored into the ground, have been one of the sweetest surprises of my adventures. They seem to be left by some anonymous explorer for use by others whose voracious curiosity demands physical immersion over simply a pretty view. At least that's what I want to believe. I imagine some are left by people involved in assessing erosion. I handle the ropes to ensure they're not brittle from sun exposure and test the strength of their anchors, then take a chance and lower myself, knot by knot, down into a fern grotto with a trickling creek or over a maze of crumbled sandstone and fallen trees.

Aptos Creek Fire Road in the Forest of Nisene Marks State Park rolls out like a thirteen-mile carpet. A single dirt road running through ten thousand acres of wooded trails, starting in quaint Aptos Village one hundred feet above sea level and climbing gradually into the Summit area at twenty-five hundred feet. I love walking its full length, but today, after several miles, I've left the fire road and gone off onto smaller trails to reach my desired destination, a waterfall a friend told me about.

I never fully understood the thrill of physical exercise when I was young. My siblings and I loved to romp in the woods when our family went camping, but we didn't play or watch sports. Well into my fifties and extending now into my sixties, I began to gain new strength and confidence while I still have the physical ability to participate. I've rediscovered the pleasures of unfettered play through walking and hiking. My life story now gets to include a chapter of fully, strenuously, joyfully occupying my body, even as I receive regular solicitations from the former American Association of Retired Persons, now known as AARP, and I've had to devote one of my desk drawers to little plastic organizers with doses to prevent repeat blood clots, keep cholesterol in check, and slow osteoporosis.

The brand of toughness I adopted when I was young is useless against the oncoming train of old age. Shrinking articular cartilage and urinary urgency cannot be outrun or intimidated. Clues that I'm getting *old* encroach daily. Body parts I didn't know I had make themselves known. Ureter? Labrum? At the medical lab, the young phlebotomists unwittingly mark my age on a reverse growth chart by no longer asking, "Would you prefer paper tape or self-adhesive Coban?" Apparently, it's self-evident that now my skin is too thin to withstand adhesive.

Among my close friends, most of our parents have died. Some have lost siblings. We attend more memorial services than we'd been accustomed to. We are poignantly aware that in our sixties and seventies, we are standing in the foothills of an inescapable avalanche of loss.

Even as I'm brought to my knees with this startling awareness that my skin, once too thick, is now too thin, and it's the vessel I must rely upon to keep my physical body contained, I'm visited with feelings of contentment, self-possession, and confidence that I could not have known to hope for in my younger years. I didn't even know they were on the menu.

I move between moments of simple, unabashed joy and roiling thoughts. Elaborate homemade picnics and grab-and-go snacks. Jaw-dropping awe and rigorous exercise. I don khaki-colored waders with built-in boots and slog through rivers and creeks to gain hands-on knowledge of how water moves through our community.

As the project progresses into the mountainous areas of the county, daunted by steep roads, I count my steps to distract myself and avoid facing the incline ahead. I take a hundred steps, then stop and look back to prove my progress to myself. As the hills become more familiar and less intimidating, I grow to cherish the challenge of conquering a steep rise. It has become a sensory craving, the need to pound out long strides, grit through taxed quadriceps, tame my breath while my heart drums against its walls. My increased physical endurance and my passion for exploring the world have grown in complement to each other.

In the same way that I often find myself saying "I am small among the trees" when I'm in a state of wonder out in the forest, I hear the words "I'm moving in!" when I'm physically engaged in walking fast, climbing, or wading into cold water, exuberant to be fully inhabiting my body.

Occasionally my newfound physical confidence is tempered by a humbling reminder of its limitations. The rope climb in Aptos has led me to a lush green trail where a fallen redwood is blocking my path. I can't see a way to maneuver around it because it has landed in an area of dense vegetation, including plenty of poison oak. But I'm determined to continue my hike. I look around for a large branch or a stump that I can drag over as a boost. No luck. I walk back several paces and with a running start, I charge the tree, visualizing myself somehow vaulting over it. Instead, I ram awkwardly into it and feel a little pop in my chest. After one more attempt, I manage to use the deep furrows in the bark to scramble awkwardly to the top, then slide down the other side against the rough, back to the trail. The pain from what turns out to be a tear to the cartilage connecting two of my ribs doesn't catch up to me until the next day, but it lasts weeks before healing fully. I wish I could say this has happened only once.

I try to remember to think before I act . . . look before I leap . . . curb my enthusiasm. But at times the excitement of the moment has me scrambling up a bluff, down a natural slide of sandstone, or over a cyclone fence before I've made a rational decision to do so. On those occasions I've sometimes had to swallow a moment of mounting panic when I realize that it's possible that I've stranded myself on a beach with a rising tide, where I was able to lower myself down with relative ease, but not able to as easily maneuver my way back up.

In the woods I experience a kind of reassuring smallness, where my worries and preoccupations are minimized, but in these moments when I've wandered too far from reason, when I've followed awe over a deep rift or daydreamed myself into precarious terrain, there's another, more unsettling kind of smallness. I could be swallowed whole by the rising tide, flung off a cliff by a loose rock, or sucked into a landslide and the planet wouldn't blink. There's a fine edge between unwitting immersive healing and sheer stupidity. I wouldn't recommend balancing along that sharp line without the outdoor skills necessary for the task, as I sometimes have, but it is also true that in some essential way, it saves me.

As a child, I always felt terribly uncomfortable in my skin, as if my body itself was an ill-fitting article of clothing. I have a specific memory of standing between the pews in church with my siblings on either side. I was shifting from one foot to the other, trying to get comfortable and wondering if everyone felt as unsettled in their body as I did. Even as a child it struck me as an odd thing to be preoccupied with.

I continued to feel out of place in my body well into adulthood. That general feeling of unease gave way to chronic back pain starting in my twenties, so I joined gyms with the intention of developing a practice of regular exercise to strengthen my abdominal muscles. Simply writing out the monthly check, it turns out, does nothing to improve one's fitness level.

When Kita was eight, I got a call from his school informing me that his teacher had determined that he needed to be in adaptive PE classes, one-on-one instruction for kids who are not developmentally on target with physical coordination or strength. I was shocked and concerned. I hadn't noticed anything amiss. After just a few adaptive classes, I got another call informing me that the school no longer had any concerns about Kita's physical abilities, that the apparent delays they'd noticed were not about any limitations on his part, but about lack of opportunity and exposure to sports and exercise. In other words, as I internalized it, it was my fault.

I immediately enrolled him in swim classes and signed him up for a soccer team, and his birthday and Christmas gifts were bats and balls and a small trampoline. I registered him for baseball as soon as I could, and in his first season he won the award for most improved player. At the first practice, he caught on quickly how to use the bat to smash the ball, but after hitting the ball he'd run to his left, making a beeline to third base, rather than to first.

The teacher who informed me of the need for adaptive PE hadn't been cruel, but she had been frank and her message required little translation. I had been an impediment to my son's physical development. It had already become clear to me that before long I wasn't going to be much help with homework, and now this. I had no experience with sports and I spent time outdoors only if coaxed by a friend, and then only if it involved bribes paid off in potato chips or cookies.

IN THE PROCESS of trying to have my back problem diagnosed in my thirties, I had X-rays and scans and learned that I had a healed tailbone fracture. This wasn't assumed to be the cause of my back pain, just an interesting artifact. I searched my memory to try to figure out when I might have broken a bone unknowingly. At nineteen when I was visiting Michele in Vienna, I practiced a judo roll on an open sofa bed and hit my tailbone square on the wooden arm of the couch. In my mid-twenties I slipped off a retaining wall of cinder blocks and landed on my tailbone. Both incidents caused considerable pain. Years later, as a child welfare social worker, I heard a lecturer at a professional conference on child abuse investigation talk about coccyx fractures in small children who are slammed down on a counter or other hard surfaces in a seated position, giving me a third potential culprit and a different kind of pain.

In general, the physical abuse I recall in our family tended to end in bruises and welts. In fact, the only broken bone resulting from an altercation that I'm aware of was when my sister Edie resisted our mother's attempt to push her down the stairs. As children, we played a game called King of the Hill, where several kids would get on top of a mound of dirt at a building site or a grassy knoll in a park and play-fight each other by pushing and shoving people off the hill until one person was left standing and won the title, King. Two well-matched players could look more like they were square dancing than fighting, both grasping each other by the upper arms and leveraging their strength, weight, and height to best position their opponent before shoving them down the hill. My mother and Edie were positioned in a similar attitude when Edie—who was the same height as my mother but much lighter in weight—forcefully, painstakingly inched her in a circle until my mother's back was to the stairs, and shoved her so that she toppled, breaking a bone in her foot in the process.

I ultimately settled on the belief that the healed fracture in my back was a result of the judo roll that I tried, showing off for Michele. The base of my spine hurt for weeks after, which is the expected course for such a fracture. But the fact that I so readily wondered if my mother might have handled me forcefully enough as a small child to cause a fracture makes me wince.

I discover that the more I walk, the more my back pain resolves. As I go from walking to climbing, reaching, crouching, and balancing over rocks and rivers and streams, I demand more of my body, and my body delivers. But growing stronger and more fit in my fifties and sixties does little to stave off aging. It's stunning how much pain can radiate from the half inch between the tip of the pinky finger and its distalmost knuckle as arthritis issues warnings of discomfort to come. Getting from sitting to standing is slower and takes more attention than it once did. Balancing across logs and rocks requires an assist, a hiking pole or a walking stick fashioned from a slender tree branch. Competition with true athletes would leave me in a dusty wake, but competing against myself at any other age, sixty-four-year-old me comes up a winner every time.

I sometimes catch myself gazing wistfully at strong young people, envious of attributes I had never noticed when I had them: the body's natural cushioning between the joints, the ability to run, jump, and walk barefoot. On particularly long walks, I mourn the days when I was the boss of my bladder instead of the other way around. Even as the walks help me reconcile the past and relax into the new depths of contentment, they also usher me into my future, into a new stage in life where I'll need refurbished tools and a whole new kind of resilience.

In my seventh decade, I feel more present and alive in my body and more motivated to get outdoors and move than ever. Most days, I wake up to sense my lips shaping into a grin before I've even opened my eyes. I feel the morning pulling me to come out and behold its orange cast, breathe in its chill air, and seek out wonders hidden in plain sight. I can't start every day with an epic walk, but I can start it with the joy the walks and all their lessons and discoveries have instilled.

I still have to contend with the inconvenience of my human limitations. It becomes clear early on in the project that walking at every conceivable opportunity, managing a household, nurturing my relationship with Ellen, and parenting our younger son, still living at home, while working full time is horning in on my sleep. I become a simultaneous night owl and morning lark. Knowing that I'll be creeping out of the house before dawn to squeeze in several miles before work, I spend hours the night before cleaning and preparing monster batches of pesto and towering containers of homemade chicken stock so we'll have healthy home-cooked meals that I can prepare quickly during the workweek. I frequently climb into bed at one or two in the morning, where Ellen sleepily folds me into the warmth of my cherished place beside her, only to get up four hours later and slip out the door.

As a result of these exertions, I wake up one afternoon in the driver's seat of my car to the far-off sound of shouting and honking horns that draw gradually nearer. I open my eyes to find a man pounding on my car window and realize I'd fallen asleep waiting for a traffic light to turn green. It isn't the sound that has moved closer to me, but my level of consciousness rising from sleep back to wakefulness that has brought me closer to the sound.

The guy at my window is a cartoon depiction of an angry man, his eyebrows a sharp V, his full dentition exposed to the molars until, with what looks like an agonizing last push, he gives birth to the word "GO!" from somewhere behind his tonsils and storms away. Even before the man slams himself back into his car, I have to acknowledge that the pace I'm trying to maintain is unsustainable.

Relief arrives disguised. Two years into my project, Ellen has an opportunity to apply to become the director of the social services agency within which we have both moved up the ranks over the course of our twenty-year-plus tenures. She's become the assistant deputy director and I'm a child welfare program manager. We are made aware that this change of position might be perceived as a conflict of interest, as it would put me directly within Ellen's chain of command, so we are confronted with a decision: Ellen can remain in her position as assistant director or I can leave the agency.

We've each devoted ourselves fully to our work, and neither of us wants to be the one who gets to keep her job at the expense of the other missing out on opportunities. After much discussion, some bitter arguments, and more than a few therapy sessions, we arrive at the conclusion that the best option for our family is for me to retire and for Ellen to pursue the directorship.

The idea of a break is more than a little alluring. I've been working in a stressful environment for more than two decades, preceded by six straight years of academic rigor, and before that I'd endured a chaotic early life that prepared me for the field of child welfare every bit as much as my formal education did. But losing my salary, my benefits, and the ability to continue amassing retirement income rekindles an old fear that I'll end up destitute, eating cat food out of cans in my dotage. Worse, the potential loss of a role that I've worked hard to earn, and with which my very identity is interlaced, raises an almost palpable golf ball in my throat.

Working in the child welfare system is taxing, but it can also be rewarding. It's not all about prying wailing children from their mothers' arms or witnessing the grotesque physical and emotional fallout of severe abuse, as movies and television tend to depict. Though most social workers who have been in the field for a time have some horrific memories etched in their psyches, the great majority of referrals to child welfare agencies are for neglect of basic needs, such as food, clothing, and shelter. And the great majority of families involved with the system are living at or well below the federal poverty level, often facing generational poverty, trauma, institutional racism, or all three.

The work unfolds within a tangled web of limited resources, politics, complicated laws, and numerous stakeholders with strong opinions, all of which must and should be heard and considered: parents, children, attorneys, advocates, law enforcement, relative caregivers, foster parents, educators, judges, and local, state, and federal agencies that provide funding and services, each with their own pile of regulations and requirements. Difficult and life-changing decisions must be made within impossibly short time frames. Stress runs high and interventions and outcomes rarely feel completely right. It's a steep learning curve with high stakes, and staff turnover is always a lurking concern.

Years into my career, I was given the opportunity to participate in designing and eventually directing a program to address the developmental needs of children and families involved in dependency drug court due to complications related to parental methamphetamine abuse. Along with a skilled and expansive interdisciplinary team, I helped to secure a substantial federal grant that allowed us to bring innovative therapies to our community and provide comprehensive supports to families in their homes, based on their individual needs and focused on their strengths.

I was so excited when I received the voicemail telling me that we got the grant that it took three attempts before I could calm myself enough to press the right buttons on the phone to return the call. And I was so tongue-tied when I reached the official I was responding to that I wondered if she might reconsider the decision. I felt as if our little team, the two social workers and I who managed the day-to-day work of the program, was concretely and authentically helping families—and our outcomes bore this out. The feedback we received from participants was uniformly positive. The work reinvigorated me as a social worker. The grant funds ran out after four years, but fourteen years later the program is still running and successful. This program will be one of the hardest parts of my job to leave behind.

Ellen gets the directorship and I retire on my fifty-fifth birthday and accept a part-time position as a hospital social worker. I have barely a flash of time to wallow before my schedule opens, my stress level plummets, and the major facets of my life—parenting, relationship, friendships, work, cooking, and walking—all come into balance, along with markedly more sleep. I was not happy about the trajectory of my career being taken out of my hands. I would not have left if I could have stayed without putting Ellen's career at risk. But as soon as I experience a less hectic life, it's hard to imagine going back. I quickly reach a point where I am spending as many waking hours outdoors as in, and my heart, mind, and body are in sync.

ON THE TRAIL, I edge along a steep rocky stretch and take a spill when my right foot gets trapped under a raised root obscured beneath forest duff and the rest of my body complies with gravity. I stand up quickly, brush off my now-skinned hands, and assess a small tear in the knee of my jeans, smirking at myself that even alone, the habit of not wanting to appear vulnerable or injured is so deeply entrenched. Predators are more likely to prey upon the sick or vulnerable. It's true among wild animals and it's true among some humans. I've always understood this. It is perhaps the crux of my striving for toughness and the reason letting go of that part of my identity has felt so denuding.

I'm eager to reach the waterfall, so I've been walking faster than I should when covering terrain that requires some degree of strategy. The only constraint on my time is the wish to be in my car heading home before the hooting of owls and the howling of coyotes replace traffic sounds, so I slow way down and turn my full attention to each step until I'm back on a groomed path.

In motion again, I take a telephoto shot of a red-shouldered hawk landing in a distant tree. I snap the shutter only half-heartedly, realizing that the bird is too far away, then I continue my uphill trudge. I glance up in time to see the same bird swooping down and heading in my direction. It flies within inches of my head. I can hear the *whoosh* of its suddenly massive wings. Close up, its talons look like sharp tools. The hawk retreats and returns several times, diving at me as I quickly pace up the hill. It's coming at me like a fighter jet, making direct eye contact. I hold my camera bag on top of my head for protection and yell at it, "*Leave me alone, bitch! I didn't do anything to you!*" I'm enraged beyond reason.

Finally, I reach some boundary, invisible to my eye, that it seems to determine renders me no threat. I shake off my fear after a bit, finding my way back to a smooth rhythm of breathing and walking.

Only later, with the crisis of being attacked behind me, do I register that the bird is likely a nesting mom and my big telephoto lens must have resembled a giant eyeball landing its sight on her eggs or her babies, her eyases. She was doing her job, fiercely protecting her young. And I was a thoughtless, bumbling visitor in her home.

I'm no stranger to hypervigilance in the face of a suspected foe. As a child, I developed the irrational belief that if I remained alert to danger, I could keep it at bay. My belief became so deeply embedded in me that it continues to impact me significantly to this day. Of course, I understand intellectually that allowing myself to feel safe does not equate to inviting danger, but my physical body has never fully caught up to this.

When I'm alone overnight, after locking all the windows and doors, I move furniture in front of my bedroom door to prevent anyone coming in or at least to alert me if someone tries to get in. I get into bed fully dressed. I keep a weapon and a phone close at hand and if I sleep at all, I sleep very lightly. This has been such a source of shame and embarrassment my entire life that until recently only close friends have ever been aware of it.

As a young adult, I continued to see myself as tough, and I worked hard to project that image to the world by day, needing not to appear vulnerable. At night, however, I was hostage to my own debilitating fear and went to great lengths to avoid being alone. When it was unavoidable, I chanted a simple affirmation over and over—"I want to be safe. I deserve to be safe. I am safe"—and clung to the words like a lifeline. If that didn't do the trick of calming my nerves, I'd sleep on the floor behind a couch, or in the bathtub, hoping I could foil an intruder by being somewhere unexpected. Nighttime was endless.

The severity of my fear is something I'd expect to see in someone who had been kidnapped, raped, or chained up in a windowless room. None of these things happened to me, but I've always struggled against the feeling that I am acutely unsafe at night. After years of talk therapy and even more years of *walk* therapy, I believe multiple smaller traumas accumulating over my life resulted in my building layer upon layer of protection.

When I talk about "smaller traumas," Ellen thinks I'm minimizing what I experienced. There is probably some truth to that. After thirty years of working with people who have faced a wide range of traumas, some that I can scarcely comprehend, my continuum is undoubtedly skewed.

IN THE EARLY '90s social service providers weren't shy about looking at individuals through the lens of the "problems" we assessed them to have. We even filled out report sections with the preprinted heading *Problem Statement*. As the concept of trauma-informed care caught up with the field, we moved away from the question of "What's wrong with you?" toward one of "What happened to you?," trying to take the sense of shame and blame off the involuntary recipients of our services.

In his book *The Myth of Normal*, Dr. Gabor Maté describes trauma as "an inner injury, a lasting rupture or split within the self due to difficult or hurtful events. By this definition, trauma is primarily what happens within someone as a result of the difficult or hurtful events that befall them; it is not the events themselves. Trauma is not what happens *to* you but what happens *inside* you."

Thinking about trauma in these terms, it's easy to go to a place of regret and self-blame. Could I have saved myself decades of living with a chronically dysregulated nervous system? Could I have turned my attention toward learning another language? Playing an instrument? More disturbing, did I spend three decades providing support, education, and advice to people facing trauma while leaving my own elaborate defensive mechanisms fully assembled? I'm afraid so.

Fortunately, I do believe that even though it took years to fully explore my own past and heal, my lived experience made me a better social worker.

The good news, as Maté puts it, is that "seeing trauma as an internal dynamic grants us much-needed agency. If we treat trauma as an external event, something that happens *to* or around us, then it becomes a piece of history we can never dislodge. If, on the other hand, trauma is what took place *inside* us as a result of what happened, . . . then healing and reconnection become tangible possibilities. . . . Facing it directly without either denial or overidentification becomes a doorway to health and balance."

Rereading Dr. Maté's words, I realize that I have created such a doorway to health and balance for myself by syncing mind and motion and letting memories float into a calm walking-mind, bobbing and whirling in unforced thought. When painful memories surface, I keep walking and let them visit me quietly. When I manage to do this without pushing them to the back of my mind, or trying to justify the intentions of those involved, or recasting them to make them less hurtful, or dramatizing them, I can see them for what they are, without either denial or overidentification.

I'M SIX. I've done something to make my mother mad. She sends me out to pick a switch from the willow tree in the front yard. When I bring one back, I quiver inside and brace for its sting against the backs of my legs. Later, I stand at the mirror and crane to see the long intersecting red welts across my thighs and the backs of my knees. I don't feel any pain. I feel nothing but cold curiosity about the lines.

I'M SEVEN, on the shore of Lake Merritt in Oakland, at Fairyland, where we like to visit the shoe-shaped house of the old woman who had so many children she didn't know what to do. I lean over a low fence, throwing breadcrumbs into a tiny pond for the mallards and geese. Suddenly an adult presses up against me, rubbing his body against my back. I can feel the distinct shape of his male parts. I feel an edge of fear, but also resignation. I have felt this before. In the same instant, the man is gone, and my father is standing beside me. I'm relieved to see him. I tell him, "A man was squeezing against me." My father shushes me and says, "You're OK," with a wink.

I'M ELEVEN. My best friend, Melinda, and I are sleeping on the top bunk and wake up to a bloodcurdling scream from my little sister Margaret on the bunk below. I've just started to hurl myself down to get to Margaret when I see the outline of a man scooting out from underneath her bed. For a second I reflexively draw my legs back up so I am securely on the top bunk. I need to help her but I'm terrified. Margaret says, through heaving sobs, "A hand was trying to touch me." The man had squeezed himself under her bunk, reached his arm up between the bed and the wall, and started to grope her. Margaret experienced it as waking up to a detached but living hand in her bed. She is terrified beyond soothing, bobbing her head and stretching her little neck like a turtle gasping for air above the waterline.

Her scream wakes up others in the house. A guy who's "crashing" at our place, likely a friend of one of my parents, comes into the room, ostensibly to find out what's going on, and my father comes in right behind him, which is surprising since his bedroom is upstairs at the opposite end of the house. We rarely see him downstairs.

"He was under Margaret's bed!" I yell to my father.

The man denies it.

He and my father start hurling questions at me: "What did he look like?" "How big was he?" "Did he say anything?" The questions feel designed to confuse us more than to make us feel safe.

I have to admit to my father that I only saw his back when he rushed out from under the bed and fled the room. I can't identify him.

My father settles the problem by telling the guy that he needs to go back out to the family room, fewer than ten paces away, and "stay put" for the rest of the night. My father leaves, apparently satisfied with his degree of intervention. There's no door on our bedroom.

I don't sleep.

I'M ELEVEN. I hear my sisters Edie and Cathy crying. My mother is beating them with a large wooden spoon. They were caught stealing food from the grocery store. I creep up the stairs from the first floor, barefoot, until my eyes are level with the living room floor. I can see that my mother has stepped out of the room and Cathy, fourteen, and Edie, twelve, are side by side on the couch, dreading her return. I feel their trembling anticipation as if it's my own flesh bracing for another round of blows.

I can see on their faces that she's returning before I can

see her. She prods them down the hall, shoving one, then the other, toward the bathroom, where she's left the bathtub faucet running, then storms back to the kitchen, noisily pulling the levers on metal ice trays, then back to the bathtub, dumping the frozen cubes into the water. My sisters, still shaken from being brutalized, protest as they step into the freezing water and sit down. Only as an adult did it dawn on me that the cold bath was likely not simply further punishment but an attempt on my mother's part to try to reverse any injuries she left on their bodies, as they were both covered in raised welts.

THE COUNTLESS MEMORIES I revisit and uncover during my walks are valuable to me, as a way to finally begin to feel like a person with a history—a story—rather than the disjointed, rootless feeling that comes from practiced and honed emotional detachment. The stitches of rough sinew with which I lashed my pieces together have softened into a new textile. The walks are a loom, each memory a thread. A weighty, intricate tapestry emerges, imperfect but whole.

Early in the project, each walk that starts out in the dark or finds me alone on unpopulated roads or out in the woods begins tentatively, me on high alert. Each unfamiliar sound seems a potential threat, leaving my nerves frazzled. I frequently stop, frozen at full attention, heart pounding, to see who or what is lurking just out of sight. As I become more practiced at moving past that initial fear, the world opens before me. I hadn't known that squirrels have distinct sounds or that large flocks of wild turkeys can stir up a virtual concert with their quavering voices and raking in the forest duff. But I come to decipher their sounds from the more subtle rustling of scrub jays in the dry brush.

Over time, the three-syllable demand of the quail—"I *need* you! I *need* you!," its *need* so expressive as to set its apostrophe chapeau in motion—the buzz of hummingbirds like surging electrical lines, or the water-down-a-pipe knock of the raven rises above the din like the well-known laugh of a friend in a crowded place. The world is growing safer. I have the odd sensation of feeling maternal and protective toward a more vulnerable part of myself. As if I am the proverbial mama bear, claws out for anyone who would dare try to mess with me.

I become a corporeal barometer. My senses grow attuned to different weather in the forest. The sunlight that manages to break through contrasts alluringly against the perpetual shade of the woods. The wind sneaks up, startling me with a sudden and sustained *whoosh* that stirs everything inside me. If it's raining, I don't even know it under the trees, where the dense canopy can delay moisture reaching the ground. After the rain stops *outside*, the droplets continue to roll branch to branch like clearies down a marble maze, filtering rain on me hiking below. There's something singularly quenching about being the recipient of this conifer-infused secondhand rain.

One night, after everyone has gone to bed, I sit at my computer and type into a search engine, "Are there tree gods?" and then begin reading about nymphs, hamadryads who die when the tree they occupy dies, and Nang Ta-khian, a female spirit in Thai folklore who haunts Ta-khian trees, which are rarely used for lumber because the spirit can become enraged and continue to haunt the wood even after it's been milled and used for building. I trace the significance of trees in ancient China, India, and Sweden, where Old Tjikko, a 9,550-year-old Norway spruce, is rooted, believed to be the oldest living clonal *Picea* tree in the world. *Picea* refers to a genus of temperate and arctic evergreen trees. *Clonal* refers to trees that reproduce asexually and grow in colonies where individuals are genetically identical, connected, and interdependent, sharing water and nutrients. My search leads from gods and mythology to specific colonies like Pando in Utah, with a root system estimated to be 80,000 years old, possibly the oldest living organism, and the oldest nonclonal tree in the world, the Great Basin bristlecone pine Methuselah, in California. But the presence of the trees and my newfound tree gods aren't always protection against having to contend with old fears.

I can hear the burble of water flowing over rocks. I've almost reached the falls, so I pick up my pace, eager to see the waterfall and unpack my little picnic. I'm hungry after eleven miles of walking and scrambling. A sudden movement causes my heart to jump; I freeze mid-inhale. On the side of the trail, just ten feet ahead, a man's rounded spine unfurls as he moves from crouched to standing. He's slender and moves in an unearthly way. Surges of cortisol and adrenaline collide as when an incoming and an outgoing wave crash into each other and erupt above the crest in a giant scallop, amplifying their individual effects. I reach into my pocket and put my thumb on top of the canister of Mace I always carry on hikes.

In almost the same instant, I register that this is not a human but a fern that has been weighed down by rain and is simply rebounding to its full height of three or four feet as the water spills from its fronds. Eventually, I settle back into my former reverie.

It takes several instances of experiencing this kind of pronounced yet fleeting fear before I begin to absorb its lessons. I am experiencing fear in the way that the human body is designed to experience it. An unfamiliar sound or motion triggers an immediate stress response. Once I assess that the stimulus is not a threat to my safety, I return to my previous calm state. Or, in the rare instance when the stimulus *does* pose potential danger, such as when a pack of coyotes stood in the middle of a trail and stalked me for several paces as I retreated, I remain in a state of heightened awareness until I get myself to safety.

These distinct incidents of momentary fear followed by swift recovery pose a stark contrast to the sense of compounding panic when I'm alone at night that has plagued me as far back as my memory can stretch. They help me acknowledge the severity of my hypervigilance. I begin trying to replicate the experience. If the house creaks when I am alone at night, I acknowledge that it startles me, identify the source of the noise, and ask myself, "Am I safe right this minute?" If my answer is yes, I try to relax into that moment of safety and trust myself to rise to the occasion if and when an actual threat surfaces.

I train my ears to stop straining into the void of a quiet house for signs of danger. Eyelids help us filter out excessive light, facilitating sleep. Why, I wonder, don't we have earlids? I talk to myself as a parent would a child, explaining how I'd internalized a belief that the world was unsafe and I'd become so focused on being ready to defend myself against danger that I'd missed out on important things, like rest and peace. I tell myself that there is nothing useful about waiting to be harmed. I feel foolish and ashamed about the need to hand-hold myself through this basic training, but I do it again and again until I feel the shift not only in my brain as it more fully grasps the concepts, but in my physical body. I feel the burden lifting as I disentangle myself from the cellular belief that only by being on guard can I possibly remain safe.

I finally reach the falls, where I take off my hiking boots, eat my lunch of a homemade BLT with thinly sliced green apple, avocado, and a sprinkle of coarse salt, and take a quick dip in the one-person, crystal-clear plunge at the base of the cascade. I sit perfectly still, letting the cool water settle around me, then make a churning motion with my hand below the surface and watch as sunlight and water cast waves and ripples and eddies of light on the rock face. I wait for the motion to stop again, then pat the skin of the water so the light breaks into a frenzy of horizontal lines, like the EKG ticker tape of a wildly beating heart.

Each time the display approaches flatlining, I revive it with a light tap of the surface. For moments, there is nothing but this water and this light projecting onto the sandstone.

Refreshed, I step out of my private pool and stretch out on my back in the dirt and duff, using a boulder like a wall at the gym to stretch my legs up at a forty-five-degree angle, heels reaching for the sky, giving the blood in my feet a chance to circulate more fully and giving my tight calves a good, if slightly painful, stretch. Once sufficiently tortured by this pose, I fold up my sweatshirt for a pillow and doze off under the trees with the low roar of the waterfall for a lullaby, waking several minutes later with my eyes softly focused on the leafy canopy overhead. I organize my gear, put my bag over my shoulders, and trundle off sluggishly for a series of trails that will circumvent the area where I used the ropes to reach the falls. I have a few hours of walking ahead of me, depending on how many salamanders, purple brittlegill mushrooms, or butterfly wings call out to me en route, but it's largely downhill and all on groomed trails.

My mind wanders back to the fern that startled me earlier in the walk and I ask myself judgmentally, "What is wrong with me?" Quickly I rephrase it to "How did I get so scared?" Instead of brushing the question aside, I decide to spend some time consciously thinking about the root of my fears.

This line of inquiry requires that I set aside my usual cynicism. A friend of mine once told me, by way of explaining why he'd behaved poorly, "My mother didn't breastfeed me as a baby." I laughed, sputtering out the mouthful of

Diet Coke I'd just taken, certain he was joking. But his hurt look clued me in otherwise.

I don't know how to think about this without feeling like a bad person, but that friendship didn't last. It couldn't. I'm not proud of this, but I can barely hear a child refer to their mother as "Mommy" without my skin crawling. They might as well say, "I'm needy. I'm helpless. I'm counting on you," which, of course they are, but admitting it so openly for everyone to hear? What are they thinking? Where's their armor? But an adult crying over literal spilled milk? Can't do.

So I have to forgive myself for my cynical default, swallow my pride, and eat some crow before I can make a straight-faced attempt to make sense of the unreasonable degree to which gripping fear has followed me like a shadow all my life.

And I have to acknowledge the disconnects caused by my tendency to emotionally detach from pain. As I follow the narrow dirt hiking trails back toward Aptos Creek Fire Road, an example comes to mind: In 2018, Ellen and I took Miles and one of his friends to Kauai. Walking down a set of wet stairs to the beach, I slipped and fell, dislocating my shoulder, breaking a small bone, and tearing my labrum, the cartilage that stabilizes the ball and socket.

At the emergency room, my shoulder was placed back into its socket and my arm was put in a sling. Over the course of our weeklong vacation, with my arm largely immobilized, I developed frozen shoulder syndrome. Medical follow-up after we returned home included surgery to repair the labrum and "manipulation," a benign-sounding euphemism for forcing the joint to move under general anesthesia followed by months of physical therapy.

I wasn't surprised to find myself feeling shaky when I went up and down stairs as I was recovering from the fall. It's a common response to injury. But what started as mild tentativeness became an outright phobic reaction to stairs. For the first time in years, the obsessive thoughts that plagued me as a young adult resurfaced in full force. I kept visualizing myself falling down a flight of stairs and hearing the words *I fall. I fall. I fall* . . . looping through my brain like a mental tic, picking up speed and volume until I wanted to peel off my skin and escape the cage of my body. I tried to use the tools I'd learned in therapy so many years ago. I talked to a couple of close friends about it, and when it finally reached a point where it was disrupting my ability to sleep, I worked with a clinical psychologist, Lucie Hemmen, who practices EMDR (eye movement desensitization and reprocessing), an approach that uses specific eye movements while processing traumatic events to help relieve symptoms.

I can only think of two occasions in my life when I've cried sheets of tears. Sitting on Lucie's couch talking about the injury was one of them. I was perplexed, dumbfounded, and embarrassed by this uncharacteristic eruption of emotion. But after a single session, I was able to effectively get myself back in check enough to scale stairs without my limbs seizing up or my brain bugging out.

Still, it isn't until months later, during a walk, that it

finally strikes me that maybe sustaining a significant injury by accidentally falling down a flight of stairs could have triggered overwhelming emotions because of childhood incidents of experiencing and witnessing physical violence on and around the stairs in our home. It's the kind of connection I make frequently, almost autonomically, while working with families facing generational violence, but my emotional remove from my own experiences prevents me from drawing such a simple, straightforward conclusion about myself. In a sort of self-protective snobbery, I tend to think of myself as above such rudimentary emotional equations.

Terms like *inner child* work like a supercharged reflex hammer on me. I can scarcely be held accountable if my tendons rebound violently against the utterer. But if I want to talk about the ways I'm changing on a cellular level, if I want to continue to try to bend my epigenome back in my favor, I need to find language I can live with. I need to admit, at least quietly, to myself, that I was a vulnerable child. I need to be able to use words like *abuse* and *neglect* in reference to my own childhood without feeling like I'm conceding to an opponent.

I've wandered off my intended trail, but having downloaded my maps before I left home, I easily find my way to the amusingly named Pig Trail, which leads me to the edges of White's Lagoon, a small body of water within the state park that intrigued me when I saw it on the map and left me hoping it would be a good swim spot. When I get there it's covered in slimy green swamp plants and I don't know how to assess its fitness for immersion. Still, I stop for a short break for water and a snack and explore the marshy edges.

I've developed a habit of looking for what appears to be a drab, boring spot of earth, marking out a perimeter of a few feet or so, and challenging myself to find something of interest within it to photograph. In the lowest light of late afternoon, I might find gravel-size rocks casting shadows many times longer than the rocks themselves. Sometimes there's a broken wing from a moth or a crane fly. Or shapes of sandstone or decomposing redwoods that look like scale-model metropolises. Once, in Davenport, within such self-imposed parameters, I watched a Jerusalem cricket emerge from its molted skin. Another time, in Capitola, I watched a hermit crab move out of one shell and into another.

Within my chosen patch of trail, I notice a gathering of ants and swap out my 35mm lens for a macro, then lie down on my stomach, propped on my elbows, to get as close as possible to the action. The ants are gathered around a dead honeybee, and over the course of a few minutes, I watch them convey it several inches toward the opening of their nest. One ant stands on the fuzzy back of the dead bee, looking like a foreman or a scout. There are two ants behind the bee, each with their mandible pincers locked around a leg, pushing at the body while another pulls from the front. Multiple other ants arrive on scene looking disorganized and wander around the bee as if considering helping but then leave, so the primary work rests with the three movers and the foreman. I wonder how much my presence affects their behavior, take a few more close-ups, then carry on with my walk, leaving them to their task.

I've recovered from post-nap sleepiness and focusing on the ants has given me a break. It dawns on me that Ellen won't be there when I get home tonight. She's visiting family in Virginia. Miles won't be home either. He recently started attending the University of Colorado Boulder and Ellen and I are adjusting to the empty nest.

I wonder about the wisdom of thinking about fear before what will undoubtedly be a long night with little sleep. But as I step along the path, my mind shifts. I have the feeling that landing on some way to explain it to myself will help me defuse it. Of course, like all doggedly rooted coping mechanisms, the causes and consequences are multifarious and difficult to fit into defined slots.

But I believe the broad strokes are a combination of developmental progression, concrete things that happened to me directly or that I witnessed happening to my siblings that created a feeling of physical unsafety, things that I surmise based on stories from my older siblings but don't specifically remember, and the particulars of my personality and the ways I found to cope, some of which were perhaps ultimately as problematic as the root problems they were designed to protect me against.

Feeling afraid and vulnerable at night is common for children, often starting in the toddler years. The darkness and quiet of night can create a blank slate upon which their budding imaginations project any number of monsters or fantastical scenarios or recaps of things they've seen or experienced. If they make their fears known by crying out or going to a caregiver for comfort, and they have an adult who has the bandwidth to talk through their fears with them and demonstrate to them that they are indeed safe, this period of fear will hopefully be a phase, an adjustment to their ever-expanding world of good and bad possibilities.

If bids for comfort and connection don't render a response, children eventually learn to manage their fears internally. This is what my father would call "growing hair on your chest." Both of my parents felt certain that toughening a child up was preferable to coddling them. An understandable if unfortunate stratagem for young parents of eight who had multiple stressors, including trying to make basic ends meet.

I grew up in a time and in a home environment where sexual freedom was a new and liberating idea. With more perspective as an adult, I can see that my parents' practice of having multiple sexual partners coincided with the sexual revolution of the '60s and '70s, a movement that challenged assumptions about sexuality and interpersonal relationships and factored into paving the way for important social change that I value and that I have personally benefited from. But as a child living in a more conventional suburban neighborhood, I was aware only that my family was weird and different, and that having extra adults in our house made us all the weirder. I didn't know about a larger movement or that there were other families like mine. The fervor for sexual freedom unfortunately extended to young teenagers and children in ways that I don't believe those supporting the sexual revolution intended. My siblings and I were exposed to sexual language, innuendo, and overtures in ways that caused confusion and discomfort and, for me, made the world feel even less dependable. Unfortunately, the guise of sexual freedom and liberation sometimes blurred boundaries in ways that created a smoke screen for sexual abuse.

WHEN CHILDREN UNDERSTAND what might trigger a parent's anger, they can make an informed decision to help avoid repercussions. When they understand what's expected of them, they can adjust their behavior accordingly. But when the code is too complicated for children to decipher and anger appears to erupt unprompted, it's impossible for them to feel like they are part of the equation, like they can have any small degree of control over outcomes.

Typically, when we think about the impacts of family violence on children, we think about violence between partners or spouses in front of their children. But increasingly, the impact of witnessing a sibling being abused by a parent is recognized as a form of childhood adversity that can have lasting impacts on mental health, learning, and memory and can be every bit as damaging as witnessing domestic violence, which has long been established as harmful to children's healthy development. My memories of seeing or hearing my siblings being abused are as troubling as my memories of being harmed myself.

Maté's description of trauma refers to a "lasting rupture or split within the self due to difficult or hurtful events." Applying this to my nighttime fears, I can look at the internal rift between my diurnal self and my nocturnal self, especially when alone, as a way that I experienced, and continue to experience, such a split within myself. This gives me a concrete way to think about it and a new hope that the rift can heal.

I've made my way back to the wide fire road. After hours of seeing no one, I cross paths with hikers and cyclists every few minutes. Everyone smiles and nods in greeting with looks that seem to say "Lucky us to be outdoors on this gorgeous day." I'm tired and overready for dinner but also a little proud of myself for thinking deeply about a problem that has always felt immutable and now feels like something that could possibly budge. Bolstered, I'm OK about a night alone. My car is a welcome sight when I finally reach the parking lot. I lean against it while I half-heartedly stretch out my calves and hamstrings, then click open the lock and take a seat.

Once home, I make myself a simple dinner (think Cheerios and milk), read a book, and go to bed, where I try to fall asleep. Unsuccessful, I get up and stand at the glass door of our bedroom that opens onto the backyard. With a clear night and a new moon, the sky is a confetti of stars. I flip the thumb-turn dead bolt and my heart jumps with the sound of the unlocking. As I step into night, I imagine that this must be akin to what it takes for an agoraphobe to step over the threshold.

I participated in one of the first Take Back the Night marches in the United States, a peaceful demonstration against sexual violence in San Francisco in 1978. Hundreds of women and men flooded the streets chanting and carrying signs. I felt emboldened fearlessly walking down the middle of the road in a sea of people who cared about women's safety.

Over forty years later, clad in flannel star pajamas, with bare feet, I organized my own political action, standing alone in the night, gazing at the sky before stepping back into the house and tucking into bed with a depth of contentment to rival cinnamon-sugar toast with loads of butter. Then I sleep, radically.

Chapter 12

Meeting the Neighbors

***

fugacious *adjective* \fyü'gāshəs\: lasting
a short time: evanescent

***

WHEN THE PROJECT first starts, I intentionally walk alone and rarely interact with the people I cross paths with. I'm eager for silence. But that quickly changes. As my vision and attention adjust to looking more closely and I grow increasingly spellbound by the world around me, fellow humans come into focus in new ways, and I find that the quality of the exchanges I have with them when I'm in the unhurried state of mind that walking brings about is rich and textured. I've come to think of these fugacious connections as micro-friendships, and I always feel a twinge of sadness when I walk away.

ONE OCTOBER EVENING after a particularly hot day, I walk in a welcome breeze along East Cliff Drive and have a conversation with an artist, an array of spare paintbrushes threaded through her straw hat, while she paints a colorful image of the boardwalk beach after a king tide. Walking in Watsonville, I meet a woman watering her lawn with a blue-headed parrot on her shoulder. On the upper west side, I chat with a man who's considering starting a project of photographing manhole covers, then taking a road trip to visit the foundries where they were made. In Davenport, farmworkers heading out to pick strawberries request that I take a group photo of them. And on King Street in Santa Cruz, a nine-year-old walking with his mother tells me that he wants to be a "photo-grapher" too.

When I walk in the rain, many people stop and offer me a ride. On a particularly hot day, I'm given a bottle of water by a man on Summit Drive in Bonny Doon, northwest of Santa Cruz. On Skyline Boulevard, the Santa Claus who manages traffic flow at a popular Christmas tree farm gives me a candy cane. I have numerous chats with perfect strangers about various aspects of Santa Cruz history, architecture, wildlife, cave systems, trails, ghosts, trains, and waterways.

Walking down Dellview Avenue, a very short street in a suburban neighborhood known as the Banana Belt, I feel the stored heat of a summer day issuing from the asphalt and stratifying the air as an early evening chill descends. An elderly gentleman tending his yard asks me what I'm up to. I tell him about my project. He has a suggestion for my photograph for his road. He reaches overhead and pulls down a branch from a massive tree. On the branch is a stunning flower with lime-green petals, butter-yellow pistil and stamen, and a bright orange line mimicking the flower's shape. He picks the flower and gives it to me as he reminisces about purchasing the tree, a true tulip tree, and decades ago planting it as a sapling. I take a close-up of the flower, thank him, and carry it for the rest of the walk.

That night, before I drift off to sleep, I see in my mind's eye the flower in full color and detail. The next day, I brag to Ellen that I am so smitten with the old man's gesture that I can actually see the flower when it's not there. I tell her, "I didn't just describe it to myself. I could visually *see* the flower with my eyes closed!"

She seems perplexed that I am so excited. She asks, "Isn't that how you visualize things?" When she tells me that she can close her eyes and "see" anything, I'm skeptical.

I remember a number of occasions throughout my life when I was told to close my eyes and picture something. I tried but I never saw anything. Over time, I figured that I was taking the words too literally and I began translating in my mind until *visualizing* or *picturing* something came to mean simply trying to imagine it by describing the thing to myself.

I never realized that when some people talk about seeing something in their mind's eye, they can actually see a thing in shape and color. This is staggering news. I start conducting an informal poll and learn that some of my friends and family can deliberately see things when they close their eyes. Others can see only rough outlines or silhouettes. A few, like me, may occasionally see an image, especially in the event of intrusive thoughts, but can't conjure them intentionally.

I learn that the inability to visualize was first described in 1880, by Francis Galton, who did not assign it a specific name but referred to research subjects as either "non-imagers" or "visualizers." Francis Galton was a cousin of Charles Darwin, and he was the man who developed the concept of eugenics, the despicable, racist pseudoscience focused on increasing the occurrence of desirable, heritable traits with the goal of improving the human race. During the twentieth century, eugenics was finally acknowledged to be both dangerous and unscientific, but not before it was used in Nazi Germany to justify obliterating millions of lives.

After Galton's initial description, the topic of the ability to visualize went largely unexplored until 2015, when University of Exeter professor Adam Zeman released a paper on the inability to voluntarily form mental images and coined the word *aphantasia*, drawing on a term used by Aristotle to describe the power to form mental images. The condition is not considered a disability or a disorder but simply a cognitive characteristic that runs along a continuum. It's thought that up to 4 percent of people have no ability to voluntarily form mental images. However, as the topic has resurfaced over the past decade, tens of thousands of people have reported a lack of ability to visualize, and many of them note that they had always assumed that concepts like counting sheep and picturing yourself winning a game were strictly abstract, so 4 percent may be a gross underestimation. My own informal poll of family and friends puts it close to 50 percent.

This discovery, stemming from a single flower proffered by a kind stranger, deepens my understanding of the range of human perception and my own small orbit within it. Time after time on my walks I've had the electrifying experience of feeling my world expand. Sometimes it's discovering a plant or an insect that I've never seen before. Sometimes it's a brief interaction with someone I would not have encountered if I wasn't out exploring. Other times, it's having a meaningful experience and then letting the wind blow me from clue to clue, expanding my understanding of the experience, like a treasure hunt.

When there is a treehouse, no other object has a chance of being the representative photo for a given street. Every time I spot one, whether it's a full-fledged home replete with lighting and curtains or a bunch of nailed-in two-by-four "stairs" leading to a plywood platform, it takes restraint to not jump up and down and clap my hands. I don't remember knowing anyone as a child who had a treehouse, but somehow they imprinted in my mind as the ultimate expression of a contented childhood, right up there with peanut butter and jelly sandwiches cut on the diagonal.

One particularly crisp morning I spot a treehouse between two houses, squeezed into a space some might have written off as too small. As I stand admiring it, the man who built it for his sons comes out of his house, a steaming cup of coffee in hand. He is not only friendlier than I would

be about finding a stranger outside my home taking photos, but he invites me to go up into the fort to get a better
look. He reminisces about sleepovers his sons enjoyed in
their treehouse, and we lament the inevitable abandonment
of beloved playthings.

"It's been leaning to one side for some time," he tells
me. "It's going to have to come down soon." We stand there
side by side, perfect strangers, looking up at his tree, the
commonality between us that our little boys have grown
and we are still a little shocked to find it so.

During a long walk in Scotts Valley, I make the acquaintance of two adorable little girls who are selling "glass
gems" and seashells under the watchful eye of their big
brother. I ask them how much it would cost for a glass gem,
and one of the girls tells me it will be "twenty-five cents for
one or twenty-five cents for two or a dollar each." I suggest
a dollar for two and they both agree that's fine. They pick
the colors for me, which takes time and extensive delibera-
tion between them, but in the end, I purchase two pieces of
sea glass, one blue and one green.

Another day, I stop on a bridge above the stream in the
town of Boulder Creek. It is autumn, and the damp ground
is carpeted in colorful leaves. I want to capture a photograph of that feeling you get watching a leaf travel through
space. I've tried many times to take a photograph of that
descent, the zigzag right and left, the surprise lift and tum-
ble on a barely perceptible breeze. I stand mesmerized, always too slow to raise the camera and grab the shot. Today
I'm determined to get a good one.

I gather a pile of leaves and set them at my feet. I hold my camera with my right hand, and with my left throw a few leaves at a time out over the water. I am so absorbed in my task that I don't notice a woman walking toward me until she's close enough to ask, "Do you need an assistant?" I smile at her and reply, "Yes, please," and she starts handing me individual leaves, commenting on their colors and textures. I shoot one after the next for a few minutes. When the pile runs out, she says goodbye and continues on her way.

In Capitola, I am walking along looking for something to photograph when I see some women gathered in a garage. They're sitting on the floor in a circle. I walk up to see what's going on and ask them if I can take photographs as they cook, using a fryer set up on the floor between them. They gamely oblige and offer me some of their lentil fry bread. They are a group of sisters who, like me, are from a sibling set of five sisters and three brothers. They tell me that they were born in Kenya and grew up in both Africa and India. They're cooking in preparation for their brother's sixtieth birthday celebration that evening and they invite me to attend and take photographs, which I sadly decline because I already have plans. I snap a photo of the five sisters. Some months later, I run into one of them and learn that the eldest sister had passed away. I bring her a copy of the photo; she gives it a good long look and thanks me.

Walking in the Summit area, I stop and talk with a couple who are brimming with historical information about the region. They tell me about a railway tunnel in their neighborhood. Following their directions, I find my way to a dirt path between two homes that opens onto a hiking trail, crossing two trickling streams and passing over the top of the tunnel. The path winds down until I face a cement facade with the date, 1908, barely visible under the moss and vines. I stand near the entrance of the tunnel and feel dank history exuding from its walls. Only later, reading an article about Wrights railroad tunnel, do I learn that in 1879 thirty-two people, primarily Chinese men who had toiled for more than two years to dig through granite, perished in a raging fire twenty-seven hundred feet into the mountain, when their foreman attempted to light the fuse of a dynamite charge and ignited a massive pocket of gas. The men were buried near the tunnel in unmarked graves, without ceremony.

These men, immigrants who put their lives at risk and labored in unimaginably physically taxing and low-paying jobs, were treated poorly in Santa Cruz and scapegoated for the recession and high unemployment rates of the time.[*]

Many months later, covering Harvey West Boulevard near downtown Santa Cruz, I walk through the historic Evergreen Cemetery and find a gravesite acknowledging these men and others who suffered similar fates. When you stand alone at the mouth of the tunnel and feel the heavy

---

[*] Ryan Masters, "The Horrors of the Summit Tunnel," *HillTromper Santa Cruz*, December 18, 2014, hilltromper.com/article/horrors -summit-tunnel.

chill of the damp granite, you can sense the unsettled spir-its. History, I begin to understand, is so much more than dates and names to be painstakingly remembered. It's the pulsing story of the *now* of *then*. My task is to discern which versions of recorded history to trust.

On one stormy afternoon, I watch a photographer at the jump-in point at Steamer Lane catching action shots of surf-ers. He's standing on a narrow cliff that juts out into the water. With surf crashing wildly on either side of this tiny peninsula, he appears suspended among the waves. The morning light hits him just so through the spray, giving the scene an unearthly feel. I climb over the fence that typically separates the surfers from the rest of the world and go out to join him. I show him photos I took of him through the crashing waves and agree to send him copies. He shows me a compelling street photograph he took in San Francisco and describes an image he tried to capture but missed.

We start talking about missed shots like fishermen with stories of the ones that got away. We stand in the spray as he recounts trying to take a shot of a beautiful young child staring off into space at a bus stop, dappled light from a nearby tree playing on her face. He hesitated for a second and the bus pulled up, obscuring his shot. I told him about spotting a red fox on Summit Road sitting on a pile of iron-rich orange rocks with a background of a tree-studded mountain in the distance, across the canyon. I was afraid she would dart if I moved, but she just sat staring at me. When I finally raised my camera, she turned and disappeared into the brush. He and I grow more animated with each exchange, one-upping each other with our photographic missteps and miscues and laughing like old friends.

I've had very few male friends. Since I came out as a teenager, my social world has been narrowly concentrated around other women. From age sixteen to twenty-one, I was rageful toward men. I resonated with the idea of lesbian separatism. Having a community of women served as a sort of incubator for me, a refuge from fear. I don't regret that time in my life, but I see now that it limited me in ways I hadn't anticipated.

At a women's music festival in 1984, sitting around a campfire, holding baby Kita wrapped in a blanket, I was approached by a woman who asked whether my child was a boy or a girl. When I replied that he was a boy, she insisted I leave. She pointed out that I was in the lesbian separatist camp and male children were not welcome, no matter how old. And just like that, lesbian separatism was a part of my past.

I've never looked back, but my social network—besides my sons and my brothers, whom I love profoundly and trust implicitly—still consists primarily of women. Over the course of the walking project, this began to shift. I puzzled over the fact that most of the people I stopped and talked to on my walks were male. These small connections with men throughout my community, I realized, were helping me understand that it was never *men* that I feared, but *bogeymen*. Tragically, bogeymen do walk among us, most often, I'm afraid, in the shape of a man, but they are much fewer and farther between than I once understood.

Suddenly, in my fifties and sixties, the population of people with whom I could imagine having meaningful conversation or taking a long walk fully doubles. The effects of the project expand my world once again. I am happily and solidly married. Romantically speaking, I am as queer as a three-dollar bill. And I'm not at a time in life when I'm looking to expand my social life, but finding my peace with a huge segment of the population, even if only in spirit, makes me feel a part of a larger humanity from which I have been sidelined and have sidelined myself for much of my life.

Most of the city of Los Gatos is in neighboring Santa Clara County, but there is a sliver of it that edges into Santa Cruz County, an area called Skyland, with stunning vistas from which you can look down the mountain and see thick billows of fog settling over trees for miles. I am delighted to find in Skyland a beautiful little church with stained-glass windows nestled between orchards, gardens, and long stretches of quiet road.

I spot an old-time vehicle and a gentleman picking apples and putting them into metal buckets. As I pass, I ask him about the trees. He tells me that he planted them more than fifty years ago and has been tending the orchard since. His primary crop is a variety of apples, but he points out a few pear trees too.

He tells me that he's harvesting apples to trade for fresh fish that his friend is out catching, even as he picks. As we talk, the man gathers his buckets and puts them in his car, then straps his orchard ladder along the length of the vehicle.

There's something about his manner that reminds me of my beloved father-in-law, Bill, a lifelong Virginian. He strikes me as kind and self-possessed in a familiar way. His intelligence is evident without being showy. I start walking away but turn back and ask, "You don't happen to be from Virginia, do you?"

He looks slightly taken aback, but confirms that, yes, in fact, he is. It's heartening when you guess right about someone based on clues that you can scarcely articulate.

Near the boardwalk in Santa Cruz a man who appears to be living on the streets looks up from his spot on the sidewalk and asks me to take a picture of him. I snap a photo of him huddled among his meager belongings. I ask him how I can get a copy to him. He replies, "There's no way of knowing where I'll be, I don't have a phone, and I don't need a copy. I just want to have my photo taken." He smells of stale pee, alcohol, and sweat. His clothing is stained and dirty and his untied shoes are several sizes too big for him. If he hadn't asked me to take his photo, I might have walked right by. He thanks me and we exchange smiles that for this moment transcend the expanse between our worlds. I later have the photo printed as a sort of physical manifestation of my wish for his well-being.

In Watsonville I meet a man in the middle of a wood-working project in his garage. I ask him if I can photograph his collection of hundreds of tools from his native Portugal. He tells me that in the town he comes from, he had no electricity, so he worked with simple tools, most of which he and his family hand forged.

In the mountains near Felton, I spot a little building, a chapel built of California redwood. I try the door and find it unlocked. I walk in and settle myself onto a wooden pew in the empty sanctuary and give my feet a break. I gaze out the window just behind the altar at a stand of redwoods encircling the chapel so closely that it's not a stretch to imagine I am perched in a holy treehouse. The gnawing questions *Do I belong here? Am I trespassing?* haunt me in many aspects of life, but never more so than in a church, leaving me torn between comfort and concern.

I'm a spiritual orphan. I momentarily grow full Catholic around chubby white candles lit in prayer, but the smell of frankincense makes me queasy. I'm pagan for whole eggs baked into bread, but I recoil at syrupy, goddess-y sentiment. I feel intrigued and moved by the mezuzah on the door of my former foster mother's home, but I don't touch it because I don't belong to it.

"Are *you* my God?" I ask the presence I sense or imagine in the chapel. "Are *you* my God?" I ask the smoothed pebble in the riverbed and the broad ocean and the apple orchard.

Why, yes, I answer for them.

I feel indignant, almost offended, when people deny the presence of God. Please. Have you never seen a red fox in snow or choir-of-angels sunlight streaming through clouds or felt the buoyancy of an ocean swim? The evidence is everywhere. The taste of pickled ginger. Wild cucumber tendrils reaching and grasping. Sun-bleached animal bones on the beach. Yet my internal devotional compass seems always to pull reflexively back to atheism.

Rested, I rise from my pew, take a last look, and then leave, closing the door behind me. I walk slowly through the drizzle, sidestepping earthworms along the now-soaked sidewalks, and ponder holiness as I make my way back to Graham Hill Road and manage to reach the beginning of Big Basin Highway before drizzle gives way to downpour. I duck into Johnnie's Super to preserve my camera, now hastily clad in a plastic produce bag, from the rain and call Ellen, hoping that she is available to honor one of the custom free-ride coupons she made for my birthday. She is home and agrees to pick me up at Johnnie's and drop me back at my car at the base of Graham Hill Road.

While I wait under the eaves with a cup of hot soup, I chat with a gentleman as he shakes rain off his umbrella. I tell him about my visit to the chapel—the Mount Hermon Memorial Chapel, I learn—and he smiles broadly. "My wife and I were married there!" He tells me that his wife wanted to marry in a church, while he had hoped for an outdoor wedding. When she brought him to the Mount Hermon Memorial Chapel and showed him the surrounding redwoods, he readily agreed to tie the knot there. "I'm not religious," he confides, "but you can't really sit in a chapel ensconced in a forest and not feel something stirring in your soul, right?"

ON A STRETCH of road on the east side of town, pedestrians can comfortably meander along a sidewalk above the surf. I take a detour down a stairway to the beach, where I meet a man in waders, standing in a deep tide pool, reaching under rock ledges and pulling up grumpy-looking monkey-face eels and blobby purple sea cucumbers. I stand and watch as he serves up sea creature wisdom. He has been rewarded for his sharp eye with a shark's tooth and a portion of a whale vertebra, which he shows me eagerly. "My wife will disown me if I come home with another whale bone," he says, and hands me the section of spine. It's a strange and dazzling gift.

Inspired by his enthusiasm, I find a pool of my own and study its edges. Among the tide pool mainstays—urchin, anemone, crab, and sea star—I find a tiny lime-green fish, a spotted shrimp, and a nudibranch, a kind of mollusk. I announce each new find to my tide pool neighbor, and he updates me in kind.

Spotting movement in a nearby mound of seaweed, I look closer and find a tiny white octopus, a heavy-headed Martian scooching across rocks and eventually plopping into a pool where a sea cucumber has inked the water bright pink. The man in the waders slogs himself out of his trench and we sit on rocks, transfixed, admiring my cephalopod until we realize that the sun is about to run out of light.

Walking on Tipping Way in Ben Lomond, I ask a man standing next to his banana-slug-yellow truck whether it's OK to continue walking up part of the road that has a NO

TRESPASSING sign posted. He tells me that he doesn't live in the neighborhood and is there to paint a house, so he's not sure whether it would be frowned upon. He asks me about my camera, and I explain my project while he listens with interest. I decide to take a chance and walk the rest of the road, stopping to take a photo of the setting moon, then move on to the next street.

Several months later, I take a weekend photography workshop through our local community college. I immediately like the instructor, Nick Borrelli, a skilled photographer and adventurer. He shows the class some slides of his photographs, including extreme surfing shots at Mavericks, a surf break near Half Moon Bay, a small coastal town about fifty miles north of Santa Cruz, where waves can crest as high as sixty feet. He talks not just about photographs but about the process of photography with contagious enthusiasm. At the end of the first class, Nick approaches me and says, "I think I've met you before."

He doesn't look familiar to me. "I don't think so," I say. But he is certain.

We go through a few of the standard how-would-I-know-you questions: Where do you work? Do you have kids? A small crowd of students mill around to ask technical questions or learn more about the format of the workshop. I step back to give others a chance to talk to the instructor.

"Wait," Nick says as I start to leave. "Are you the one walking all the streets?"

Instantly I realize who he is. "You have the bright yellow truck!" I am gleeful that this man I met randomly in the mountains is teaching me about my most cherished pastime.

Long after the class is over, I walk in Aptos, making my way along side streets off Soquel Drive, including Merrill Road, where, in front of a lovely home, I see a bright pink garden bench and a pair of larger-than-life ceramic slippers, painted in the same pink, beside the bench. As I marvel at this surprise, the owner of the home, who is working in her garden, notices me and invites me to stroll through the impressive landscape.

My photo for Merrill Road, not surprisingly, is of the bench and slippers. I post it on my social media page and Nick comments, telling me that the owner of the home is a good friend of his mother's and that he painted that bench.

As the project ends, Nick tells me that he knows how to gain access to one of the private, gated roads that I want to walk but have reluctantly written off as inaccessible. He offers to walk the road with me. Growing up, he spent a lot of time on the road as the tagalong younger brother of a Girl Scout with their mother, the troop leader.

We arrange a day to walk it, and as we amble down the road one late afternoon, he points out landmarks and tells me little bits of history about the area. Just where the paved road gives way to powdery dirt and the trees grow denser, I spot a tiny blue butterfly like the one I saw months ago on Mountain Charlie Road, then another. Nick takes a step and a cloud of these beauties flutters up from the dirt. We laugh in wonder, then stand and watch as they settle in clusters back on the path. We walk around them and make our way to a creek cascading over branches and brambles and climb over rocks and fallen trees to reach a pool at the base of a waterfall. We notice a tiny bird on a branch. As we stand admiring it, it trills a song with piercing volume and clarity, effortlessly overpowering the sound of the waterfall. Nick shows me how to take a photo that makes a white silk scarf of the running river: long exposure. A curved section of the river surrounded by moss-covered rocks with maple leaves glowing green above. Walking with one's photography teacher can render creative miracles. Ellen had the photograph from this walk framed. It is the only image I've taken that hangs in our house.

I NO LONGER own a single pair of jeans that don't have ground-in grass and mud stains or holes in the seat and knees. Occasionally, I'll buy a new pair and promise myself that I'll keep them out of the dirt—a promise as futile as kids swearing they won't get their clothes wet at the beach. I'm always careful at first, but then I find myself lying flat on the ground to see the underside of a mushroom, or climbing up onto a high tree stump to spy on a banana slug having a lunch of leaves and dewdrops, or edging down a bluff to visit a hard-to-access beach. In these moments, the condition of my clothes is the furthest thing from my mind. Only later, digging through stacks of clean laundry for something casual but tidy-looking to wear, do I roll my eyes and chuckle at myself before I pull on one of these collaborations of dirt and denim and wear them like proud art, a second skin fitted to the contours of my body and my life.

After our trip to the waterfall, I invite Nick and his wife, Kate, to take a trip to see lesser sandhill cranes at the Merced National Wildlife Refuge, and we spend a day standing in awe as the sun goes down and thousands of cranes crowd the sky in overlapping strands, making a sound that's part mewl and part high-pitched call at such a volume that their song continues to ring in our ears well after we've started the long drive back to Santa Cruz.

Again and again, the eyes of perfect strangers offer windows into broader worlds. After sharing bread with the five sisters in Capitola, I went home and called each of my own sisters. Seeing the older brother of the little girls who sold me glass gems in Scotts Valley made me think about childhood moments with each of my brothers. The man in Watsonville with a garage full of handmade tools made me miss the father I knew and loved before I learned more about him.

For the most part, I know next to nothing about the people I've met throughout the project besides the details they shared with me. That one of them built their mailbox as a replica of their home, or that they're eighty-nine years old and have lived in the same house since the day they were born, watching the community build up around them from open farmland to shopping malls, or that they live on the site of an old tourist destination, Magnetic Springs, active through the late 1800s, that was said to possess curative waters and still have the last vestige of it, an old barn, on their property. But every one of them lives fully in my heart as a stitch in a quilt that I will pull tightly around my shoulders through all my remaining winters.

Chapter 13.

Reconnecting

THE WINTER HOLIDAYS are a wrap. After days of cleaning, cooking, decorating, wrapping, and celebrating, I claim a Sunday in the new year for walking. I consult my maps and decide on an amble in the mountains. I lay out my adventure clothes, including a thick sweatshirt and a windbreaker, stock my camera bag with a spare battery and an SD card, pack a lunch and snacks, stow them in the refrigerator, and get to bed early so I can jump up at the sound of my 5:30 a.m. alarm, get dressed fireman style, grab my gear, and bound out the door.

I park at the crossroads of Highway 236 and Highway 9 in Boulder Creek and start walking up 9, the two-lane road that runs thirty-five miles from downtown Santa Cruz all the way into Santa Clara County, bisecting the Santa Cruz Mountains.

There's no traffic yet but I'm crossing the road repeatedly to take advantage of the best shoulder options and avoid walking into blind curves. I wander down a side street and spot a hollowed-out tree trunk with a blackened interior—the one-person cathedrals that dot forest landscapes—and think of my elder brothers, who would find trees like these when we were camping and sleep in them.

As a child I was awed by my brothers' bravery, sleeping "out in the wild." There was no saying what they might encounter. But now, out wandering, I begin to wonder whether they had actually slept in those tree trunks at all or if that was just another of their tall tales.

They came by it honestly. My father also loved a playful ruse. He repeatedly told us that our "dear uncle Auto" had established businesses all over the country. Driving around Oakland, for example, heading to a special mass at a Bay Area church, or visiting our Nana Floyd, my mother's grandmother, my father would point out the window and affirm, "There's one of your uncle Auto's stores!" Sure enough, there was his name in big letters: AUTO GLASS. Over time, I developed a vague resentment toward this uncle. Did he think he was too good for us? He certainly had plenty of money rolling in with all the stores—and yet I could discern no apparent effort on his part to help our part of the Glass family. We never even got to meet him.

I'm moving a beat ahead of my natural pace—faster than a stroll and slower than a clip—and wallowing in morning light as it filters through the trees. There's visible moisture in the air but it's so soft and airy and quiet that it can't quite be described as rain. I smirk and shake my head about Uncle Auto. The joke was on me. It wasn't until I was seventeen, after my father died and I hadn't thought about my wayward uncle in years, that I walked past an auto glass store in San Francisco, realized the joke, and laughed out loud. To this day, it's almost impossible for me to drive by an auto glass store without mentioning my old Uncle Auto, and when a friend recently named her dog "Otto," I, in all seriousness, asked her, "Why the unusual spelling?"

I follow the narrow shoulder along 9 until I reach Kings Creek Road. I spot a point where I can easily make my way to the creek and head down to walk its edge. I notice an amphibian swimming alongside me. "Who are you?" I ask, and I stop to watch it cruising through the water, a minuscule dinosaur, forelimbs flush to its sides for hydrodynamics, its tail an impressive rudder. It's a newt. I've seen them before, but I hadn't realized that they live a good part of their lives in the water. As I study the one at my feet, I hear splashing sounds and turn to see a thrashing ball of about a dozen intertwined newts, a living, breathing Escher print. I've just moved closer, intrigued by the commotion, when two, clearly mating, break away from the tangle and swim off double-decker while the others, dejected, slowly disperse.

From the edge of the creek, I see a twig with small sacs of eggs attached to it submerged in the water. I wade in to get a closer look. To get the best view, I'll need to fully sit down in the creek, which means taking off my jeans and tossing them onto the bank, then stepping carefully over slippery rocks in my cotton skivvies with my winter legs exposed to the world, hoping that one of the few residents in this isolated area doesn't pick this moment to take a drive along the creek.

Only when I settle down into the water to study the egg sacs do I notice two eyes peering back at me. The mama newt is wrapped around the twig, keeping watch over her eggs. I am overcome with the beauty of this tiny creature standing guard. I desperately want to take a photograph, but shooting directly into the water is trickier than I expected. Moving around and trying different angles, I figure out that by casting my own shadow over the area I want to photograph, I block distracting reflections and more easily see below the surface.

There are several newts within inches of me. I think, *They must have some kind of defense system because they don't shy away from me at all.* I grin to myself and whisper, "Good thinking!" I'm giddy over the great fortune of spotting these remarkable creatures in such numbers and so utterly spellbound that when I finally decide to stand up, my toes are pruned and my knees are rusty hinges. The cashmere drizzle from earlier has turned to garden-variety rain and I have to pull on drenched pants and continue down the road in soaking shoes.

I wander under a handmade wooden sign at the entrance to a Tibetan Buddhist retreat center at the end of Kings Creek Road, which reads in engraved gold lettering MAY ALL BEINGS BE HAPPY, and my thoughts turn immediately to my siblings.

They are often on my mind as I walk, but more so than usual today because we've begun talking regularly as a group and we had a long conversation just yesterday afternoon. After years of walking and thinking about the ways our family life impacted me, I want to get a better understanding of how each of my seven siblings experienced our family. I also want to let them know that I'm doing a lot of writing about my project and my childhood and give them a heads-up that I'm seriously considering trying to have a book published. As we visit from across three states—California, Washington, and Oregon—the conference-call screen makes a *Brady Bunch* scene of our faces. We all got out our cell phones to snap rare photos of the entire clan. The Ogdoad, the eight.

Over the past few weeks, I've talked to each of them individually. I knew that talking as a large group would make the level of nuanced discussion I hoped to have all but impossible, so I asked each of them if they would allow me to interview them about their childhood, and they all graciously agreed.

We've had too many close calls to believe that we will remain an unbroken set forever, too many middle-of-the-night phone calls over the years—a stroke, a heart attack, a suicide attempt. When Jerry had open-heart surgery in San Francisco many years ago, those of us who were able to came to the hospital, where we commandeered the family lounge and spilled into the hallway, singing to our brother as he was wheeled to the operating room. Ellen got all of us a shared hotel room near the hospital and most of us crowded into the one small space for a restless night of giggling fits, which then degenerated into streams of tears that required no explanation. Cathy stayed at the hospital overnight so there would be a familiar face close by when Jerry opened his eyes. Losing our father many years before was disruptive to each of us in different ways, but the prospect of losing our eldest brother gave grief new depth and dimension.

For our group conversations we settle on a format of reading a chapter from an early draft of this book, then discussing it, after which we spiral into stories. We fill in blanks, leaving each of us with a much fuller understanding of our childhoods. Hearing from the four eldest—Jerry, Debbie, Cathy, and Kevin—is especially helpful. In many ways they have a broader context. They lived in different houses and saw our parents at different points in their lives and careers. They went to Catholic schools. Jerry was a teen when we moved into the two-story house, and he lived upstairs in the bedroom across the hall from my parents until he was kicked out at age seventeen. He'd never realized the depth of the chaos and filth downstairs.

The youngest four are in disbelief to hear that our mother once sewed and baked birthday cakes. The older four got more attention from her. They also got more abuse. Our mother was their primary caregiver, whereas we younger kids were also cared for by our older sisters. The elder siblings didn't know that our father's drinking had gotten out of control in the last few years of his life. And the younger ones didn't know that the locked downstairs freezer once stored not only hot dogs and cartons of ice milk, but

LSD, one of many artifacts of the era of the hippie counter-culture we unearth from our childhoods.

With our tendency to talk all at once, we Glasses try to take turns posing a question to the group, then answering one by one. Some questions are lighthearted: "If you could meet anyone in the world, who would it be?" or "What was your favorite toy as a kid?" Others dig a little deeper: "Did anyone notice that you were being hurt at home?" or "Did anyone try to help you?" Only a few of us had adults in our lives who tried to help. When Jerry was a young adult, a couple who had been friends of my parents told him, "We knew something was wrong, but we didn't know how to help."

Edie talked about how our neighbor Mrs. Sutherland was in the grocery store when she and Cathy were caught stealing, and Mrs. Sutherland appealed to the security guards to release them to her rather than calling our mother. Edie had the feeling that Mrs. Sutherland understood there were problems in the Glass home. Hearing Edie's story, I had to tamp down a flash of jealousy about Mrs. Sutherland trying to help her. She was my person! The same feeling arose in me when John talked about living with the Rogerses, the family I lived with briefly when I was fifteen. After our father died, John moved in with them and they became family to him. His picture hangs in the hallway of their home right along with those of their daughters and grandchildren.

The questions "Who belongs to me?" and "To whom do I belong?" are the fodder of the basest, ugliest parts of me. Envy and jealousy are alligators I've wrestled all my life. Apparently I'm not alone in this among my siblings. When I was in my fifties, shortly after our mother died, I bought something I'd yearned for since I was a small child, a charm bracelet, and I decided to consider it a gift from my mother. I showed it to Margaret and said, "Look what Mom got for me." Margaret's face fell like a sunken soufflé, and I felt like a complete asshole. She later told me that she'd had an immediate and massive stab of envy and felt as if she was five years old again.

During our gatherings, we post images on the screen of the few photos and documents that we have from childhood. A newspaper clipping of my eldest sister, Debbie, raising the flag in front of her elementary school while her classmates, hands over hearts, recite the Pledge of Allegiance. A business card from our father's handyman business that my sister Cathy kept. A photo of someone's first Communion.

During one call Cathy tells a story about wrapping a Christmas gift for Jerry in layers and layers of paper and boxes; as she watched him unwrap it, she became increasingly worried that her gift wasn't as meaningful as the wrapping made it seem and he'd be disappointed. She got so worried that she started to cry. This story led to others and soon we were all telling stories about how important Jerry, as the eldest brother, has been to each of us. He was visibly moved by the stories. Having a large group of brothers and sisters with shared history and the courage, trust, and willingness to explore its impacts on each of us made the experience of reconciling the past less daunting and less lonely than it would have been without them.

We talk about what it was like for those of us left behind whenever an older brother or sister left home. Cathy, the third born, tells John, the seventh, that when our eldest sister, Debbie, left, Cathy found him curled up in a chair crying. "I feel like a part of me is missing," he told her. Decades later, we share a held breath imagining our curly-haired baby brother feeling so unmoored. It never dawned on me that in the same way Edie became a parent figure to Margaret, Debbie played a similar role with John until she left home.

Kevin recounts an early memory from when he was seven years old and he spotted some easily accessible marshmallows in the kitchen. He went to his room to get a T-shirt and returned to take a handful of marshmallows to roll into it. Before he could make his way back, our mother caught him. She grabbed him by the hair and when Kevin tried to break free, she yanked harder and came away with a handful. She became irate that he had "made" her "rip his hair out," slapped his face, and kicked him repeatedly. When she finally finished, Kevin went back to his room and passed out. Hours later, he woke up, his body aching and his scalp on fire with sharp pain. He knew he had been injured but, confused and groggy, he had to reconstruct what happened. He stayed in bed until he had the strength to get up and the courage to be in the same room with our mother again.

The rest of us on the call are silent, heartbroken for that

little boy and by the ways Kevin's story mirrors our own memories.

During one call, as I read the story of Edie and Cathy getting caught stealing food from the grocery store, I look up from my reading and see that Edie is crying. I stop and we talk about how living with someone whose emotional outbursts were unpredictable and violent affected us as children. As we talk, I see on my siblings' faces that each of them is back in their own moments of having a parent turn on them without mercy. I worry that I have hurt them by revisiting the past, but they reassure me that they feel validated by what I've written and by our conversations. We remind each other that it's all right for any of us to bow out of the conversation or change the subject if the discussion becomes too painful, and to use a therapist, partner, or friend to support us.

Looking back on our childhoods, it's easy to define the impact our mother had on each of our lives. She was brutal, physically and emotionally. And when she decided she was done being a mother, she left us and barely looked back.

With our father, it's a harder story to tell. While he had his own fits of rage—his face turned red when he was angry, the veins in his neck pulsed and protruded, and he wielded his leather belt capriciously—he also had a certain charm our mother lacked. He loved Halloween and went to great lengths for it. One year he built a hinged coffin for my brothers, who, dressed as vampires, would rise out of it as unsuspecting trick-or-treaters approached.

He also at times made efforts to create order in our

house. Once he fashioned a bookshelf using two metal elbow brackets and a piece of plywood and installed it at the top of the stairs. On it he placed a complete set of the *Young People's Science Encyclopedia*, a gift from his boss, the electrician my father worked for, whose own kids had outgrown it. Each binding was a different color with a big number on it that made it easy to keep them in order—in the event anyone in our family ever wanted to put them back correctly.

A complete set: the books with their worlds within worlds of gems, jet planes, and the deep sea. And me and my siblings, the young people for whom they were intended: a complete set. We were the Troops, the Brood, the Menagerie, or simply the Glass kids, depending on who was talking to or about us.

I'VE BEEN WALKING in wet, squelching shoes and I can feel blisters rising on my big toes. Rather than continuing onto the alluring road ahead, I decide to start the trek back to my car and go indulge in my favorite meal at Zameen at the Point.

Over a warm bowl of pearl couscous with chicken, currants, and yogurt sauce, I pull out my phone and start to read about newts. They are classified as part of the Pleurodelinae subfamily of Salamandridae. All newts are salamanders, but not all salamanders are newts. Some are fully aquatic, others terrestrial. There are arboreal newts, which spend their entire lives in the high canopy of the forest.

And they do, in fact, have a system of defense. In the case of the rough skinned and California newts most common in the Santa Cruz Mountains, their aposematic coloration, the scientific term for the bright orange of their underbellies, serves as a warning to other animals. Newts secrete neurotoxins from their skin that can cause serious neurological damage or death to other animals. They are one of the most toxic animals in the United States.

Newts' limbs and even their organs can regenerate when damaged or severed. Our hearts, and even our souls, I have learned, can also regenerate. Newts can help. Newts are hardy, traveling miles to reach the water. They're squishy and vulnerable but they have enough poison in their little bodies to kill a horse. By most accounts, they are not a grave danger to humans, unless we eat them. I'm grateful I already have lunch plans.

I HAVE ONLY one photograph of myself as a child. I'm eleven years old. There's a galaxy of freckles spanning the bridge of my nose and spilling over onto my cheeks. My thick, wavy hair has amber tones and my dimples are still distinctly discernible where now they hide among echoing lines. As a young adult, I once asked my mother what I had looked like as a younger child.

"How the hell am I supposed to know? There were

eight of you!" she snapped, irritated, as she often was by my curiosity and sentimentality.

As it happens, there was only one of me. But my siblings and I do joke that taken for parts, we Glasses could patch together one wholesome, healthy, functioning body and soul—a full Glass. During our calls, when we tell stories about our childhoods, I imagine us an eight-headed being speaking as one, the Glass in the aggregate.

Between us, we have nineteen children and nine grand-children. Some of us raised our children as single parents, some as part of a couple. Some decided not to have chil-dren. We placed one of our children for adoption. Three of our children have died.

When our father died, we each got a few hundred dol-lars, one sister got the cookie jar, another our grandmoth-er's Victrola. Our mother got the house and my father's impressive collection of tools that were part of his handy-man business. My two eldest brothers fought hard to get her to agree to use some of my father's assets to benefit the younger kids, to no avail. When our mother died, we inher-ited a single-paragraph electronically generated goodbye letter.

To our aggravation, what we did inherit is our parents' combined dismal health. I had my first deep vein thrombo-sis at the age of twenty-three. Margaret had a heart attack and simultaneous stroke and pulmonary embolism at thirty-three. Jerry had open-heart surgery at fifty-six. Cathy has had two strokes, to say nothing of our combined three heart attacks, three strokes, four deep vein blood clots, and two pulmonary embolisms since. We do our part to keep anticoagulant manufacturers in business.

Three of the eight siblings have a diagnosis of bipolar disorder. Two have made serious suicide attempts resulting in major health complications, including a prolonged coma. Two of the eight have had a leg amputated: one resulting from a jump from a two-story building, the other from being trampled by a half-wild horse. Two siblings have permanently damaged arms, one from a stroke, one from an accidental fall. One, my brother Kevin, uses a power wheelchair and lives with a feeding tube due to a cascade of health complications. Four of the siblings have had cancer, and of them, one has had two distinct types of cancer. Two have diabetes.

As children, we flinched against flying fists, switches, and dishes, and as young adults we continued to flinch even at well-intended gestures by friends and partners: a hug, a handshake, a pat on the back. We no longer flinch. We were subjected to our father's sexual boundarylessness with not-so-subtle comments, to cloying physical overtures, and to more serious offenses. Some of us learned about this abuse as young children and teenagers when we were subjected to it. Some learned about it during early adulthood when a sibling confided in us, and others learned about it during these calls. Some of us remember the abuse viscerally, some don't remember abuse, and some scarcely remember having been a child.

WHILE THERE'S NO DOUBT that heredity is at play in our family's collective health, as a social worker, I can't ignore that other factors are at work too. I first learned about the Adverse Childhood Experiences (ACE) questionnaire through my work as a child welfare social worker. The development of the tool, now broadly used in education, social services, and the justice system, stems from a large-scale, landmark study by the Centers for Disease Control and Kaiser Permanente, which examined the long-term impacts on the health and well-being of individuals who faced certain specific experiences during childhood.

At a work conference I attended, trainers handed out the questionnaire and had everyone complete one—then proceeded to outline all the potential deleterious impacts on health and development for people who have a combination of the adverse experiences as children. A score of 4 or higher correlates with increased risks related to several categories of health and well-being in adulthood, including social issues like decreased opportunities related to education, occupation, and income, and serious health issues such as cancer, diabetes, and early death. Information about what can be done to ameliorate the health risks associated with adverse childhood experiences appeared to be addressed only as an afterthought, triggered by a question from the audience. At that time, hypnotherapy was the primary intervention that seemed to show promise.

The questionnaire has its shortcomings. The early iteration didn't factor in ethnicity or class and many of the questions ask whether certain experiences, such as being hit, sworn at, or provided insufficient food, happened "often," providing no guidance as to what constitutes "often."

An individual who was brutalized once or twice over the course of their childhood might answer no to question two: "Did a parent or other adult in the household often push, grab, slap, or throw something at you or hit you so hard that you had marks or were injured?" But someone who was spanked regularly as part of a conscious (though unfortunate in my mind) approach to discipline, might answer yes.

All the same, it was a helpful guide around which to organize discussions with each of my siblings. While I felt some hesitation introducing a clinical tool into informal conversations with my brothers and sisters, the questionnaire also felt validating, to me and to them, as it put a name to the constellation of circumstances that comprised much of our childhoods, and all but certainly compromised our health and well-being.

I wasn't surprised that there were plenty of details over which we disagreed.

Was it a condiment container or a dinner plate that Mom threw toward the glass door? We let Debbie settle that one, since she was the subject of the rage that sent the bottle of hot sauce hurling in her direction and crashing through the sliding glass door that led from the kitchen onto a deck.

Was it Dad or Jerry who fashioned the spiderweb-shaped patch to cover the resulting damage? Jerry clarified this one. He made the patch from cardboard and duct tape and he did a good job. It remained in place for years.

Was it only a few days that we stepped around the resulting pile of glass or did it stay on the kitchen floor for weeks? We never settled that one. But we all agreed that it was a while before anyone dared walk through the kitchen barefoot.

The ACE questionnaire poses ten questions on topics such as a caregiver's mental health issues, drug use, witnessing domestic violence, parental divorce or separation, and neglect, and follows a simple scoring system from 0 to 10, with each yes answer increasing the score. Among my siblings, we scored between a low of 5 and a high of 8. Six of the siblings scored a 7 or an 8.

As I sorted through my siblings' comments and tallied our ACE scores, I wondered what my parents would have scored had the same instrument been around to measure their childhood experiences. Trying to complete the questionnaire for my father, I was reminded how little I knew about his youth and upbringing. I didn't have enough information to take a guess at his score. I calculated my mother's score as 9.

TOGETHER WE TELL our stories and compare notes. We express our gratitude that we have people with whom we share a common history, and we venture beyond our common experiences and tell stories specific to our own lives, many of which I have never heard before.

Jerry tells us about being in an industrial accident at the wallpaper factory where he worked as a teenager. Debbie tells us about being so angry as a teenager when she was told that she couldn't be in the Miss Fremont pageant because she didn't have enough poise that she crashed the contest by showing up at the event. Cathy shares that she once got to sing onstage with the Doobie Brothers. Kevin tells about being fired for standing up against racism directed at his coworkers. Edie talks about the time she was shot in the leg by a child with blessedly bad aim as she walked home from the night shift at a convenience store in Sacramento. We were all aware of this tragic event, but she filled in details (some of the siblings hadn't heard about her begging the court for counseling and rehab for the kid rather than jail time). John tells the story of being in the navy at seventeen aboard the aircraft carrier USS *Midway* in the Balabac Strait as the Panamanian merchant ship *Cactus* collided with it. Margaret reminisces about dancing in *The Nutcracker* at the Paramount Theatre in Oakland as an eleven-year-old foster child. Jerry tells her something she'd forgotten: He was in the audience watching the performance.

Debbie and Edie each tell of occasions when they had to insist that they raise their voices, even as they quavered, to speak to congressmen or senators. Debbie spoke about the struggles of single mothers and about her personal experience with gun violence, while Edie, when she was briefly married to a man in prison, spoke about prisoners' rights.

WE TALK FOR HOURS, weaving between shared memories and updating each other on our lives in the decades since we shared a roof. Tears flow, laughter rings. And there are even long moments of silence—a rare occurrence among the Glasses.

Moving from this world to the next—in parts, like sections of a citrus fruit pried from its pith—will be excruciating. We will tremble at the momentary loss of our whole, the haecceity of our particular eightness, but we will emerge into stardust, or heaven, or a timeless redwood forest, or nothingness, our quirks and quiddities intact and redoubled, and we will find each other.

We will find each other, I am sure, and we will make a formidable ghost, our songs braiding the wind, and travel to all the places we never got to see. We'll bounce from cloud to cloud concocting elaborate games of tag, riding bikes one-foot-two-foot, doorbell ditching the angels, and looking down onto estuaries and blue whales and flamboyances of flamingos. We will spy on our earthbound children and grandchildren bellowing out our songs—"Johnny Verbeck," "In the Boarding House," "Sons of God"—while blistering the corn tortillas just so for our favorite childhood tacos. All limbs intact, cushioned, and oiled, our skips and stomps and gallops, our furious unfettered joy, will register on a seismograph and break it.

We will make a formidable ghost

I wrote that as I was trying to imagine the unimaginable loss of one of my siblings. Trying to fathom what shape our circle could possibly take with any one of us missing.

Months later, in November of 2023, in the middle of my workday at the hospital, I got a call from Margaret, whom I could barely understand through sobs. She was on her way to the hospital in Sacramento. Edie was in the cardiac catheterization lab after suffering a massive heart attack at work; she was brought to the emergency room by ambulance (though she had put up a valiant fight with the coworker who called 911, insisting that she could drive herself).

All the siblings who were able descended on the hospital to join Margaret and Edie's youngest daughter, Amy. The rest of the family stayed in touch by phone. We understood intellectually that the news was not good, but the degree to which we allowed ourselves to understand that we might lose our sister varied from moment to moment and from person to person, not always set to the same clock. We stood vigil at her bedside in small groups, surrounded by the beeps and alarms of the ventilator that kept her with us for the moment.

With the doctor's first attempt to remove her breathing tube, Edie was combative, so she was heavily sedated and the process delayed. When she started rousing again, several hours later, she opened her eyes and registered who was standing around her bed. She looked at each of us and held direct eye contact for several long seconds, smiling around the mouthpiece of the endotracheal tube. The doctor came in to start prepping to try again. Edie became visibly anxious. I leaned in close and said, "Please try to stay calm so they can take the tube out." Edie rolled her eyes and I whispered, "Don't roll your eyes at me, bitch!" She smiled extravagantly, beamed her eyes at me, and coughed. I was speaking her language. I was rewarded with a priceless, loving look from Edie and a stern reprimand from another sibling, reasonably so.

Cathy and Jerry are both nurses, and they helped translate what was happening for the rest of us. Cathy stayed with Edie for the extubating process, which was more successful this time with a loved one close by. Each of our respective coping mechanisms appeared as we faced the hellish limbo of waiting to see how Edie would respond to breathing on her own. There were so many feelings. So many unspoken needs. I didn't know how to make room for all of it. I felt as if all the skills I've learned as an adult for communicating clearly, listening carefully, being flexible, supportive, patient, kind, and good collapsed inside me like a long, snaking row of dominoes. I was a joke. A fraud. I was a mess.

Messes can be cleaned. Cleaning has been a long-standing coping mechanism for me. The idea that I could clean Edie's apartment gave me a renewed sense of purpose, and I resolved to spend the next day not in the hospital with family, but at the apartment alone. Cleaning. Coping.

Edie and I could go weeks without talking to each other over the years, then go through periods where we talked a couple of times a week. I was grateful that in the month before her heart attack we'd been talking a few times a week, so I had an idea of what was on her mind. Besides her youngest child, who was living with her, Edie's kids were spread from Scotland to Oregon to Texas. She had three very young grandchildren, two of whom she hadn't yet met, and her daughter and son-in-law were going to come to Sacramento from Scotland for Thanksgiving so she could finally meet them.

Edie was undone with excitement. She bought absurd quantities of toys for the kids at secondhand stores. Easily a third of her living room was piled with Duplos, ride-on toys, and dinosaurs. She bought stacks of tableware at the dollar store in fall colors. She asked me if I would pick up Karin and her family and drive them to her home in Sacramento, and reviewed details of car seats, pit stops, and toys for the trip a million times. She recounted every phone "conversation" she had with her grandchildren (many consisting of babbles).

She told me that she planned to clean her apartment floor to ceiling to make sure there was no lingering smell of cigarette smoke and that the kids could safely play and crawl on the floor. She planned to clean carpets, curtains, every surface. But she was feeling depleted and unable to take on the tasks.

The focus of our phone calls turned from her excitement about the grandbabies to concerns about her health. She told me that she thought she was seriously ill and that her doctor couldn't find a pulse in her foot. I told her to go to the emergency room, but she said she had already been and the doctor had told her there was nothing that could be done, so she'd made another appointment with her regular doctor to follow up. The last time we talked, she told me she was going to work in the morning even though it was painful to walk. I begged her to take time off until she could see the doctor. She insisted that it was impossible to take a day off. After several rounds of arguing, finally she agreed to take one day off. The following day she went to work. Margaret's call on her way to the hospital came that afternoon.

I LINED UP my cleaning supplies and went to work. I removed every curtain in the house, opened the windows, filled bathtubs and sinks and toilets with cleansers, pulled up carpets, moved everything I could manage outdoors to be aired. I moved furniture to ensure every inch of the floor underneath was scrubbed. On my hands and knees I cleaned the floor, I stood on a ladder to clean the walls and the ceilings, and I crouched under the sinks and cupboards. Each swipe of my rag reinforced her heartbeats. Each spray of bleach pushed blood through her arteries. I was keeping her alive, frantically saving her. Soon she'd be home in her freshly cleaned bed. My siblings and I would arrange an around-the-clock schedule as she recovered. We'd all stay for Thanksgiving and would be there when she met her grandbabies. Everything was going to be OK. I got an update from the hospital that Edie was talking, even joking. I kept scrubbing madly. It was working.

When I finally took a break in the late afternoon, I realized that I'd had nothing to eat or drink all day except an obscene number of twelve-ounce cans of Diet Pepsi. I texted Margaret and said, "If you guys get something to eat on the way home, can you please pick something up for me too?" I got an instant reply that said simply, "Come now."

I dropped everything and got in my car. Margaret's son Josh called me and asked if I wanted him to come get me. I told him I was already driving and asked, "Is she dying?" He hemmed and hawed and I said, "Tell me, Josh!" more harshly than I intended. He confirmed what I feared and told me they were trying to keep her alive until we were all there.

To drive safely I had to go to a cold, detached place inside. I called Ellen and Jesse and made them talk to me about boring subjects that offered distraction without requiring concentration.

Twenty minutes later, I got to the parking lot and made my way into the hospital, where there was a line of people waiting for visitor badges. I tried to sneak by but the man at the front desk told me to get in line. I went to the desk and asked the people at the front of the line if I could please cut in front of them. They looked at me as if I'd dropped down from Mars. "My sister is being kept alive for me," I blurted, then gushed an involuntary stream of tears and ran for the elevator. This time, the guard didn't try to stop me.

Edie's room was crowded with people trying to revive her. I wanted to scream at them, "Leave her alone!" I wanted to get closer to her but was told to step back. I stood with

Cathy, and after a couple of minutes the doctor came out and told us, "We did all we could." We all went back into the room and stood around her bed, holding her hands, crying, singing, trying to reach her important people on the phone so they could be there with us.

My sister Margaret and my nephew Josh had been with Edie that afternoon when she had a massive seizure. Up until that moment, she had been communicating clearly. Margaret believes that Edie left this world when that seizure started. She's probably right, and I think Edie would have loved for her last moment to be with family and for it to have involved laughter. But I also need for her to have been alive when I got there, so that I had a last moment with her that day, too, even though I know that if Edie heard me say that, she would roll her eyes so far back into her head that they'd be stuck under her lids.

I knew it would be brutal to lose a sibling, but I didn't understand how fully interwoven our fibers were until one thread was pulled and seven edges frayed. The loss of any of my siblings will unravel me, but in the case of Edie, we lost our Beetle Bug (one of many nicknames we had for her)—ensconced in amber. More than any of us, she preserved the spirit of our childhood scrappiness. She held a critical part of our collective identity, and just as little John felt when Debbie moved out, we all wander lost for a while, feeling like a part of us is missing.

A friend suggests that I take Edie on a walk with me, so we head out onto the cliffs, along the northern coast of the county, high enough that we're eye level to passing lines of soaring seagulls and pelicans, scanning the sheer rock walls below for the shy pigeon guillemot with its bright orange feet and watching scoters, sea ducks that surf the waves, waiting for a ride. I stand close enough to the cliff's edge to feel the pull of frighteningly spacious nothingness, but back far enough that the dirt won't crumble under my feet. I won't step off. I don't want to die. But I'm gutted by the ache of staying here on earth without Edie, and the sensation that stepping off could somehow join me with her leaves me trembling. I wrench myself away and trudge home, a nascent ghost.

I want to write my siblings into my skin so I can keep them. I've designed a tattoo to be etched below my thumb, along the radius bone, so I can hold up my hand and read it like a sentence, a line of eight simple symbols representing each of us, youngest to oldest.

In the months since Edie died, I've searched for ways to keep her with me. I first learned about wind phones many years ago when a friend told me about Itaru Sasaski, a Japanese man who'd put an old telephone booth in his garden with a disconnected phone as a way of coping with the death of his cousin. He'd call to talk to his cousin "on the wind." Shortly after he installed the wind phone, his community faced a massive earthquake and he opened the phone booth up to the public so those grieving friends and family members lost in the disaster could "call" their loved ones. People all over the world were moved to follow suit, and there are now a few hundred wind phones around the world, including around 150 in the US.

After we lost Edie, I was going through some of my project photographs and noticed the one I'd taken of the red phone booth on Rider Ridge Road. I wondered if it had been a wind phone and resolved to go back and look. A couple of days later, I made the thirty-minute drive, eager to get the receiver in my hand and call my sister. The phone wasn't in the spot I'd seen it many months before, but I drove the length of the road and spotted it on someone's private property. I'd hoped to find a sign on it inviting people to use it, but there wasn't one. I sat debating with myself whether to just make my call anyway but ultimately it didn't feel right. Dejected, I headed home.

The next day Ellen and I visited a giant antique fair in Alameda County and I spotted a rotary dial phone from the 1940s for sale. My heart flipped for joy and I decided on the spot to make a wind phone for bereaved people in Santa Cruz. I'll need to figure out the logistics of where to locate it, how to build a phone booth, all the practical aspects that surface after an idea has a chance to settle in. In the meantime, the phone sits on a table in my home office and I call Edie whenever the whim strikes. I called her on her birthday and wished her a happy sixty-fourth. I call her each time I communicate with one of her kids or grandkids. I called her to tell her about her symbol in the tattoo design.

She never answers. I can finally get a word in edgewise.

Conclusion

eudaemonia *noun* \yüdē'mōnēə\: well-being,
happiness, human flourishing

I N A LECTURE I attended on brain development and attach-
ment, the speaker demonstrated his definition of attune-
ment. He asked for silence and waited patiently for the
whispering, shifting, and shuffling of papers to stop. He
took up a violin and bow and played a single, stirring
note, letting it hover, powerful and invisible, on the air of
the enormous hall. Then, with our absolute attention, he
started his lecture.

This project created in me that same quality of silence,
resonance, and space within which to experience attune-
ment with the natural world.

Over the course of several years, I am repeatedly swept
into a kind of breathtaking awe. I kneel reverently at the
edges of tide pools and watch egrets in the shallows gripping hanks of seaweed and shaking them vigorously to release hidden fish, snatching them up in their beaks. I marvel
at fallow purple thistle flowers giving way to fairy weeds

for wish-making, rattlesnake grass named for the reptile whose tail it resembles and its percussive qualities when dried, acorns with fitted, removable caps.

There are skinks with their startling flash of cobalt tail. By the time my brain does the split-second work of registering and categorizing them, they dart out of sight, leaving me with a lingering eyeful of electric blue and a yearning for a closer look. I am charmed by pink meadow grasshoppers, dazzled by the works of fine art on the backs of beetles and spiders and bees. In sufficient doses, walking and steeping myself in nature, whether in a neighborhood garden or on a mountain pass, becomes medicine and begins to palliate my wounds. If my soul is a glass pitcher, I have now filled it up repeatedly, rinsing it with bits of beauty until stagnant water finally runs clear. I change my life story by adding to it until the good stuff and the beauty dilute my challenges, until joy outpaces fear.

The walks, with all their sights, sounds, smells, and revelations, continually churn a voracious appetite for learning more. My bedside stacks start to resemble a series of stalagmites reaching from the floor to the book-covered nightstand until we have to install new bookshelves in my office. Paper pages, electronic books, audiobooks, and online searches lead me hopscotching from amphibians to Aristotle, caterpillars to composition, mushrooms to Marcus Aurelius, pollywogs to politics. I devour details in a way that might appear disjointed or indiscriminate to an onlooker, but to me it all reads like smooth silk. I tell Jesse about this learning approach and in her Jesse way she produces a fitting quote:

> We do not receive wisdom, we must discover it for ourselves, after a journey through the wilderness which no one else can make for us, which no one can spare us, for our wisdom is the point of view from which we come at last to regard the world. The lives that you admire, the attitudes that seem noble to you, have not been shaped by a paterfamilias or a schoolmaster, they have sprung from very different beginnings, having been influenced by evil or commonplace that prevailed round them. They represent a struggle and a victory.
>
> —Marcel Proust

I remember saying to Miles when I was in the throes of falling madly in love with the world during that first walking year: "I know it's not true, but it really feels like time is going much faster."

He replied, "Of course it is, relative to how long you've been alive and how much time you have left." He immediately realizes that this could be taken as "You're old, Mom," and adds, "The same is true for me. For all of us."

I'd never thought of it that way. Suddenly, "Live every day like it's your last" seems less like a sappy saying and more like a pressing assignment.

As I get close to finishing up walking the roads and trails in Santa Cruz and trying to figure out where my feet will take me next, I wake up from a dream where I've declared dramatically to an audience of thousands that I am almost done with my project of walking every street in the world. I toss and turn in that place between sleep and wake, thinking, *What am I saying? I haven't even started on China yet!* I'm so relieved when I fully awaken and realize that the crowds were not real and that the scope of my project is achievable.

JO AND I didn't meet until we were young adults living in Santa Cruz, but we quickly discovered that our paths had almost certainly crossed many times during childhood. We'd both grown up in Fremont and attended the same schools. We'd both been raised in large Catholic families and went to the same churches. We grew up with the expectation that we would not go to college and decided later in life to do so. Jo pursued a degree in social work. A few years later, I did the same. Jo got a job in Santa Clara County, and when I finished school I applied with the same department. I got the job and was assigned a worker number. By sheer coincidence, it was the same worker number Jo was given when she was first employed at the agency. One day, I showed up for work and a coworker took a long look at me, laughed, and asked, "Did you and Jo plan this?"

"Plan what?" I asked.

My coworker replied, "I'm not going to tell you. Go find Jo and you'll immediately see what I'm talking about."

When I found her, we were dressed in precisely the same outfit. Collared, short-sleeved white blouses with geometric designs embroidered in black thread on the front placket, long green skirts, and low black shoes. We were both glad we weren't in any shared meetings that day.

We've discovered dozens more similarities between us over our four decades of friendship, and, of course, plenty of differences. What we learned as we started walking the California coast is that we are twins for a particular type of adventure. We put one foot in front of the other and watch the world kaleidoscope around us. Whether we're walking in the tracks of a coyote over miles of open beach somewhere between Pigeon Point and Half Moon Bay, tracking a bright pink sun rising through fog overlooking the Golden Gate Bridge, or watching droves of woolly bear caterpillars being somersaulted by the wind at Tomales Point—where we also find carpets of blue self-heal flowers, yellow wallflowers, pink seaside daisies, and cobwebby thistle, and observe a herd of tule elk—we walk in joy and verve and we simply do not get bored. Ever.

Walking along a creek in Sonoma, we hear a hawk cry from a nearby tree. We look and look but can't spot the raptor, only a lone blue jay. But as we stand there, the jay opens its beak and out comes the unmistakable sound of a hawk. Walking near Point Arena, we come upon otherworldly landscapes of massive sinkholes, wind-sculpted rocks, and colorless rainbows, or fogbows, as we learn they are called.

On San Diego beaches, we watch seagulls repeatedly flying straight up in the air, then swooping back to the sand. After observing them at length, we figure out that they are picking up tiny bean clams off the beach, carrying them in their beaks, then dropping them back onto the ground to break them open so they can eat them. Along some of the beaches in Los Angeles, we are country mice gawking at the wealth. There are enormous houses set high on cliffs with long private stairways down to the sand, and multilevel houses right on the beach with infinity pools. We stare slack-jawed at a hot tub that appears to be made of pure glass and hung like a gigantic sconce on a concrete wall. At some point during every single walk, one of us earnestly announces, "This is my favorite of all the walks," as if we've never said it before.

We have walked 664 miles along the edge of California as of this writing. We head inland when we must, but we stick to the sand and clifftops as much as possible. We're working on three distinct stretches, two south of our homes and one north, allowing us to choose our destination based on weather. When we have unremitting floods in the central and northern regions of California, we take our southern path, which currently runs from the Tijuana River Valley in San Diego to El Matador State Beach in Malibu. And when the thermometer threatens to pop its top in Southern California, we head for one of our northern routes, either the stretch from Point Lobos in Monterey County to the tiny town of Inglenook, population 128, in Mendocino County, or the one from the California-Oregon border to the Crescent City Harbor.

When we begin the project, on each trip we drive to the spot where we last left off, walk all day, and drive home. But soon, the drive to get to our last point takes hours, so day-long trips give way to three-to-five-day expeditions, and the coastal walking project gets more complicated but also more exhilarating. We stay in a yurt at the Tijuana River Valley Regional Park Campground, sleep in our cars in redwood forests, share a two-star hotel room at Pacific Beach steps from the water, and occupy a bell tent on a farm in a Southern California town called Valley Center. We camp in state campgrounds, RV parks, and private lands. We travel by Uber, taxi, or bus, or we leave one car at each end of our intended route. We've even hitchhiked a couple of times. We bring food and water but also stop to sample local fare at delis and farm stands when opportunities present.

Kita was tiny the first time I heard him use the word *climate*. Curious as to his understanding of the concept, I asked him what it meant. He considered for a moment and replied, "It's the texture of the weather."

Jo and I both love to feel *the texture of the weather*. On one of our camping trips in Los Angeles County, we woke before sunrise to pouring rain and strong winds. Jo stuck her head out of her truck and yelled, "Let's go!" and off we went. We wrapped ourselves and our gear in garbage liners and started walking into the storm. Our makeshift rain gear whipped around us so loudly that we could hardly hear each other speak. A photo of us in those moments before the sky cleared could have been used in a dictionary beside the definition of the word *glee*.

Sometimes we walk side by side, catching up on our respective lives, looking back and reminiscing over the past forty-some years of friendship, doing some lighthearted philosophizing, or just stepping together through awe. Other times we're absorbed in our own thoughts and move at our own paces. On a beach in San Diego, I spot a large group of what I later learn are wavy turban snails, the largest sea snail in California, whose shell can grow up to six inches long. Jo is way ahead of me, so I have to shout at the top of my lungs. "Jo, come back," I yell, "it's a seashell emergency!" She returns and we marvel together. Later, Jo finds some flat, roundish, smooth-edged shell pieces that share the same mother-of-pearl look as the inside of the turban shells on one side, and a ridged texture on the other. We surmise they must be a separate part of the same shell and as soon as we have a chance, we research these giant gastropods and learn that the pieces Jo found are called the operculum or "trap door." They serve to protect the snail from predators. I've come to adore sleeping in my vehicle, and the operculum makes me think of the keen sense of security that washes over me when I snuggle into the shell of my car, then pull my operculum—the door—closed behind me.

The intrusive thoughts I wrestled with in my twenties still rear up from time to time, but I can usually get the upper hand almost instantly using the tools I learned many years ago. Recently, though, they've gained a little traction. I have a sense of impending doom around the longevity of my teeth. Their shifting has caused a slight change in my speech. The way the hygienist cleans them, as if they're crafted of translucent bone china, only fuels my worry. The fear of social isolation brought on by shame, however self-imposed, plunges me into a whirlpool of despair and holds me under. I have to snap myself out of thinking about it obsessively. I occasionally allow myself to wallow in the belief that I should be spared the whole painful process of watching my body slowly deteriorate. I mean, I finally got my shoes on the right feet.

When I start to spin out, I ask myself, "Am I OK right now?" The answer is almost always yes. So I relax into the moment and allow that to suffice. I remind myself that I can still hold my own on a hike with twenty-four-year-old Miles, at least when he's being merciful.

When anxiety flares, I close my eyes and imagine standing shoulder to shoulder with Jo on a raised walkway around the King Harbor in Redondo Beach, pointing out stingrays, octopuses, common loons, and bright orange garibaldi fish. Or I imagine taking the two-and-a-half-mile walk with Ellen from our home to our local cinema for five-dollar movie night and holding hands with her while I indulge in salted popcorn and root beer. Or the true tulip tree flower the old man on Dellview Avenue handed me. I now have a seemingly endless trove of breathtaking moments to draw upon that can help me shift gears smoothly from troubled back to contented.

Aristotle used the term *eudaemonia* to describe a sort of pinnacle of human flourishing. I don't think he meant sitting in a tiny post office eating hippie popcorn while waiting for a bus that never comes, or making hats out of sea palms and frolicking in the sand, or sitting in plastic chairs outside middle-of-nowhere country liquor stores eating Dove Bars or mint It's-Its, or lolling around in an obscure highway-side graveyard, resting our feet and using round pretzels and malt balls to make extra sets of eyeballs to layer over our own and holding them in place by squinching our eyes around them. Human flourishing has many faces. Some have malt-ball pupils.

A few months before Edie died, she asked if she could join Jo and me on one of our walks. She made it clear that she had no intention of walking with us, but she wanted to make us a campfire and feed us macaroni salad, potato salad, grilled hot dogs, and s'mores when we reached Little River in Mendocino County, one of her favorite places. Jo, of course, was game.

We'll reach that point on our journey soon. I'll bring my wind phone with me. And some potato salad.

I FEEL CAUGHT UP. I see my holes, my missing pieces, my troublesome quirks, but they no longer look like deficits. They look like spots along a continuum of humanness that I can lament or embrace, strive to change or continue to endure.

Ellen and I walk together along West Cliff Drive. She catches my hand mid-swing and says, "We've spent forty-three percent of our lives together." Geese fly over our house every day in the late afternoon. We stop whatever we're doing and listen to their noisy honking. I see lines of them reflected in the glass top of our dinner table as they pass overhead. On my office wall hangs a handsomely framed, hand-colored 1950 Thomas Bros. map of Santa Cruz County. A gift from Ellen. She gave it to me shortly after I finished the project so I'd have something tangible in the house to remind me always of this transformative journey. Every time I look at it, I feel nerdily proud to be a person with a framed map on my office wall. I gaze at it as I might a mirror and see a shy glow of accomplishment reflected back. But mostly, when I look at it, I feel a flush of gratitude for having a partner whose unwavering support, love, and patience enabled me to *do my work.*

Ellen and I recently became grandparents to the daughter of Kita and his partner, Yafah. The baby, Vida, which translates to "life," is named for her maternal great-grandmother. She has a storm of black hair, a ready smile, and boundless curiosity. A family friend of Yafah's brought Vida a bouquet of sunflowers, and I was there to witness her eyes pop like those of a tarsier, the tiny primate of Southeast Asia whose eyes are larger than its entire brain, as she seemed to strain to absorb and make sense of the shocking beauty.

She may be a budding botanist. At six months old, she's captivated by leaves and flowers. We have to check her little fists for leaf litter, nicked on the fly if we walk anywhere near a plant. I crunch up dried leaves near her ear and we exchange smiles when she turns toward the sound. I open my hand and we marvel as the wind lifts and carries the organic confetti. A few flakes land on her perfect little feet like scrambled alphabets writing her into nature's story.

I have a feeling of wholeness that derives from developing a more cohesive narrative of my own life, which in turn impacts my regard for others. The simplest interactions take on new meaning. I'm much more apt to make eye contact, nod a greeting, or say hello to everyone I cross paths with and to cherish the cumulative effect of returned greetings. You're here. I'm here. Our paths have crossed. That's enough. I've become more openhearted. More authentically giving. More trusting.

My visual perception has changed. By becoming immersed in photography, I have learned to look more closely, to see subtle changes in light, shadow, reflection. I have learned to look for depth and dimension. I exhaust myself with the effort of noticing every detail until this way of looking becomes my basic vision. The world becomes more faceted, nuanced, and radiant.

When I walk deep into the woods, I'm acutely aware that I'm among sentient beings. I feel benevolently watched over by the trees. They hold the burden of vigilance while I go on studying the forest, picking up samaras, winged seed pods, and watching them helicopter back to earth until something else catches my attention, maybe a length of curved bark, blown from its tree in a storm, still bearing a pattern of rounded holes where a woodpecker once stored its loot, angling it to catch light and cast its holey shadows on the dirt path. Here, even with all my flaws laid bare, I am utterly accepted. The trees don't care what I know, where I've been, or what clothes I wear. They teach me about inclusion and belonging while I rest my nerves and play freely under their tender watch.

My range of emotions has expanded. I overcorrected for the chaos of my childhood by morphing into a spirit level, constantly trying to keep the bubble balanced between the lines, keep my emotions closely controlled, and project confidence. Amid crises on the job, coworkers frequently remarked that I was "unflappable" or that I had "nerves of steel." I could be overwhelmed, tattered inside, while maintaining an outward appearance of utter calm. The process of moving through challenging emotions as I walk and the joy of immersing myself in nature have tilted the level. The bubble now has an infinitely broader traveling range.

Acknowledgments

Gratitude to my late parents, Fred and Barbara Glass. I thank them for my life, my siblings, and my songs. And to my brilliant, beloved, funny, feisty, formidable siblings—Jerry Glass, Debbie Hamilton, Cathy Glass, Kevin Glass, Edie Evans (in memory, FK!), John Glass, Margaret Lewis—who listened to each chapter and gave their full and cherished blessings. And to my dearly loved foster sisters, Sabra Saperstein and Sophia Gutierrez, and their mother, my foster mother, Sue Saperstein, who modeled the craft of choosing family and has remained family to me all these years.

Having never written a book, I am gobsmacked and humbled to learn all that goes into each aspect of the process of making one. I thank my agent, Bonnie Nadell, for the coaxing—"We get what you *think*, but how did x, y, or z make you *feel*?"— and for her patience as I wriggled out of my blind spots. I love that Diana brought us together. Elizabeth Wood, you were a bridge between two worlds for me. Thank you for that. Jake Morrissey I thank for working his magic on my manuscript, tossing some superlative new words my way (*elegiac, buffeting*), and guiding me through a complex universe. I appreciate all the support, assistance, and availability of those I had the pleasure of working with at Riverhead, including Patricia Clark, Nora Alice Demick, Amanda Dewey, Viviann Do, Laura Ellsessar, Alison Fairbrother, Shailyn Tavella, Delia Taylor, and Helen Yentus. Frances Key Phillips helped me frame the story and edited the earliest draft, while aiding in the search for my missing voice. Bridget Lyons also helped with edits of the earliest drafts and was game for meeting in motion as we walked and talked through her input. The word *kindred* comes to mind when I think of her heart for nature. Andy Couturier, writing teacher and author, helped me place the first stone in the river.

Thank you, Annigoni to Zachary, for walking with me for a block or twenty-six miles (or anywhere between) even when your shoes were tired:

Jacqueline Annigoni, Daniel Bayen, Nick Borelli, Deborah Bresnick, Jesse Burgess, Consuelo Chavarria, Theo Glass Clare, Melissa Delgadillo, Sandy Dueck, Donna Glass, Jerry Glass, Kita Glass, Sophia Gutierrez, Emma Herceg, Melissa Herceg, Debby Humolsky, Ken Johnson, Michele Landegger, Alexis Lewis, Margaret Lewis, Peter Meehan, Kirsten Mehl, Jennifer Meyer, Jerilyn Munyon, Treco Munyon-Burgess, Bruce Murphy, Julie Murphy, Jo Plante, Ann Carney Pomper, Jay Rorty, Jim Schoonover, Ron Slack, Jeanne Sofen, Susanne Teichman, Bill Timberlake, Ellen Timberlake, Izzie Bella Timberlake-Glass (in memory), Miles Timberlake-Glass, Nancy Virostko, Abby Wexler, Mathew Zachary

. . . and Burgess to Virostko, for reading a few paragraphs or an entire early draft and giving your invaluable insights:

Barrie Davenport Burgess, Jesse Burgess, Allison Claire, the Glass sibs, Jen Hastings, Samara Marion, Dana McRae, Catherine Newman, Jo Plante, Ann Pomper, Jay Rorty, Max Rorty, Sue Saperstein, Lindsay Steigner, Evi Strauss, Ellen Timberlake, Patrice Vecchione, Nancy Virostko

. . . and **Alvarez to Zueck, for chatting with me when we crossed paths out on the roads and trails:**

Anita Alvarez, Wallace Bain, Mary Cahill, Jacki Carillo, Jimmy Cook, Trevor Davis, Georgina Dews, Kelly Forman-Allari, John Foy, Laura Garnette, Kita Glass, Celia Goeckermann, Fred Koehler, Roberta Mervis Krenz, Paula Marcus, Susan Mauriello, Dana McRea, Jasmine McRca, Isaiah Miles-Davis, Malachi Miles-Davis, Lynn Miller, Julie Montoro, Richard Nanas (in memory), Frances Orland, Davina Polanco, Alex Polland, Scott Polland, Ann Carney Pomper, Rick Roberts (in memory), Wendy Roberts, Lucero Robles, Pat Shea, Emily Simoni, Rae Gwyn Smith, Heather Stratford, Scott Stratford, Nan Toy, Katie Tripp, Cheri Turner, Sharmaine Vindanage-Cheleden, Abby Wexler, Lance Wexler, Maya Wexler, Nate Wexler, John Zueck

. . . and **Bain to Wexler, for creating opportunities to share my project and my photographs or for making art that reflects it back to me:**

Wallace Bain (*Santa Cruz Sentinel* article), Melanee Barash (Science Night at the library), Mike de Boer (Bay Photo), Antara Brewer (ceramic), Liz Broughton (2020 Vision Exhibit at Santa Cruz Museum of Natural History), Tauna Coulson (Eloise Pickard Smith Gallery), Kathy DeWild (Santa Cruz County Arts

Commission Spotlight Awards), Doug Erickson (New Tech MeetUp), Catherine Sonquist Forest (Coyote Crossing), Allison Garcia (Open Show), Laura Garnett (Youth Resources Bank auction), Jim Greene (fine art painting), Marie Henley (photos on Slow Adventure website and introduction to DM), Diana Marcum (in memory, *LA Times* story), Monica Martinez (permanent display at Encompass Community Services), Ellen Ortiz (Kiwanis), Jo Plante (unSCruz), Joseph Carr Ritchie (California Color), Michael Rubin (*Neomodern* blog), Leslie Scanagatta (Santa Cruz County offices), Robbie Schoen (installation at Encompass Community Services), Jefree Schroepfer (Lululemon's Locals Loft display), Lindsay Steigner (permanent display at Encompass Community Services), Jamie Taylor (Special Edition gallery), David Terrazas (city council presentation), Shmuel Thaler (*Santa Cruz Sentinel*), Ellen Timberlake (all-around promoter), Melissa West (Peet's Coffee display), Lance Wexler (private business use), Claudine Wildman (quilty as charged), Nancy Wolosyn (fine art painting)

. . . and Aiello to Yokel, for cheering me on:

Laurie Aiello, Chris Bratt, Beverly Brito, Tomas Cleary, Sherra Clinton, Melinda Costello, Heather Duffy, Margie Erickson, Maria Gitin, Cathy "Aqua Bitch" Glass, Jerry Glass, John Glass, Kevin Glass, Kita Glass, Gail Groves, Sophia Guttierez, Edie Hahn (in memory), Debbie Hamilton, Evelyn Hengeveld-Bidmon, Anita Jain, Kamini Jain, Lochlann Jain, Patrice Keat, Hiranya Kleisch, Andrea Landis, Margaret Lewis, Paul Lewis, Patty Partch Lovato, Bridget Lyons, Samara Marion, Melinda Martindale, Keith McHenry, Steve Mentor,

Jan Mitchell, Dinah Philips, Irene Reti, Mardi Richmond, Robin Roberts, Sabra Saperstein, Sue Saperstein, Lea Scarpelli, Lu Ellen Schafer (in memory), Sarah Schmudlach, Bill Timberlake, Darla Timberlake, David Timberlake, Miles Timberlake-Glass, Samuel Torres, Patrice Vecchione, Claire Wesley, Judy Yokel.

Glossary

dehisce *verb* \də'his\: to split along a
   natural line

epigenome *noun* \,epə'jēnōm\: the
   complement of chemical compounds that
   modify the expression and function of
   the genome

eudaemonia *noun* \yüdē'mōnēə\: well-being,
   happiness, human flourishing

formosity *noun* \fȯr'mäsətē\: beauty or a
   beautiful thing

fugacious *adjective* \fyü'gāshəs\: lasting
   a short time: evanescent

grace note *noun* \'grās 'nōt\: a small addition
   to make something more beautiful
   or interesting

griffonage *noun* \¦grifə¦näzh\: careless
   handwriting: a crude or illegible scrawl

haecceity *noun* \hak'sēədē\: that property
of a thing by virtue of which it is unique
or describable as "this (one)"

omnium-gatherum *noun* \‚ämnēəm-
'gatḫərəm\: a miscellaneous collection

quaquaversal *adjective* \¦kwākwə¦vərsəl\:
dipping from a center toward all points
of the compass

saporous *adjective* \'sapərəs\: of, relating
to, or capable of exciting the sensation of
taste: having flavor

sororal *adjective* \sə'rȯrəl\: of, relating to,
or characteristic of a sister

terebrating *verb* \'terəbrāting\: boring;
perforating

welkin *noun* \'welkən\: the vault of the sky:
firmament